The Strategic Constitution

Law and Society Series
W. Wesley Pue, General Editor

The Law and Society Series explores law as a socially embedded phenomenon. It is premised on the understanding that the conventional division of law from society creates false dichotomies in thinking, scholarship, educational practice, and social life. Books in the series treat law and society as mutually constitutive and highlight scholarship emerging from the interdisciplinary engagement of law with fields such as politics, social theory, history, political economy, and gender studies.

A list of titles in the series appears at the end of the book.

The Strategic Constitution
Understanding Canadian Power in the World

IRVIN STUDIN

UBCPress · Vancouver · Toronto

© UBC Press 2014

All rights reserved. No part of this publication may be reproduced, stored in a retrieval system, or transmitted, in any form or by any means, without prior written permission of the publisher, or, in Canada, in the case of photocopying or other reprographic copying, a licence from Access Copyright, www.accesscopyright.ca.

22 21 20 19 18 17 16 15 14   5 4 3 2 1

Printed in Canada on FSC-certified ancient-forest-free paper
(100% post-consumer recycled) that is processed chlorine- and acid-free.

Library and Archives Canada Cataloguing in Publication

Studin, Irvin, author
    The stategic constitution : understanding Canadian power in the world /
Irvin Studin.

(Law and society, 1496-4953)
Includes bibliographical references and index.
Issued also in electronic format.
ISBN 978-0-7748-2714-0 (bound). – ISBN 978-0-7748-2715-7 (pbk).
ISBN 978-0-7748-2716-4 (pdf). – ISBN 978-0-7748-2717-1 (epub)

    1. Constitutional law – Canada. 2. Canada – Politics and government. I. Title.
II. Series: Law and society series (Vancouver, B.C.)

KE4219.S78 2014	342.71	C2014-900397-8
KF4482.S78 2014		C2014-900398-6

Canadä

UBC Press gratefully acknowledges the financial support for our publishing program of the Government of Canada (through the Canada Book Fund), the Canada Council for the Arts, and the British Columbia Arts Council.

This book has been published with the help of a grant from the Canadian Federation for the Humanities and Social Sciences, through the Awards to Scholarly Publications Program, using funds provided by the Social Sciences and Humanities Research Council of Canada.

UBC Press
The University of British Columbia
2029 West Mall
Vancouver, BC V6T 1Z2
www.ubcpress.ca

IN MEMORY OF MICHAEL GRIESDORF,
FRIEND, COLLEAGUE,
AND WORLD-CLASS CANADIAN STRATEGIST

Law and strategy are not merely made in history ...
They are made of history.

– PHILIP BOBBITT, *THE SHIELD OF ACHILLES*

Contents

Preface and Acknowledgments / ix

Introduction / 3

PART I
The Conceptual Framework for Assessing Canadian Strategic Power in Constitutional Terms

1 Framing Some Key Concepts / 13

2 Diplomacy / 29

3 The Military / 38

4 Government, or Pure Executive Potency / 46

5 Natural Resources (and Food) / 55

6 National Economic Might / 68

7 Communications / 81

8 Population / 94

9 The Strategic Constitution as Conceptual and Analytical Framework / 103

PART II
Applying the Conceptual Framework: Four Policy Case Studies

Case Study A: Canadian Strategic Leadership in the Americas / 109

Case Study B: Bona Fide War / 120

Case Study C: Arctic Sovereignty / 135

Case Study D: National Security/Counterterrorism since 9/11 / 151

Conclusion / 169

Notes / 175

Bibliography / 235

Indexes / 248

Preface and Acknowledgments

I came to the study of constitutional law not as a lawyer but through my primary intellectual and professional interest in international affairs. The first-born of détente Jews from Odessa in the former Soviet Union, born in Rome and raised in Toronto's French schools and on its soccer pitches (swearing in some twenty tongues, including both official ones), can little help but be at ease with the kinetic mixity of global politics, war and peace, and the general borderlessness of the human condition.

Of constitutional law, I knew at first only what a superficial reading of the canonical Peter W. Hogg text allowed, and I delved only as deeply as a reasonably educated former Canadian civil servant could suffer in the course of participation in a great variety of policy files – ranging from the wars in Afghanistan and Iraq to national security and democratic governance.

A careful first "professional" reading of the entire *Constitution Act, 1867* (the former *British North America Act*) required me to discover the following somewhat shocking line in the second recital of the preamble to what is supposed to be the foundational document of the modern Canadian project: "And whereas such a Union would conduce to the Welfare of the Provinces and *promote the Interests of the British Empire* ..." (emphasis added).

Few Canadians, jurists and non-jurists alike, know this line, and almost none knows what it means in today's constitutional context. The constitutionalist-poet F.R. Scott once asked, almost *en passant*, what it meant. He offered no answer. I am sure that nearly no foreign or defence policy specialist in Canada today is aware of its existence; none has ever commended it to me in discussion or debate. It is never quoted in the popular media and has little examination in the scholarly literature. In short, it is, in my view, at once the most important and the most underserviced line in the entire Canadian constitutional framework.

Yet, as a newcomer to constitutional law, and as a Canadian *tout court*, I find that this line tells me most of what seems true (and under-appreciated) about the Canadian condition: first, that, *pace* the glorification of Confederation in today's pedagogy, Canada was born *expressly* as a colony; second, that "high policy" and "strategy" (questions of major national interest) were driven out of the United Kingdom (at Westminster), whereas presumptively "tactical" questions relating to "welfare of the provinces" (or federalism) were what exercised (and ought to have exercised) Ottawa; and third, that Canada in the twenty-first century, whatever it tries to accomplish in the world, must reckon with the original "colonial" and "tactical" iron constitutional cage that arguably has dictated much of the country's logic over the past century and a half.

This third implication led me to the study contained in this book. What can Canada do in the world, given its constitutional framework (properly defined of course)? What can it not do? Can it meet the challenges of what, in my analysis, promises to be, in strategic terms, its most difficult century yet? Can Canada, in other words, strategically "over-perform" in relation to what is implied by its constitutional structure (textually and jurisprudentially)? Indeed, what is the effective strategic capacity of the Canadian state in constitutional terms?

I am indebted to many people for the publication of this book. Patrick Monahan, deputy attorney general of Ontario and former dean of Osgoode Hall Law School, was exceedingly generous in giving me the "run of the place" at one of North America's premier law faculties. He also provided numerous comments and suggestions that ultimately helped to shape the book into its current two-part structure. At Osgoode, I profited from the expertise, professionalism, and friendship of a number of superb jurists, including Gus Van Harten, Jamie Cameron, Craig Scott (then head of the terrific Nathanson Centre), Peer Zumbansen, Bruce Ryder, Brian Slattery, Robert Wai, Susan Drummond, Marilyn Pilkington, Ed Waitzer, and, among others, François Tanguay-Renaud.

Professor Fred Lazar of the Schulich School of Business, perhaps the best professor during all of my erstwhile student life (alongside the late Fred Halliday of the London School of Economics), has become a dear friend and continued source of warm critique laced with hearty encouragement. I am ever grateful to him for his support of this book and for his incisive interventions throughout its drafting.

The University of Toronto's School of Public Policy and Governance (SPPG) has been my intellectual home for the past five years. It is the best policy school in the country because it enjoys the leadership of one of the country's most talented young policy entrepreneurs in my friend and colleague Mark Stabile, the school's founding director. I am grateful to Mark for having brought me into the SPPG fold in 2009 as well as to my many long-standing SPPG colleagues: Anita Srinivasan, Ian Clark, Pam Bryant, Petra Jory, Zora Anaya, Phil Triadafilopoulos, Carolyn Tuohy, Linda White, Garth Frazer, Tony Dean, James Radner, Matthew Mendelsohn, Chaviva Hosek, Bob Rae, Ito Peng, and Michael Baker.

Mel Cappe is not only a colleague and friend at SPPG but also first hired me in the embryonic days of what has since become the remarkable Recruitment of Policy Leaders (RPL) program in the Government of Canada. Mel was Clerk of the Privy Council Office (PCO) at the time. Ever the gentleman, he allowed a reasonably green (and, granted, somewhat cocky) graduate student to march into his office in the Langevin Block across from Parliament Hill in early 2002. Mel asked: "Studin, what's the solution to the Israel-Palestine conflict?" Studin answered: "There is no solution." Cappe retorted: "You're hired."

In my time at PCO, I was exposed to some of Canada's leading policy practitioners – many of whom rained generosity on me and allowed me to get much of the exposure and immersion that were formative in the thinking that led to this book and cognate publications: Alex Himelfarb, Janice Charette, Graham Flack, George Anderson, Robert Fonberg,

Margaret Biggs, Robert Wright, William Elliott, Yaprak Baltacioglu, Claude Laverdure, Jonathan Fried, Ben Rowswell, Neil Bouwer, Allen Sutherland, and many others.

Ed Morgan and Douglas Sanderson of the University of Toronto Faculty of Law were kind enough to comment on early drafts of the manuscript. Michael Byers of the University of British Columbia provided invaluable advice for the Arctic case study in Part II of the book.

If I have often been a fierce public and scholarly critic of the quality of Canada's foreign policy thinking, debate, and practice (for reasons made plain in this tome), I nevertheless believe that Canada's legal or juridical classes are arguably without par. In the context of my research for this book, the lawyers whom I have come to know at the federal Department of Justice are consummate professionals who are masters of their craft. I speak in particular of Warren Newman, Stanley Cohen, Ron Stevenson, Joanne Kellerman, Alan Kessel, and Ken Watkin.

A number of exceptionally hard-working research assistants were invaluable in helping me to solve some of the factual and conceptual puzzles of this book: Misha Munim, Zach Paikin, Jaclyn Volkhammer, Sarah Carpenter, and Steven Wang.

Finally, I am always blessed by the indulgence and love of my beautiful Allochka (Alla), my wife, life partner, and mother to the three other loves of my life who have succeeded in making the final proofing of this book a breathless and sleepless affair. My old and dear friend Sam Sasan Shoamanesh, of the International Criminal Court and managing editor of *Global Brief* magazine (if I may, by far Canada's premier international affairs magazine, with a heavy global readership), was pivotal in getting my juices flowing about constitutional law. I am ever grateful to him for his friendship, loyalty, and kindness.

Sincere thanks to Randy Schmidt, Holly Keller, Nadine Pedersen, and the terrific team at UBC Press for allowing such books to be published. If not them, as the rabbi once said, then who?

The Strategic Constitution

Introduction

In Canada, after the English and the French, the most significant historical solitudes are arguably the Constitution and Strategy. Indeed, while Canada's constitutional framework and its various constitutional debates give ample expression to the first two solitudes, they are largely silent on strategy and strategic power, which deal, in the classical international or foreign relations sense, with "strategic" instruments of state employed for "strategic" effect in the world.[1]

This constitutional silence is hardly accidental. The little-read second recital of the preamble to the *Constitution Act, 1867*[2] (once the *British North America Act, 1867*, and hereafter the "1867 Act"), reads that the "Union would conduce to the Welfare of the Provinces and promote the Interests of the British Empire." The only provision of the 1867 Act that explicitly references foreign affairs is section 132, though it speaks to the implementation by Canada of *imperial* or British Empire treaty obligations. I will return to section 132 later. For now, I can propose with reasonable certainty that both the character and the paucity of explicit language on *strategy* in the text of the founding legal document of the modern Canadian state betray a fundamental reality: that Canada, *constitutionally speaking*, was *never* intended or expected to be a power player of any note in the world. Rather, Canada was constituted as a strategic appendage or "auxiliary kingdom" of the British Empire – its instruments and interests subsumed to the strategic designs and direction of Westminster.[3]

Canada's *a*strategic constitutional conception finds expression in both Canadian constitutional scholarship and constitutional jurisprudence. Canadian constitutional scholars and courts have historically been exercised, first and foremost, by concerns of federalism or federal-provincial division of powers, largely exclusive of foreign or strategic affairs. For the sake of simplicity, one can call this realm of focus the "federalism school" of Canadian constitutional scholarship. And, since the advent of the *Charter of Rights and Freedoms* in 1982, Canadian constitutional scholars and courts have increasingly focused on questions of civil liberties, as part of what one can call the "rights school" of Canadian constitutional scholarship. (Much like the text of the *Constitution Act, 1867*, the text of the *Constitution Act, 1982*,[4] hereafter the "1982 Act," in which the Charter figures prominently, is conspicuously silent on foreign affairs; the domestic realm is king!)

International relations scholars or strategic analysts in Canada, in turn, are little concerned with the Constitution.[5] They focus primarily on the international order and typically see the Canadian domestic order – politics, really, far more than the Constitution – as relevant only at the level of strategic decision making or praxis by the federal government: to go or not to go to war; to provide more or less funding for defence or foreign affairs; or to give development funding to, or conclude an international treaty or trade agreement with, country X rather than country Y, or group of countries A rather than group of countries B. Some "realist" international relations scholars, borrowing heavily from the neoclassical theory of the firm in economics, even fancy the domestic order altogether irrelevant.

So one comes closer to the core *problématique*: the constitutionalists are radically inward looking, while the strategists are, with few exceptions, constitutional philistines. Yet, conceptually speaking, the Constitution and strategy are but flip sides of the same Canadian enterprise (the Canadian state) – or at least the legitimacy of that enterprise. The Constitution, concerned as it is with law, is representative of the *internal* legitimacy of the Canadian state, while strategy, concerned as it is with power, is representative of the *external* legitimacy of the Canadian state.

British historian Michael Howard says as much in his preface to Philip Bobbitt's *The Shield of Achilles*:

> This is Bobbitt's starting point: "Law and strategy are mutually affecting." There is a constant interaction between the two. Legitimacy itself "is a constitutional idea that is sensitive to strategic events" – not least to a "strategic event" so cataclysmic as losing a war. Nevertheless, although wars may create and mould states, it is the State that creates legitimacy both domestic and external, and it is legitimacy that maintains "peace." If states can no longer maintain their legitimacy, or if their capacity to do so is called into question, then there will be another war, the outcome of which will create a new legitimacy.[6]

Henry Kissinger, for all intents and purposes, alludes to the same dyad of constitution and strategy when he defines the state as "by definition the expression of some concept of justice that legitimizes its internal arrangements and of a projection of power that determines its ability to fulfill its minimum functions – that is, to protect its population from foreign dangers and domestic upheaval."[7]

Question: if there is logical or conceptual interdependence between the two faces – the first internal, the second external – of the legitimacy of the Canadian state, then why does this interdependence find such little expression in the psyches of its principal Canadian interpreters?

Since the *Statute of Westminster, 1931*[8] at the official earliest, though more likely, in practical terms, by the start of the Second World War, when the Canadian government's (and Parliament's) declaration of war was at last differentiable – if only slightly – from that of the United Kingdom, Canada has effectively acquired the trappings of a proper and serious player in international relations, including an independent diplomacy and an independent capacity to declare (or not) and wage war. Although Canada had no formal diplomatic capacity at Confederation, it did have a modicum of military power projection against the Americans – specifically, volunteer (non-professional) land and naval militias that acted in support of British regulars, for all of which, under section 15 of the 1867 Act, the "Command-in-Chief" was "declared to continue and be vested in the Queen" (in whom "Executive Government and Authority of and over Canada" were vested under section 9), and legislative responsibility for which lay with Parliament under section 91(7), the so-called militia and defence power. However, the Canadian militias, whether mobilized for domestic strategic purposes (such as insurrection, rebellion, or other emergency) or, to the extent possible, deployed internationally – more probably continentally – were, in accordance with the said constitutional preamble, to be in the strict service of the interests of the British Empire. (To which the Canadian constitutionalist F.R. Scott adroitly replied: "[W]hat does 'promote the interests of the British Empire' mean in law?"[9]) But when independent diplomatic and military capabilities – strategic capabilities – eventually did accrue to the Canadian state in practice, one could not deny that Canada was at last a state that could project or attempt to project independent power – strategic power – in the world. Such independent strategic capabilities (or strategic *means*, as it were) now allowed the Canadian state to pursue strategic interests (or strategic *ends*, as it were) of various descriptions and intensities, depending, *inter alia*, on the culture, preferences, and chutzpah of the government of the day.

This leaves one with the remarkable paradox of Canada being able to project strategic power in the world despite the *prima facie* absence of any explicit textual reference to any particular strategic capabilities in either the *Constitution Act, 1867* or the *Constitution Act, 1982*, or in any other Canadian constitutional text, for that matter.[10] Canada's Constitution, unlike that of, say, Australia,[11] a reasonably comparable former British colony, has no explicit foreign affairs power. And, as for the said militia power of section 91(7), perhaps because it was not intended to be understood outside the context of British imperial power, it was, according to the late great Canadian jurist Bora Laskin, scarcely developed and "never authoritatively defined"[12] in the constitutional jurisprudence.

Therefore, one can be easily forgiven for presuming, at first glance, that Canada's Constitution – the essentially parochial "iron cage" that frames its internal arrangements – has little to say about Canadian strategic power, notwithstanding the said conceptual interaction between the state's internal and external authorities; or, in other words, that modern Canadian strategic affairs effectively exist *outside* the conceptual – though certainly not the legal – orbit of the Constitution. Indeed, many constitutionalists and international strategists seem to have concluded thus – often implicitly or even instinctually, if not explicitly – thereby concretizing the two aforementioned solitudes. However, they have so concluded in error, as I will demonstrate in this book, for deep in the bowels of the Constitution, by dint of either genius or serendipity, lie many of the essential building blocks of Canadian strategic power.

I will argue first that these strategic building blocks can be identified and second that, notwithstanding the Constitution's astrategic original design, and despite ostensibly astrategic interpretation of that Constitution by judges and scholars alike, the Canadian state has emerged with a solid, indeed powerful, strategic core – one that, in theory, is *constitutionally capable* of projecting substantial strategic power in the world. Praxis, as mentioned, is a different matter – and this for a variety of historical-political-cultural reasons. In this book, I will illustrate the parameters of this theoretical constitutional capability. In other words, the task at hand is to explain *Canadian strategic power in constitutional terms*. Or, in still other words, I will embark on a unique exercise in what might be called "constitutional statics" to demonstrate ultimately how a domestically oriented "supreme law" underpins, informs, and conditions, in theory and then in practice, Canada's performance in affairs strategic. In so doing, I hope to outline the conceptual parameters of a new, *third school* of Canadian constitutional scholarship: call it "strategy and the Constitution" or, better still, *The Strategic Constitution*.

Structure of the Book
The book is divided into two parts. Part I develops a conceptual framework for assessing and interpreting Canada's strategic power in terms of, or according to, the Constitution. The fundamental argument mobilized is that Canadian strategic power can be distilled from an audit of the Constitution and that this Canadian strategic power, in such constitutional terms, is significant, notwithstanding any practical appearances

to the contrary. Chapter 1 explains what is meant by strategic power, defines Canada's Constitution, and, most importantly, introduces a central, *de novo* construct called "the Strategic Constitution," which contains all the elements or factors of strategic power contained in the Constitution for the purpose of the subsequent strategic audit. Chapter 1 also stresses the importance of federalism (including the Quebec question) and even Aboriginal rights to a proper understanding of Canadian strategic power.

Still in Part I, Chapters 2 through 8 comprise the strategic audit of the Constitution, as anticipated by the Strategic Constitution construct outlined in Chapter 1. Chapter 2 deals with the diplomatic instrument of Canadian power. Chapter 3 discusses the Canadian military instrument. (As explained below, each of the diplomatic and military instruments is also, in and of itself, a manifestation or output or tentacle, as it were, of Canadian strategic power; that is, Canadian strategic power can be evaluated in terms of the potency of the diplomatic and military instruments, properly defined, of the federal state.)[13] Chapter 4 deals with the potency of the executive branch of the federal state as a third factor of strategic power. Chapter 5 addresses Canada's natural resources (and, less centrally, food). Chapter 6 treats the national economy. Chapter 7 deals with communications. And Chapter 8, finally, assesses the demographic or population factor of Canadian strategic power.

Part II applies the conceptual framework developed in Part I to four different policy case studies that are, in this early twenty-first century, of significant strategic moment for the Canadian state: Canadian strategic leadership in the Americas (as first proposed by the Canadian government in 2007) (Case Study A); bona fide war (as was the case in Korea and, until recently, Afghanistan) (Case Study B); Canadian Arctic sovereignty (Case Study C); and counterterrorism in the post-9/11 security environment (Case Study D). Each case study shows the Strategic Constitution in action or, in other words, the constitutional underpinnings of key (practical) Canadian decisions and actions in strategically important scenarios.

Parts I and II together allow one to conclude that Canada enjoys and profits from a highly flexible national constitutional framework that, though not consciously designed – and, in many cases, not jurisprudentially interpreted – for the purpose of meaningful performance in international affairs, may in practice be applied, with great effect, for considerable national strategic achievement. This central *constat* lends itself – perhaps counterintuitively – to the suggestion that many major *practical* Canadian strategic achievements – including those that might await in this new century – can be interpreted through, and explained by, a national Constitution that quietly harbours the seeds of national strategic potency.

PART I
The Conceptual Framework for Assessing Canadian Strategic Power in Constitutional Terms

Framing Some Key Concepts 1

What Is Canadian Strategic Power?

A state's (external) power can be defined as its *capacity* to intentionally make a foreign party – usually another state or group of states and non-state affiliates – do (or not do) something that the party would otherwise not have done (or would have done). As already suggested, my principal interest in Part I is in power as *capacity*, not power as *exercise*, except insofar as the exercise helps one to define the capacity. (Exercise, to be clear, is a decision for governments, whereas capacity can, on my argument, be explained in constitutional terms.) For purposes of the Constitution, this definition of state power is to be distinguished from any notion of "soft," so-called Nyean power[1] that might be projected or, in the legal parlance, "transplanted" by a state such as Canada indirectly or inadvertently in virtue of, or through, its constitutional regime – for instance, through the Charter or some specific decision of the Canadian courts – something tantamount to a "signalling" or "demonstration" effect on the behaviour of other states. It is also to be distinguished from the *negative* power – or "drag" or "rigidity" – associated with the numerous *processes* of constitutional building, bargaining, and negotiating that have marked most of the life of the modern Canadian federation. Strategic power is power used by the state in the pursuit of strategic interests (*ends*) – such as security, sovereignty, territorial integrity, wealth, or prestige – or, more readily, power pursued by *means* of strategic instruments, the most classical and important of which are diplomatic and military instruments (properly defined). So, *constitutionally speaking*, one can posit that the character of Canada's strategic power can be explained at least partially not so much by the strategic interests (*ends*) pursued by the state – which have been and continue to be many and variable, depending on policy choices made by governments – but by the key strategic instruments, the *means* – in particular, and ultimately, diplomacy and the military – used over time by the Canadian state in aid or service of such interests.

Naturally, since I am interested in the nexus between strategic power and the Constitution, I ought to emphasize that the relevant type of strategic power, for my purposes, is that exercised through *constitutionally legitimate* channels – that is, channels permitted by the Constitution. (States can and often do exercise strategic power through constitutionally illegitimate channels.) Leaving aside the numerous and broadly understood possible benefits of federalism for purposes of *domestic* administration in a country as vast and complex as Canada, and leaving aside the obvious need for a robust rights framework that can control the arbitrary use of government power, I will assume, as a general rule, that the more powerful the federal executive – the "strategic centre," as it were, of the Canadian state – in respect of the *factors (or elements) of strategic power* discussed below, the greater the strategic potency of Canada's diplomatic and military instruments and therefore the greater the aggregate strategic power of the Canadian state. Moreover, notwithstanding the recent string of minority federal governments in Canada, I will also assume, for all intents and purposes, that the more expansive the legislative powers of Parliament in respect of a particular factor of strategic power, the greater the power, *in most cases*, of the federal executive (the "strategic centre") in respect of the same factor of strategic power.[2, 3]

The Constitutional Elements of Canadian Strategic Power
I should be precise about what I mean by the term "constitution." For the Constitution of Canada, properly understood, is far more – and more complex – than just the *Constitution Acts* of 1867 and 1982, even though

these acts are clearly the cornerstones of the "written" or textual Constitution, as defined in section 52(2) of the 1982 Act.[4] Indeed, a more labyrinthine body of principles, conventions, and, critically, judicial decisions (jurisprudence) comprises the "unwritten" parts of the Constitution – some of them more "constitutional" than others. Writes the constitutional scholar Patrick Monahan:

> There are ... many enactments or rules of a constitutional nature that are not included in the definition of the Constitution of Canada in section 52(2). These "unentrenched" documents include all the pre-Confederation constitutional documents such as the *Royal Proclamation of 1763*, the *Constitutional Act, 1791*, and the *Union Act, 1840* ... Constitutional conventions, ordinary statutes of an organic character, and treaties with Aboriginal peoples [or land claims agreements] are likewise not referred to in section 52 ... Since these enactments or rules are not [strictly speaking] part of the Constitution of Canada, they are not subject to the procedures for amendment established by Part V [of the *Constitution Act, 1982*].[5]

The *Statute of Westminster, 1931*, which, as discussed above, speaks to the legislative equality of the Parliament of Canada with that of Westminster, as well as the capacity of the former to legislate extraterritorially, is doubtless a part of the formal Constitution – item 17 of the schedule to the *Constitution Act, 1982*, referenced in section 52(2)(b). The *Letters Patent Constituting the Office of the Governor-General of Canada, 1947*, however, which empower the governor general of Canada, *inter alia*, to approve the credentials of foreign diplomats, are not, strictly speaking, part of the Constitution, according to the list of instruments in the schedule to the 1982 Act. Still, on a broader conception of the Constitution, one might well regard these letters patent as an integral part of Canada's effective constitutional framework, given their genetic connection to the representative of the head of the Canadian state.

The 1867 Act is by a considerable margin the most important part of the Constitution for purposes of assessing Canadian strategic power.[6] Despite its provincial – or "colonial" – design, if one is creative, key elements or building blocks of strategic power can be identified within its framework. Specific sections – which can be called *strategic sections* – of the act effectively deal with determinants of power that can have material influence on the potency of the two central strategic instruments of the Canadian state – diplomacy and the military – and therefore on the aggregate strategic power of the state. These strategic sections implicitly or explicitly address diplomatic and military capabilities per se as well as factors of strategic power such as the pure potency of the executive branch of government, convertible natural resource potential, national economic might or industrial capacity, communications capacity, and national population (quality, quantity, and distribution). Granted, these categories are stylized, even crude. They are also not mutually exclusive or, for that matter, exhaustive: other factors, such as geography (Canada has the world's second largest land mass)[7] and national morale or psyche or geist or character, come to mind, but they are all too abstract, over-inclusive, or otherwise too diffusely treated in the Constitution; as a consequence, they are less susceptible to serious examination. Technology, broadly conceived, would also appear to be strategically material for a modern state such as Canada; it is arguably subsumed, however, in the more "discrete" natural resources, communications, and economy factors of power. So the contention here, in the apparent absence of *deliberate* strategic architecture in the Canadian Constitution, is that the identified elements of power may be usefully "mined," as it were, to obtain a more meaningful, *implied* picture of the strategic power latent in Canada's constitutional makeup.

I have already mentioned two sections of the 1867 Act in which the military instrument finds explicit textual expression – sections 15 and 91(7). To these one can add the lesser known section 117 (an executive power), which reads that the provinces retain public property that is not treated in the 1867 Act, subject to the right of Canada to "assume any Lands or Public Property required for Fortifications or for the Defence of the Country." There is also, to be pedantic, the schedule to section 108 (the third schedule to the 1867 Act), which enumerates as federal property at Confederation strategic assets such as military roads, ordnance property and armouries, drill sheds, military clothing, and munitions of war.

For its part, the diplomatic instrument, as established near the outset, finds no support in an explicit foreign affairs legislative power. However, it is indirectly addressed in the jurisprudence on section 132, the imperial treaty power – most notoriously in the still-contested *Labour Conventions*[8] decision of 1937, discussed below. And section 9, which, as mentioned, vests in the queen executive authority over Canada, applies more broadly, via the royal prerogative, to both the diplomatic and the military instruments as manifestations of executive strategic power.

The *royal* or *Crown prerogative*, which provides the essential constitutional underpinning for the conduct of foreign affairs by the Canadian federal executive, is pivotal to an understanding of the constitutional treatment of the diplomatic and military instruments. This prerogative, which exists at common law, is said to be a vestige of the arbitrary or discretionary power of the sovereign. It implicitly finds its place in Canadian constitutionalism by virtue of the influential first recital of the preamble to the 1867 Act, which declares that the dominion is "under the Crown" and that the Constitution is "similar in Principle to that of the United Kingdom," as well as in the aforementioned sections 9 and 15 of the same act.[9] In the United Kingdom, it was the *sui generis* character of international relations or foreign affairs that commended the domain to the exercise of the royal prerogative. Of this, legendary British jurist William Blackstone wrote:

> The Crown, therefore, enjoys the sole rights of appointing ambassadors, diplomatic agents, consuls and other officers, through whom intercourse with foreign nations is conducted, and of receiving those of foreign States, of making treaties, declaring peace and war, and generally of conducting all foreign relations. Such matters are entrusted in general to the absolute discretion of the Sovereign, acting through the recognized constitutional channels ..., unfettered by any direct supervision, parliamentary or otherwise.[10]

The Charter – the centrepiece of the 1982 Act – also has a small handful of scarcely obvious strategic sections, even if it is a self-consciously *domestic* document; that is, a document not meant to have conspicuous strategic consequence. Section 4(2), for instance, speaks to extension of the life of Parliament (and a legislative assembly) "[i]n time of real or apprehended war, invasion or insurrection." The mobility rights in section 6 can be seen, *inter alia*, as a proxy for assessing the power – or, more likely, the lack of power – of the state in determining population placement or distribution. There is the section 7 "right to life, liberty and security of the person," which has been invoked in a number of important Canadian cases involving strategy – cases discussed in this book – as well as the notwithstanding clause in section 33. And, of course, under section 1, all these rights are guaranteed by the Charter "subject only to such limits prescribed by law as can be demonstrably justified in a free and democratic society."

I have yet to discuss a good number of strategic sections in both the 1867 Act and the 1982 Act, but it is sufficient to say here that, for all the strategic sections of the Constitution (as with virtually all sections of the Constitution), a mere textual reading fails to convey the actual meaning or import of the provision in question. For this, given the scope of Canada's unwritten Constitution, as Bora Laskin tried to do with the militia power, one must inevitably look to the jurisprudence on each strategic section to see how judges have defined or interpreted the section in key cases. One must also survey, in concert with these strategic sections, relevant doctrines, principles, conventions, and indeed, in some instances, certain major statutes that can be said to effectively enjoy "quasi-constitutional" status, given their potential impacts on policy-political praxis and the likelihood that they are little susceptible to material amendment or repeal in the foreseeable future.

Figure 1 provides a stylized breakdown of the sections of the Constitution most associated with key factors or elements of Canadian strategic power. Taken together these strategic sections can be said to make up what I call Canada's Strategic Constitution. Diplomacy and the military – for all practical intents and purposes – can be thought of as both elements of Canadian power and the pivotal instruments of this power. I presume that each other element of power, taken on its own or in combination with one or more other elements, has material influence – positive or negative – on the aggregate force of the diplomatic and

Framing Some Key Concepts 19

FIGURE 1 Canada's Strategic Constitution

Power element	Constitution Act, 1867	Charter of Rights and Freedoms (in the Constitution Act, 1982)[a]
Diplomacy	Preamble/royal prerogative; ss. 9; 91 general power (POGG); 132	
Military	Preamble/royal prerogative; ss. 9; 15; 91(7); 108; 117	
Executive strength of central (federal) government[b]	Preamble/royal prerogative; ss. 9; POGG; 91(11); 91(27); 91(29); 92(10)(c)	ss. 1; 4(2); 6; 7-14; 33; also s. 35(1) (part of the 1982 Act but not part of the Charter)
Natural resources (and food)	ss. 91(1A); 91(24); 92A; 95; 108; 109	
Economy	POGG; ss. 91(1A); 91(2); 91(3); 91(24); 91(29); 92(10); 92(13); 92(16); 121; 122	
Communications	POGG; ss. 91(29); 92(10); 92(13); 91(27); 92(16)	
Population	ss. 91(25); 95	

a The Charter provisions that make up Canada's Strategic Constitution are those most likely to come into play against exercises of government power based on the common law or legislative heads of power cited in the 1867 Act and 1982 Act. The same applies to s. 35(1) of the 1982 Act, discussed below (relating to Aboriginal and treaty rights), which usually goes hand in hand with the s. 91(24) federal head of power for "Indians, and Lands reserved for the Indians" (*R. v. Sparrow*, [1990] S.C.J. No. 49). In this sense, they cannot easily be separated into discrete categories along the lines of the various elements or factors of power listed in the first column.

b One might think it a misnomer to call this factor of power "executive strength [or potency] of central government," given that, apart from the royal prerogative and s. 9 of the 1867 Act, all the various sections underpinning this factor of power refer to Parliament's (legislative) powers and not to the powers of the federal executive. However, I have already assumed in this book that executive power follows the grant of legislative power (see *supra* note 2), in the context of both majority and minority governments, even if this dynamic is mitigated or complicated somewhat in minority government situations.

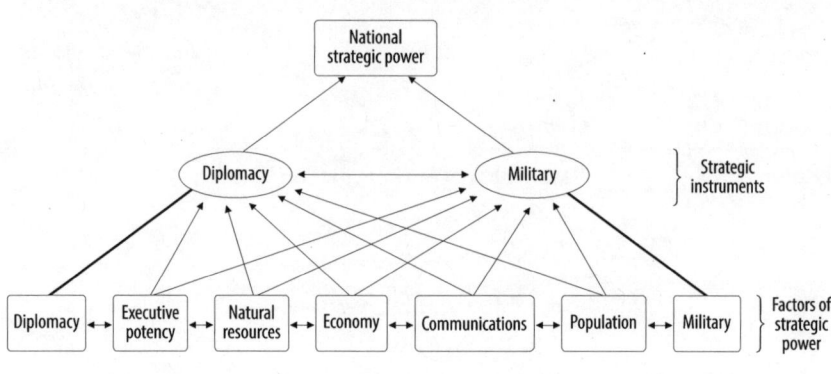

Figure 2 The factors or elements of Canadian national strategic power

military instruments.[11] The challenge, then, is to determine whether jurisprudence on each of these sections, combined with analysis of relevant doctrines, conventions, and statutes, can add meat to the (textual) bones of each of these elements of power – the bones of the Strategic Constitution – to yield a meaningful constitutional picture of Canada's strategic power.

Figure 2 illustrates the interaction among the various factors of strategic power and the diplomatic and military instruments of the Canadian state as they strive to "make" Canadian strategic power. The factors of power can be seen as the building blocks of the Canadian state's strategic power, with the two instruments as the output or manifestation – or tentacles – of this strategic power. There is effective identity between diplomacy and the military as factors of power and instruments of such power. Moreover, it stands to reason that there is dynamic interaction among the various factors of power. These factors are not strictly discrete but illustrative.

Federalism

A defining characteristic of the Canadian Constitution is its federal character. Parliamentary sovereignty is divided exhaustively between Ottawa and the provinces. And notwithstanding the absence of a formal federal foreign affairs power or genuine strategic intent or teleology in the overall edifice, the *Constitution Act, 1867, textually speaking,* paints the picture of a reasonably centralized federation. On paper, the federal government can still disallow provincial legislation or, via a provincial lieutenant governor, reserve provincial legislation for approval by the federal government – even if, by constitutional convention, these capacities are widely thought to be obsolete. More relevant, however, is the fact that most of the levers of strategic power – the militia, along with significant macroeconomic, criminal law, emergency, and nationalization powers – are *prima facie* housed with the federal Parliament and government. Legislative responsibility for immigration, a key lever for increasing the quantity and quality of the national population, which in turn provides fuel for the state's military, diplomatic corps, and industrial base, is divided between Parliament and the provincial legislatures, subject to federal paramountcy; that is, provincial immigration legislation is operative only insofar as it is non-repugnant to federal legislation. Parliament also has concurrent but overriding legislative authority over agriculture, indissociably linked to food supply. (I briefly discuss agriculture and food supply in Chapter 5 in the context of my larger treatment of natural resources as a factor of national strategic power.) Yet legislative responsibility for more traditional natural resources – minerals, metals, forests, and energy goods – lies, rather astrategically, with the provinces, a fact concretized by the 1982 insertion by amendment of section 92A into the 1867 Act. (Legislative responsibility for education, among many other variables, also lies with the provinces. And though I have not identified education as a strict strategic factor or element of power, a none-too-ambitious case can be made that the training – intellectual, cultural, and other – of the national population can impact materially the quality of the diplomatic and military instruments of the state and that, conversely, the absence of such a lever for Parliament can mean, again quite astrategically, that the federal state has little direct control over the "talent" that eventually populates and runs Canadian diplomacy and the Canadian Forces.[12])

Jurisprudence for each of the above strategic areas – particularly from the old Judicial Committee of the Privy Council – has in many cases drastically altered the *prima facie* design of the Fathers of Confederation. The Canadian federation has become far more decentralized than planned. Over the course of this book, I will discuss the jurisprudence for each of the strategic sections outlined in Figure 1. For now, it is enough to note that, prior to the Charter (a largely *a*federal document), the "worldview" of Canadian jurisprudence, even in respect of matters strategic, was conditioned almost without exception by concerns of domestic federalism. It follows that commentators such as H. Scott Fairley have suggested that, "[i]n the absence of textual guidance, notions of divided autonomy gleaned from the jurisprudence of Canadian federalism, not the implications of national sovereignty [or national strategic power, for that matter], came to dominate the judicial interpretation of constitutional principle in relation to the subject of external affairs."[13]

Bref, because of the astrategic conception of the Constitution, and because, the Charter aside, the courts – the Judicial Committee of the Privy Council chief among them – have largely tended to view the "judicial process of applying the federal principle to a symmetrical distribution of legislative and executive powers [as] a *complete* and powerful account of the Canadian federal state,"[14] the serious business of *strategy* has nary been explored in their interpretation of the Constitution – at least not in a conscientious sense. This is as much a problem of constitutional design as it is of Canadian jurisprudential *culture*. Still, the implication is the same: *to date, the Constitution has not been interpreted by judges in a way that is properly sensitive to the legitimate strategic role that the Canadian state today plays and indeed may play in practice (if it so wishes)*. That is, the general inward-lookingness of Canadian jurisprudence – obsessed as it has been with questions of division of powers and, since 1982, Charter rights – has understandably failed to give proper weight to the factual emergence, in policy-political terms, of a Canadian international strategic personality. Yet I argue here that, notwithstanding this lack of strategic culture in the judicature (and among jurists at large), the constitutional structure or framework or architecture that has emerged over the years is strategically solid in many critical respects, and the Canadian state, as a result, is strategically powerful in constitutional terms.

Of course, one should also note the exceptional case of Quebec. In strategic terms, Quebec has been the greatest complicating factor in Canadian federalism and, by extension, Canadian strategic power. Like several other provinces, Quebec has an ambitious program of so-called constituent (provincial) diplomacy in which it engages, *proprio motu*, with other nation-states and sub-national units in its areas of constitutional responsibility. Indeed, since the Quiet Revolution of the 1960s, all Quebec governments, for all intents and purposes, have been guided by the Gérin-Lajoie doctrine, which holds that, in its areas of legislative jurisdiction (sections 92, 92A, 93, and 95 of the 1867 Act), Quebec's powers are not limited to the territorial province. The vast majority of this "diplomacy" is patently transactional, falling well below the threshold of what I understand here to be strategic. Having said this, Quebec has also been, *in practice*, at the core of two conscription crises and was possibly material to the 2003 decision of the federal government not to go to war in Iraq, given the historical antipathy of the Québécois to distant military adventure. Yet the province's disproportionate strategic impact on the federal state *appears* little explained, strictly speaking, by the Constitution – textually or jurisprudentially. Both the 1867 Act and the 1982 Act make asymmetric references to traditional Quebec concerns or, by proxy, French linguistic, cultural, and religious or denominational predilections and protections. Moreover, the *Quebec Act, 1774*,[15] the basic principles of which are arguably part of the aforementioned "unentrenched" Constitution, states in section 8 that, "in all matters relative to property and civil rights, resort shall be had to the [pre-conquest French civil law] for the decision of the same." Such asymmetric references might well have given Quebec *de facto*, though not *de jure*, special status in Canada, but they do not *appear*, constitutionally speaking, to pertain directly to the elements of the strategic power of the Canadian state; that is, they refer almost strictly to the internal arrangements of the state.[16]

In fact, however, Quebec is at the heart of the constitutional-strategic logic of Canadian federalism in at least two key senses. First, Quebec – then Canada-East – was extremely influential in the original division of legislative powers, strategic and otherwise, in sections 91 and 92 of the *Constitution Act, 1867*.[17] (The reference to "property and civil rights" in the old *Quebec Act* led directly to the influential vernacular of "property and civil rights" in section 92(13) of the *Constitution Act, 1867*, which, as will be explained, has been the bane of the highly strategic federal trade and commerce power.[18]) Second, commentators have suggested, not uncontroversially, that a number of decentralizing Privy Council and even Supreme Court decisions, strategic and otherwise, in the past century were much in keeping with a certain reading of political winds in Canada – centrifugal winds that often blew and indeed continue to blow strongest from Quebec. Wrote Trudeau in *Federalism and the French Canadians*: "If the law lords had not leaned in that [provincial] direction, Quebec separation might not be a threat today; it might be an accomplished fact."[19]

Canadian Strategy and Aboriginal Peoples
The connection between Canadian strategy and Canada's Aboriginal peoples, in constitutional terms, is hugely counterintuitive: consider that, to date, no foreign relations book in Canada has dealt meaningfully with Aboriginal rights, while no book on Canadian Aboriginal law has had anything interesting to say about Canadian foreign policy. This is all still largely untouched terrain in Canadian scholarship. It deserves major treatment in original research. Although this book does not give primary or exhaustive treatment to this fascinating nexus, it would be incomplete if it did not at least begin to articulate some of the basic considerations around a calculus that should before long affect – fundamentally so – Canadian strategy and strategic power as a consequence of the advent of, and jurisprudence unleashed by, section 35(1) of the 1982 Act.

Prior to 1982, Aboriginal considerations had already begun to acquire a proto-constitutional and indeed proto-strategic character from the 1973 *Calder* decision.[20] Until then, Parliament's constitutional dominance over "Indians, and Lands reserved for the Indians," by dint of section 91(24) of the 1867 Act, had made Aboriginal considerations, in constitutional terms, strategically uninteresting, with precious little jurisprudence to subvert a Canadian legal-constitutional regime for Aboriginal governance rooted largely and principally (and quite statically) in statute – predominantly the *Indian Act*[21] – and, more indirectly, imperial executive order in the form of the *Royal Proclamation of 1763*.[22]

Calder posited the existence of Aboriginal title as a legal right the premise of which was continuous, exclusive occupation from the point at which Europeans asserted sovereignty in what would become Canada. The *Calder* decision affirmed that this legal right existed at common law. The 1984 *Guerin*[23] decision reaffirmed the existence of such Aboriginal title at common law (with underlying ownership lying with the provincial, not federal, Crown[24]), adding that the *sui generis* character of Aboriginal title meant that the Crown has a special fiduciary duty in respect of (surrendered) Aboriginal lands. (*Sparrow*,[25] discussed below, subsequently confirmed this fiduciary capacity and generalized it to encompass all Crown relations with Aboriginal peoples and lands.) The *Calder* decision would cause the federal government, in policy, to launch a process to negotiate land claims agreements between the federal Crown and Aboriginal nations. These agreements would later acquire constitutional status through the protection of treaty rights afforded by section 35.

Section 35(1) of the 1982 Act reads: "The existing aboriginal and treaty rights of the aboriginal peoples of Canada are hereby recognized and affirmed." "Aboriginal peoples of Canada" is understood, according to section 35(2), to include Indian, Inuit, and Métis peoples. In addition, section 35(3) reads: "For greater certainty, in subsection (1) 'treaty rights' includes rights that now exist by way of land claim agreements or may be so acquired." Section 35(1) is not part of the Charter and is therefore not subject to section 1 or 33. Section 35(1) is also not subject to section 32(1), which limits Charter application to state actors (that is, Parliament, legislatures, and governments), so one might presume, *prima facie*, that the section applies even to private parties.[26] However, strictly speaking, this appears to be unsettled law at the time of writing, with the 2004 *Haida* case[27] discussed below indicating with perhaps the greatest certainty to date that section 35(1) does not apply directly to private parties.

Enter the 1990 *Sparrow* decision. *Sparrow* established tests and conditions for governmental or legislative infringement of Aboriginal title and rights (title being a subset or special species of Aboriginal rights[28]). In the event of infringement of Aboriginal rights, the justification part of the *Sparrow* framework had two stages: first, the objective of the law or regulatory scheme in question had to be "compelling and substantial"; second, if the objective were deemed to be substantial and compelling, the infringement had to be consistent with Crown honour or the Crown's special fiduciary duty in respect of Aboriginal peoples (with such consistency to be assessed on a case-by-case basis). *Sparrow* suggested that, to meet the standard of consistency with Crown fiduciary duty, the infringement might variously require of the Crown consultation with Aboriginal parties, minimization of harm, prioritization of Aboriginal interests over those of other parties, and, among other things, compensation in the event of expropriation. *Gladstone*[29] refined this formulation, with Chief Justice Lamer stating, at paragraph 56 of his reasons for judgment, that the dispatch of fiduciary duty depended on the "legal and factual context" of each case of infringement.

In *Delgamuukw*,[30] Chief Justice Lamer, building on *Gladstone*, suggested that the scope of constitutional validity or justifiability for government and legislative objectives that infringed section 35(1) rights was broad.[31] He wrote at paragraph 165:

> Most of these objectives can be traced to the reconciliation of the prior occupation of North America by aboriginal peoples with the assertion of Crown sovereignty ... In my opinion, the development of agriculture, forestry, mining, and hydroelectric power, [general economic development], protection of the environment or endangered species, the building of infrastructure and the settlement of foreign populations to support those aims, are the kinds of objectives that are consistent with this purpose and, in principle, can justify the infringement of aboriginal title. Whether a particular measure or government act can be explained by reference to one of those objectives, however, is ultimately a question of fact that will have to be examined on a case-by-case basis.[32]

In *Van der Peet*,[33] the Supreme Court began to put more meat on the bones of Aboriginal rights in section 35(1), the purpose of which was to "provide the constitutional framework through which the fact that aboriginals lived on the land in distinctive societies, with their own practices, traditions and cultures, is ... reconciled with the sovereignty of the Crown." This construction of section 35(1) set the effective field for considerations of Canadian strategy in relation to Aboriginal claims and interests – to wit, the intersection or tension ("reconciliation") between Crown objectives (variously defined) and Aboriginal rights (variously defined).

In *Mitchell*,[34] Justice Binnie firmly reasserted this essential field of strategic considerations, explaining that the basic tenets of Crown sovereignty made Aboriginal rights necessarily conditional and that there remained a degree of "sovereign incompatibility" between certain Aboriginal rights and certain objectives of the Canadian state. Binnie was mostly exercised by the goal of border control and territorial integrity – legitimate ends of the federal government, in his view. Nevertheless, at paragraph 153, he gave the following counterfactual, perhaps as unvarnished an articulation of the relationship between the Constitution and strategy as has been offered in all Canadian jurisprudence and scholarly commentary to date:

> [I]t could not be said, in my view, that pre-contact [Mohawk] warrior activities gave rise under successor regimes to a *legal right* under s. 35(1) to engage in military adventures on Canadian territory. Canadian sovereign authority has, as one of its inherent characteristics, a monopoly on the *lawful* use of military force within its territory. I do not accept that the Mohawks *could* acquire under s. 35(1) a legal right to deploy a military force in what is now Canada, as and when they choose to do so, even if the warrior tradition was to be considered a defining feature of pre-contact Mohawk society.

The 2004 *Haida*[35] decision solidly confirmed the Crown's duty, rooted in the honour of the Crown, to consult meaningfully, in good faith, with First Nations parties, even on the presumption of possible or as yet unproven infringement of Aboriginal rights. Where appropriate and depending on the specific facts and context, there might be a concomitant duty to accommodate Aboriginal claims reasonably, even if there is no strict requirement for the Crown and Aboriginal parties to come to full agreement, substantively, after consultation. In the companion case of *Taku River*,[36] the Supreme Court stated at paragraph 25 that "[r]esponsiveness is a key requirement of both consultation and accommodation." The section 35 duty to consult and accommodate would also apply, where relevant, to the provincial Crown,[37] though it would not strictly apply, and could not be outsourced, to private or third parties, such as energy, mining, or forestry concerns.

If the accepted field of jurisprudence today is the said intersection between the objectives, purposes, or ends of the Canadian state and an array of Aboriginal rights (including Aboriginal title), and if the duty of the Canadian state to consult is triggered even in anticipation of state infringement of Aboriginal rights in the pursuit of state objectives, then a key line of strategic inquiry that will play itself out in the coming decades is the extent to which (and the manner in which) the Canadian state's factors of power – particularly its economic and natural resource factors of power and therefore ultimately its diplomatic and military instruments – are attenuated or compromised by the accrual of strategic levers in the hands of Aboriginal groups (who are becoming "strategically relevant" actors in their own right[38]). To be sure, such a dynamic might, other things being equal, help the cause of domestic stability or even "justice," as it were, in Canada – that is, once again, reconciling Aboriginal interests with the purposes of the Crown – but it might also militate unwittingly against Canada's capacity, constitutionally speaking, to achieve a variety of ends in world affairs (including, *en passant*, domestic stability).

Diplomacy 2

Diplomacy is one of the two cardinal instruments of Canadian strategic power. The other instrument is the military. Both diplomacy and the military are also factors or elements of Canadian strategic power. As such, they evidently influence aggregate national strategic power, as expressed by the same diplomatic and military instruments. (For instance, in simple terms, a strong military influences not only the military, by identity, but can also, as with major economic or industrial capacity, greatly enhance diplomacy.) Of diplomacy, the German American power theorist Hans Morgenthau once wrote:

> Of all the factors that make for the power of a nation, the most important, however unstable, is the quality of diplomacy ... The conduct of a nation's foreign affairs by its diplomats is for national power in peace what military strategy and tactics by its military leaders are for national power in war. It is the art of bringing the different elements of the national power to bear with maximum effect upon those points in the international situation which concern the national interest most directly.[1]

Of course, with the decline of the conventional foreign ministry and the concomitant rise of internationally active "domestic" ministries (or, in the case of Canada, the effective return to the original model of the prime minister as foreign minister), it is not just diplomats who carry out the business of diplomacy. Rather, diplomacy, as I understand it here, is *broadly conceived* to include subsidiary *strategic* instruments such as, *inter alia*, treaties (including trade and investment agreements, discussed in Chapter 6 on national economic might), development aid, sanctions, intelligence, and various types of "information sharing." Diplomacy also includes strategic capabilities such as coercion, negotiation, lobbying, important (strategic) appointments, membership in key international organizations, and international deployment of certain national assets. I will treat only some of these capabilities.

Treaties, while once considered the principal and classical currency of state-to-state diplomacy, are but one of multiple instruments of strategic diplomacy today – arguably a diminishing one in Canadian politics, both in absolute and in relative terms.[2] Yet, paradoxically, because of the proliferation of scholarly commentary on the *Labour Conventions* case of 1937,[3] the constitutional debate about foreign affairs – or, more broadly, strategy – in Canada to this day is disproportionately preoccupied with the question of treaties.[4] In *Labour Conventions*, the Judicial Committee of the Privy Council, in interpreting the imperial treaty implementation provision of section 132 of the 1867 Act, conceived of the division of powers between the federal and provincial governments as "watertight compartments," thereby distributing treaty *implementation* power between the federal and provincial legislatures and governments, depending on whether a treaty subject matter falls under federal, provincial, or joint jurisdiction. Critics of this decision continue to denounce it as having emasculated not only the federal treaty implementation power but also, in practice, the federal capacity to negotiate international treaties purposefully and efficiently – a power formally and exclusively reserved for the federal government under the royal prerogative – because the federal government is often forced to pre-consult extensively, and sometimes unsuccessfully, with the provinces.[5]

From a strictly strategic perspective, the critique is not misplaced. The state of the Canadian federal treaty power stands in marked contrast to that of, say, the Australian Commonwealth (federal) government – as mentioned, a government highly comparable to that of Canada – for which the *Commonwealth of Australia Constitution Act, 1900*[6] provides an explicit external affairs power in section 51(xxix) and for which the Australian High Court decided favourably in two landmark cases involving treaty powers in the early 1980s: *Koowarta*[7] and, most importantly, *Tasmanian Dam*.[8] In both cases, the High Court affirmed that the Commonwealth government had constitutional authority, under section 51(xxix), to unilaterally implement international treaties, even those affecting areas of state responsibility. Suffice it to say that the Commonwealth government in Canberra has since been activist in strategically – on occasion, some might suggest, even colourably – levering the external affairs section and the concomitant expansive treaty power. In contrast, as a practical example of the strategic emasculation of the Canadian federal executive in respect of treaties, even at the negotiation phase, the Government of Canada to date has had considerable difficulty agreeing on a consolidated "Canadian" position on a number of aspects of major trade deals, including with the European Union (the most recent major Canadian trade negotiation), as a result of the need to regularly consult with the provinces on jurisdictional matters that would presumably affect the implementability of an eventual agreement.[9]

Labour Conventions notwithstanding, Canadian diplomatic activity, as I have defined it, remains highly concentrated in the federal executive. This is very much on account of, and consistent with, the continued dominance of the royal prerogative in strategic affairs. And while legislation in Canada has gradually clipped or displaced the royal prerogative in matters purely domestic or otherwise astrategic, in Canada there has been a distinctive dearth of legislative override of the prerogative in matters external or, to a lesser extent, strategic. (Where there is proper foreign affairs legislation, it would typically fall under the general legislative power of Parliament found in the opening words of section 91 of the 1867 Act, as a residual power.) For example, prior to the federal budget bill of 2013,[10] which merged the Department of Foreign Affairs and International Trade (DFAIT) with the Canadian International Development Agency (CIDA), the *Department of Foreign Affairs and International Trade Act*[11] was, in all, only thirteen sections long – that is, laconic and transactional (or strategically unremarkable, as it were). Moreover, until the passage in 2008 of a private member's bill (Bill C-293), the *Official*

Development Assistance Accountability Act,[12] there existed no formal Canadian legislation touching on international development assistance. That act defined official development assistance (ODA) in law and provided for specific and regular reporting requirements on Canadian ODA activities by the government to Parliament. Still, the act left much of the royal prerogative of the government untouched, which meant that CIDA remained without formal enabling legislation and that its activities continued to be largely governed by the prerogative – presumably consistent with the predilection of the government of the day; hence, one might surmise, the government's support of the (non-opposition) private member's bill.

What of intelligence? I discuss *security intelligence* below, noting that Canada does not, at the time of writing, have a pure or classical *foreign intelligence* agency. Having said this, a new (human) foreign intelligence agency, once softly mooted and later abandoned by the last federal Conservative government, distinct from the Canadian Security Intelligence Service (CSIS) and operating outside the strict ambit of both sections 12 and 16 of the *CSIS Act*[13] (itself "quasi-constitutional" on a loose understanding), could arguably be stood up on the strength of the royal prerogative alone; that is, without enabling legislation.[14] The Canadian Forces, outside the (foreign) communications intelligence capability provided by the Communications Security Establishment (CSE),[15] regulated under the *National Defence Act*,[16] already enjoy such an in-house, foreign (human), and analytic intelligence capability in the form of the Chief of Defence Intelligence (CDI) organization, which operates solely under the aegis of the royal prerogative. Similarly, to take but one more example, the existence and character of diplomatic reporting – quasi-foreign intelligence, as it were – emanating from Canadian embassies and consulates around the world, as well as the analytic intelligence capability of the International Assessment Staff (IAS) in the Privy Council Office, are also essentially extralegislative, underpinned only by the royal prerogative.

Canadian courts, for their part, like their counterparts in other Commonwealth countries, even if they have historically been given to judicial review of prerogative powers in matters domestic, until fairly recently took the royal prerogative to be largely non-justiciable in most matters strategic – particularly in relation to foreign affairs, defence, and national security. This presumption of non-justiciability was a function of both a perception by the judiciary that there was functional propriety in unfettered executive discretion in strategic matters (in foreign affairs, defence, and national security) and a corresponding reluctance by that judiciary to make decisions that, institutionally speaking, might be beyond its ken.[17]

This deference began to yield to more aggressive judicial treatment of prerogative powers in the final quarter of the past century. By 1985, the House of Lords, in *Council of Civil Service Unions v. Minister for Civil Service*,[18] had determined that, in principle, executive action was no longer immune from judicial review merely by being carried out via the royal prerogative, though certain prerogative powers or subjects – in the event, national security powers in relation to the British signals intelligence agency, the Government Communications Headquarters (GCHQ), the analogue of Canada's CSE – were not justiciable.[19] In particular, Lord Roskill stated that prerogative powers relating to making treaties,[20] defending the realm, granting mercy or honours, dissolving Parliament, and appointing ministers could not, as a rule, "properly be made the subject of judicial review."[21] In the same year, the Supreme Court of Canada, building on this House of Lords decision, levered the Charter to state more ambitiously in *Operation Dismantle*[22] that it could not "relinquish justice on the basis that an issue is inherently non-justiciable or raises so-called political questions." I discuss *Operation Dismantle* and a related line of cases in Chapter 3 in the context of the military, but suffice it to say here that the decision in that case, both in its own right and given some of the cognate cases that followed it, was, in direct *strategic* terms, still more bluster than substance. The royal prerogative in relation to defence (declaration of war and military operations) remains largely unmolested by the judiciary, and none of these decisions has meaningfully dented federal prerogative power or decision making in relation to most of the key components of diplomacy – including *making* treaties (as distinguished from implementing them), development aid, all species of negotiation, strategic policy planning, ambassadorial or ambassador-like appointments, as well as deployment of strategic national assets, including embassies, envoys, and spies.[23] Having said this, in *Council of Civil Service Unions*, the groundwork was arguably laid for creeping judicial review, over time, of the royal prerogative, including in strategically relevant cases, in terms of procedural fairness and propriety. In this regard, Lord Diplock wrote:

> As respects "procedural propriety," I see no reason why it should not be a ground for judicial review of a decision made under powers of which the ultimate source is the prerogative ... Indeed, where the decision is one which does not alter rights or obligations enforceable in private law but only deprives a person of legitimate expectations, "procedural impropriety" will normally provide the only ground on which the decision is open to judicial review.[24]

And while Lord Diplock went on to dismiss the procedural impropriety consideration in *Council of Civil Service Unions* as having been outweighed by the national security imperative of the British government, his remarks anticipated, through the mediation of *Abbasi v. Secretary of State for Foreign and Commonwealth Affairs*,[25] the underappreciated Canadian holding, many years later, in 2009, in *Smith v. Canada*.[26] In that holding, the Federal Court determined that the Government of Canada had breached the right to procedural fairness of Ronald Smith, a death row inmate in Montana, by denying him diplomatic assistance (clemency support) to commute his death sentence, contrary to the longstanding policy of many erstwhile Canadian governments. The court said that exercise of the government's prerogative in relation to foreign affairs was generally non-justiciable but that "government decisions of an administrative character which affected the rights, privileges or interests of an individual were reviewable and were subject to the principles of procedural fairness."[27] According to the court, procedural fairness consisted of the government's "arbitrary" change of approach or policy in relation to clemency support for Canadians facing execution in foreign countries. Indeed, in his decision, Justice Barnes peculiarly identified the arbitrariness of the changed approach with what he suggested was the complete absence of a new, articulated federal policy in relation to clemency support:

> Government policy is not and cannot be the sum total of contradictory public statements of its ministers and spokespersons made inside and outside of Parliament. While the Government is generally free to change its policies there must still be a tangible and intelligible articulation of any policy before it can be applied to a case like Mr. Smith's. Mr. Smith was entitled to know precisely what the new clemency policy was before it was applied to his situation. He could not be expected to discern the policy by sorting through the inconsistent versions offered by various Government representatives.[28]

Of course, patently missing from Judge Barnes's pronouncement was recognition that public policy, by its inherent nature, can manifest itself in public statements and actions that, on their face, are inconsistent or even ill reasoned. It is not the absence of a formal policy statement or document by the government – or, say, a punctilious memorandum to cabinet pedantically approved by the full cabinet – that necessarily amounts to the absence of a proper policy position, just as the presence of a statement or document is not necessarily definitive of a particular policy position. Policy is, for all intents and purposes, whatever governments decide to do or not do – conscious choice, as it were, leading to deliberate action or inaction.[29] This definition is silent on the consistency of such action or inaction (or, for that matter, the consistency of various public statements in respect of the action or inaction). Indeed, it stands to reason that inconsistency, nuance, inchoateness, or even non-articulation of policy might well be more acute in the case of policy issues that have *strategic* consequence, as in those that purport to use the royal prerogative for foreign affairs (as in the *Smith* case). And while the *Smith* case is not *prima facie* of peculiar strategic import – that is, clemency petitions have, on their face, little to do with strategic national interests – the court's ruling (unappealed by the government, for reasons unclear) actually has significant portent for future judicial review of the royal prerogative in foreign affairs cases in which the fact patterns – "administrative" or not – are strategically non-negligible, in other words, in "high policy" cases.

Although it is not quite a Supreme Court precedent, it is the senior precedent (again unappealed) relating to administrative law incursions into the royal prerogative as it concerns foreign affairs. Take, for instance, the prospect of a change in Canadian government that results in an abrupt decision by an incoming prime minister or cabinet to close a domestic military base, thereby killing numerous jobs and presumably breaking many contracts, employment and other. Or consider a sudden, unanticipated decision by a government to impose sanctions on a foreign country, resulting in lost business, expropriated assets (for example, bank accounts), foiled contracts for Canadian enterprises, and even Canadian citizens stranded abroad. Or take the more radical prospect of a new government deciding to change military alliances or withdraw from a trading or mutual investment relationship with a given country and the associated frustration of "legitimate expectations" among individual Canadian citizens. In short, though these scenarios remain counterfactuals, the *Smith* decision was clearly made with little apparent reflection on its precedential value for future strategic scenarios of their ilk; that is, it is a consequential, albeit highly unwitting, incursion into the heretofore largely untrammelled royal prerogative for foreign affairs – or, more broadly, strategy.

In the next chapter, on the military, I discuss the Charter limitation put on the prerogative in the recent series of *Khadr*[30] holdings, from which the jurisprudential dust has arguably not yet settled[31] but which also threatens to clip some of the royal prerogative in relation to strategy. Indeed, the *Khadr* and *Smith* "clips" on the prerogative in the realm of strategy are the first of their kind in Canadian history.

But if, *Khadr* and *Smith* notwithstanding, the "strategic" royal prerogative in Canada remains for now largely whole and untrammelled by the courts, legislation and federalism have arguably controlled or channelled some of the broad scope of the diplomatic prerogative. *Labour Conventions* oblige, federalism is a pivotal dynamic, for instance, in the implementation of international trade and investment agreements – even if treaty making, strictly speaking, is still a creature of the prerogative. (As discussed, the negotiation of treaties is also *in practice* greatly affected by the dynamic of federalism; in short, the federal government can decisively or "muscularly" negotiate a treaty only if it expects to be able to implement it.) As for legislation, in addition to replacing certain prerogative aspects of intelligence, it controls aspects of strategic diplomatic capabilities such as economic sanctions – in particular under the federal *Special Economic Measures Act*.[32] This act provides for the restriction or prohibition by the federal government, *independently of the provinces*, of a catalogue of activities or transactions among Canada, Canadian citizens, and Canadian companies and a foreign state or organization, including the freezing or confiscation of designated foreign property in Canada, for the purpose of punishing or otherwise influencing the behaviour of that state or organization.[33]

Still, jurisprudence, federalism, and legislation have collectively left wholly unaffected a host of diplomatic capabilities underpinned by the prerogative. They include the prerogative of the federal government to recognize or (threaten) not to recognize foreign states and governments; create, join, or leave any number of important international councils, such as the G-7, G-8, or G-20 (none of which enjoys an enabling treaty); broker international peace and security agreements; join or leave a given military alliance or coalition; and even recall an ambassador or expel a foreign ambassador, envoy, or official.

I turn to the question of the military instrument in Chapter 3.

The Military

3

Because the royal prerogative is and remains, constitutionally speaking, so dominant in the governance of Canada's strategic military affairs, including declarations of war and peace as well as troop deployments and operations, the dearth of strategically meaningful jurisprudence on sections 15, 91(7), 117, and also 108 – the only sections of the 1867 Act that explicitly reference the military instrument – is, despite the protestations of Bora Laskin, far from crippling to a proper constitutional understanding of the potency of Canada's military instrument.[1] To be fair, Laskin was probably seeking simply to better understand the legislative contours of the instrument per section 91(7). For strict strategic purposes, section 15, the more general regal executive power in section 9, and, hovering above and beyond these sections, the royal (executive) prerogative are most important. Indeed, this dearth of jurisprudence might also betray the basic fact that Commonwealth courts have historically presumed, and to this day continue to presume for the most part, that foreign and military matters – questions of so-called "high policy" – are *generally* non-justiciable; that is, that they do not lend themselves to the judicial process and that the executive is institutionally more legitimately placed to deal with these issues.[2]

In *Aleksic v. Canada*,[3] for example, the Ontario Superior Court of Justice held that tort claims against the Government of Canada for damage incurred during the 1999 NATO bombing of Yugoslavia in the Kosovo campaign were non-justiciable precisely because the decision to bomb and the identities of the targets were purely matters of high policy, just as would have been the historic Canadian decision to join the NATO alliance or any military alliance, for that matter.[4] However, what was justiciable, and the court built here on the innovative holding almost two decades earlier in *Operation Dismantle*, was subject matter that lay at the intersection of such high policy and Charter rights – claims that the bombing campaign violated the plaintiffs' section 7 ("life, liberty and security of the person") and section 15 (equality and non-discrimination) rights. Relying on the precedent in *Operation Dismantle*, the court dismissed the Charter claims, with Justice Heeney declaring at paragraph 69 that "[t]o hold otherwise would permit any citizen to, in effect, hijack Canadian foreign policy."[5]

In *Operation Dismantle*, what had been challenged was a decision by the Canadian government to allow the testing of American cruise missiles on Canadian territory – testing alleged to have been in violation of section 7 of the Charter on the ground that, by hosting the missiles on Canadian soil, the Government of Canada had increased the risk of war involving Canada. Justice Wilson's ruling, instructively, is represented in the header of the *Supreme Court Reports* as follows:

> The government's decision to allow the testing of the U.S. cruise missiles in Canada, even although [sic] an exercise of the royal prerogative, was reviewable by the courts under s. 32(1)(a) of the *Charter*. It was not insulated from review because it was a "political question" since the Court had a constitutional obligation under s. 24 of the *Charter* to decide whether any particular act of the executive violated or threatened to violate any right of the citizen.[6]

In the end, the Supreme Court ruled in *Operation Dismantle* that there was no violation of section 7 of the Charter, not least because it determined that there must be a strong presumption that government action of a *state-to-state* nature that is not directed at, or that only incidentally affects, a particular Canadian was never intended to be captured by section 7 or, for that matter, any other Charter right. Although opening the door for more Charter actions on strategic questions, particularly those touching individual rights, the court's ruling, for all practical intents and purposes, actually concretized the dominance of the royal prerogative in respect of the military instrument.[7]

Aleksic treated, somewhat parenthetically, the question of whether the Charter applies to activities outside the territorial limits of Canada. The Supreme Court, relying on its earlier holding in *Cook*,[8] held that, conditionally, it did. The *Cook* ruling, however, was eclipsed, not uncontroversially, by *Hape*,[9] which provided for a two-part test to determine when there was extraterritorial applicability of the Charter: first, the conduct at issue has to be that of a Canadian *state actor* caught by section 32(1)[10] of the Charter; second, pursuant to international comity, the foreign state on the territory of which the conduct occurs has to give its consent to the extraterritorial application of Canadian Charter or constitutional rights. The latter could evidently be presumed to be a formidably improbable condition, thereby reasserting the general immunity of military matters, and indeed of the royal prerogative in relation to military matters, from judicial control. It is highly noteworthy, therefore, that the Supreme Court, in a unanimous 2008 decision, qualified this improbable applicability of the Charter in *Khadr*[11] (henceforth *Khadr* 2008), stating at paragraph 26 that the Charter applied to Canadian officials "to the extent that the conduct of Canadian officials involved [the officials or Canada] in a process that violated Canada's international obligations." The Federal Court of Appeal reaffirmed this ratio in *Khadr* 2009,[12] upholding the decision of the Federal Court[13] early the same year. The Court of Appeal reasoned that, first, based on *Khadr* 2008, it was clear that Omar Khadr's section 7 Charter rights were violated because of Canadian officials' participation in a process (that is, the questioning of Khadr by Canadian officials, knowing as they did that he had been maltreated, via sleep deprivation, contrary to international law, by American officials at Guantanamo Bay, Cuba); second, the section 7 violation was not saved by section 1 of the Charter;[14] and third, the remedy prescribed by the court – that is, that the Government of Canada must request of the United States the repatriation of Khadr – was wholly appropriate. Finally, in 2010, the Supreme Court, in *Khadr* 2010,[15] unanimously reaffirmed the section 7 breach of Khadr's Charter rights but determined that the remedy of requiring the federal government to seek the repatriation of Khadr to Canada was not appropriate and just in the circumstances. According to the court, at paragraph 39, while there was a necessary connection between the breach of section 7 and the remedy, "the remedy ... gives too little weight to the constitutional responsibility of the executive to make decisions on matters of foreign affairs in the context of complex and ever-changing circumstances, taking into account Canada's broader national interests." The court was also concerned about evidentiary uncertainties in this case as well as the overall institutional ken or legitimacy, as it were, of the judiciary in contradicting or directing the executive on matters of foreign affairs. In privileging declaratory relief as the appropriate new remedy for Khadr, the court wrote, at paragraph 37, that "judicial review of the exercise of the prerogative power for constitutionality remains sensitive to the fact that the executive branch of government is responsible for decisions under this power, and that the executive is better placed to make such decisions within a range of constitutional options."

In the aggregate, the *Khadr* holdings, however, surely demand rapid clarification, as together they greatly muddy the erstwhile clear, prerogative-laden *marge de manoeuvre* of Canadian officials acting abroad in complex operations, the international legality of which is not always within their control (and for which there is, in the *Khadr* 2010 vernacular, considerable "evidentiary uncertainty") or indeed not always decisive in Canadian calculations in respect of where the state's strategic interests lie. For instance, returning to *Aleksic*, could one not have argued, on the logic of *Khadr* 2008 and *Khadr* 2009, that the Kosovo war was illegal at international law (*ius ad bellum*) and that the consequent activities of Canadian troops and officials in Kosovo were, on the balance of probabilities, contrary to the Charter? Or that Canadian intelligence agents collecting information on threats emerging from Iraq during the arguably illegal war in Iraq (also in terms of *ius ad bellum*) might be at risk of acting in contravention of the Charter? Affirmative answers to these counterfactual queries would surely be tantamount to meaningfully circumscribing some of the strategic potency of Canada's military and diplomatic instruments in the world.

The 2008 Federal Court *Amnesty International*[16] decision, issued prior to *Khadr* 2008 and thus relying on *Hape*, affirmed at paragraph 26 that the Charter did not apply to the conduct of Canadian Forces personnel in detaining or transferring Afghan detainees; that is, even though they were clearly Canadian state actors, the application of Canadian constitutional rights to their detainees was not consented to by the Afghan government. So while the issue, which lay at the intersection of the prerogative and a claimed constitutional right, was easily justiciable, this mattered little in practice, for the effective *marge de manoeuvre* of the Canadian Forces in Afghanistan was unaffected by the decision.[17] (This holding was roundly upheld by the Federal Court of Appeal,[18] and a subsequent application for leave to appeal the *Amnesty International* decision was dismissed without reasons by the Supreme Court,[19] notwithstanding the intervening *Khadr* 2008 decision.) *En attendant*, it must be posited, perhaps controversially, that Charter considerations, as a general rule, continue to matter little in strategic decision making by the military in Canada. In other words, *Khadr* 2008, *Khadr* 2009, and *Khadr* 2010 notwithstanding, the Charter is not a very material bar to Canadian strategic power, as manifested by the military – at least outside Canadian borders.

Of course, as already established, in addition to the courts interpreting or controlling, through the common law, the scope of the prerogative in strategic matters, legislation can also clip or eclipse or oust the prerogative. The *National Defence Act*, for instance, governs, on the strength of the federal militia and defence power in section 91(7) of the 1867 Act, the conduct of the Canadian Forces and the administration of the Department of National Defence. And to the extent that the provisions of the act speak explicitly or by necessary implication to matters otherwise coming under the purview of the royal prerogative, the legislative provisions, under the constitutional doctrine of parliamentary supremacy, trump the prerogative. Notably, section 31 of the act provides for "active service" designation by the governor in council (the executive or government), which might seem to muddy the waters of the historically untouchable royal prerogative in respect of troop deployments. In practice, however, it seems that, at least for the time being, this provision has not generally been viewed or treated as a statutory rule in respect of deployment of the Canadian Forces.[20]

In the meantime, section 32 of the act states that,

> Whenever the Governor in Council places the Canadian Forces or any component or unit thereof on active service, if Parliament is then separated by an adjournment or prorogation that will not expire within ten days, a proclamation shall be issued for the meeting of Parliament within ten days, and Parliament shall accordingly meet and sit on the day appointed by the proclamation, and shall continue to sit and act in like manner as if it had stood adjourned or prorogued to the same day.

This provision clearly adds a perfunctory measure of legislated parliamentary involvement in at least the discussion of military matters, broadly put, at the expense of the royal prerogative. However, this means that Parliament is only strictly required to meet and sit *after* a declaration of war or troop deployment and, given the absence of specific language to that effect, without a legal mandate for scrutiny – let alone control – of the strategic or tactical operations of the Armed Forces. Moreover, considering that the evidence continues to suggest that there is no constitutional requirement for Parliament to debate or vote, *ex ante*, on Canadian declarations of war or troop deployments, the prerogative for the military instrument clearly emerges unmolested – in strategic terms at least.[21]

Provincial considerations do not figure prominently or obviously in most elements of the strategic military instrument. They are important, however, in respect of various permutations of Canadian military deployment or "call-out" on Canadian soil. Classically, the Canadian Forces can be called out in aid of the civil power, governed by Part VI of the *National Defence Act*. This aid of the civil power involves the prevention or suppression of an anticipated or actual riot or disturbance of the peace that is deemed by the relevant provincial attorney general as exceeding the capabilities of provincial civilian authorities. This call-out may be requisitioned in writing by the relevant provincial attorney general, following which, according to section 283 of the act,

> The Canadian Forces or any part thereof called out in aid of the civil power shall remain on duty, in such strength as the Chief of the

Defence Staff or such officer as the Defence Staff may designate deems necessary or orders, until notification that the Canadian Forces are no longer required in aid of the civil power is received from the attorney general of the province concerned and, from time to time as in the opinion of the Chief of the Defence Staff the exigencies of the situation require, the Chief of the Defence Staff may increase or diminish the number of officers or non-commissioned members called out.

The federal government may equally trigger the domestic deployment of Canadian Forces without the provinces. This includes the ill-defined "public service" deployments under the *National Defence Act* in respect of a law enforcement matter that, according to section 273.6(2) of the act, (a) is in the national interest (a term evidently undefined in the legislation and therefore subject to executive discretion) and (b) cannot be effectively dealt with except with the assistance of the Canadian Forces.[22] More fundamentally, however (and this gets to the core of the federal state's constitutional capabilities in respect of *strategic* domestic military deployment), any threat or emergency (or indeed attack) emanating from, or materially related to, foreign states or parties could – and, depending on its assessed scale, likely would – be addressed under the *Emergencies Act*[23] (not the aid of the civil power provisions), including through declaration by the federal executive of a public order, international, or war emergency. The *Emergencies Act* triggers, or yields to, a host of potent executive capabilities and assets, including the military instrument. Moreover, as I argue below, the entire ambit of this military instrument, as afforded by the royal prerogative in the context of strategic emergencies (domestic or international), is not exhausted or replaced by this act.

The provinces also loom large in respect of section 117 of the 1867 Act, which states that "[t]he several Provinces shall retain all their respective Public Property not otherwise disposed of in this Act, subject to the Right of Canada to assume any Lands or Public Property required for Fortifications or for the Defence of the Country." This is a powerful expropriation provision for the federal government, affirmed most recently in the *Human Rights Institute* ruling[24] in 2000, which upheld the

Government of Canada's right to expropriate land from British Columbia to continue a torpedo testing arrangement with the United States near Nanoose Bay. Although section 117 is an executive power (not a legislative power), its strategic force, for the most part, is similar to that of the non-military declaratory power (a legislative provision) in the 1867 Act's section 92(10)(c), discussed at some length in the next chapter. Of course, Parliament may also enact laws under section 91(7) – the militia and defence power – that have the same effect as section 117.[25]

Section 117 overcomes the general presumption of provincial land (and resource) ownership outlined in section 109 – a key strategic section relating to the natural resource factor of power, which I examine in Chapter 5. Along with national economic capacity and population (both discussed in upcoming chapters), the natural resources factor greatly influences Canada's military instrument (and the diplomatic instrument) through generally indirect avenues. And, of course, these factors of power are greatly complicated by the federalism dynamic. This means that the strategic military instrument, while *prima facie* dominated by the federal executive, is in reality undergirded by highly nuanced federal-provincial constitutional dynamics as well as related factors of power, to which I now turn.

Government, or Pure Executive Potency

4

If the strategic capacity of the Canadian state, constitutionally speaking, is significant in the purest terms of its diplomatic and military instruments – and this in spite of the astrategic design and, for the most part, strategically indifferent interpretation of the Constitution – then these instruments are only buttressed, as a rule, by "subsidiary" strategic elements of the Constitution. Perhaps the most important among these elements is the federal executive per se, specifically its general potency, flexibility, and efficiency. (In Canadian constitutional law, executive power follows the grant of legislative power.[1] As mentioned, notwithstanding the distinct possibility of minority government rule in Canada, given the frequent identity between executive and legislative branches in the context of majority and even minority governments in Westminster systems [party discipline oblige], a given federal legislative power should more often than not be seen as indicative of an accompanying executive power. The reverse is evidently often not true.)

The emergency powers or capabilities of Parliament and the federal executive are perhaps the most obvious manifestation of the link between pure executive potency and strategic power. On this matter, the remarks of Craig Forcese are instructive:

> There will … be threats so far in excess of the normal state of affairs and so immediate that the state will treat them as emergencies. Such

a state of emergency may change the institutional structure within which ... law operates ... [D]emocracies are built on a system of checks and balances that constrain the exercise of power. Yet, emergencies often, if not usually, require the exercise of power. Moreover, this power must be implemented swiftly and with resolution. While law applicable in normal situations diffuses power, emergencies concentrate it.[2]

Historically, the general or residuary power to make laws for the peace, order, and good government (POGG) of Canada under section 91 in the 1867 Act has provided the most apparent constitutional underpinning for federal legislation and actions in cases of emergencies, including war or threats of war.[3] This broad emergency power – or, technically, the emergency branch of the POGG or general power – was famously invoked by the federal government in proclaiming the *War Measures Act*[4] in the 1970 October Crisis. It has since arguably been disciplined to a great extent by legislation in the form of the *Emergencies Act, 1988*.[5] (The *War Measures Act* was repealed in 1988.) The *Emergencies Act* defines a "national emergency" in section 3 as "an urgent and critical situation of a temporary nature that (a) seriously endangers the lives, health or safety of Canadians and is of such proportions as to exceed the capacity or authority of a province to deal with it, or (b) seriously threatens the ability of the Government of Canada to preserve the sovereignty, security and territorial integrity of Canada." This definition makes clear that certain *temporary, prima facie* sweeping executive emergency measures are essential, in certain situations, to restore the capacity of the government to pursue strategic interests – described as sovereignty, security, and territorial integrity. These measures ("orders and regulations"), depending on the nature of the declared emergency, include everything from prohibitions on travel to requisition or seizure of property, control of specified industries, and removal from Canada of noncitizens. (Some of the act's orders and regulations clearly coincide with the federal quarantine power in section 91(11) of the 1867 Act. The limits of this power have not been properly established to date by the jurisprudence, even if the Canadian SARS emergency of 2003 gave it renewed strategic relevance.)

The act proposes four possible categories of national emergency, each of them carrying a certain strategic import: public welfare, public order, international, and war, respectively with renewable expiry dates of 90, 30, 60, and 120 days. Moreover, the act requires non-binding "consultation" between the federal executive and affected provinces prior to a declaration (on "reasonable grounds") by the former of a national emergency under the auspices of the act as well as *ex post* parliamentary supervision of the declaration and associated temporary special measures taken by the executive to deal with the emergency. (Tracking the logic of the federal defence aid of the civil power provisions, the federal government might not, in the case of a public welfare or public order emergency in which the direct effects are confined to, or occur mainly within, a single province, declare an emergency in the absence of affirmation from the lieutenant governor of the affected province that management of the matter at hand exceeds the capabilities of that province.) Parliament, in a similar vein, has the authority to revoke a declaration of emergency. Federalism oblige, the act states in section 8(3)(a)(i) that federal orders and regulations made under its auspices may not "unduly impair the ability of any province to take measures ... for dealing with an emergency in the province" or, in respect of command and control, that nothing in the act should be construed or applied "so as to derogate from ... the control or direction of the government of a province or municipality over any police force over which it normally has control or direction."

Since the act has never been invoked by the federal government to deal with an emergency, the extent to which it circumscribes in practice, or indeed channels, executive power under the emergency branch of the POGG power in dealing with pure strategic issues such as military or national security threats remains unclear. Some have argued that, while in practice "Parliament's constitutional authority to respond to emergencies cannot be defined by, or made to conform to, the terms of an ordinary statute, the definitions of emergencies found in the *Emergencies Act* would surely be relevant in any future constitutional litigation involving use of the emergency branch of POGG."[6] This seems to suggest that any litigation on an emergency – naturally slow off the mark – would typically occur *after* the response of Parliament (or the government) to the emergency – swiftness of executive response oblige – and as such would have limited opportunity to credibly circumscribe, in real time, the emergency response of the government, requiring it instead to justify its response *ex post*. Nonetheless, as is often the case, and depending on the gravity of the strategic emergency in question, it is conceivable, if not probable, that the government's response would be conditioned in part by such expected litigation, thereby somewhat affirming the controlling power of the legislation. (It is worth mentioning that the *Emergencies Act*, like all statutes, and as is explicitly mentioned in its preamble, is constitutionally controlled by the Charter. The fact that the act does not in and of itself provide for any derogation from the Charter in some sense makes it fairly tame emergency legislation.)

Legislation, after all, is only legislation. It can be so significant as to be quasi-constitutional on a broad conception of the Constitution, but it is not strictly constitutional in status. So one can reasonably argue that the gap between what is strictly permitted in or by the *Emergencies Act* and what is *constitutionally* permissible is identifiable with an emergency (royal) prerogative enjoying effective constitutional status – albeit existing, strictly speaking, at common law. This prerogative hovers over the *Emergencies Act* and is supported by cases such as *Burmah Oil Co. v. Lord Advocate*,[7] which affirms the constitutional right of the executive to defend the sovereignty of the country. *Suresh*, perhaps on a more micro level, referring as it does to "extraordinary circumstances" (yet to be defined), also intimates the existence of such an emergency prerogative.[8] Indeed, this prerogative power can be viewed as embodying the contested doctrine of constitutional necessity, canvassed in *Re Manitoba Language Rights*,[9] in which necessity is occasioned by extraordinary strategic circumstances – such as an overwhelming military or terrorist threat or attack or, in the *Manitoba Language Rights* case, a massive legal vacuum threatening the rule of law and therefore requiring extraordinary or even ordinarily "illegal" measures to protect or preserve the state. Such extraordinary measures would be strictly *within* the Canadian constitutional framework, with the "principle of necessity [viewed] either as an autonomous source of law or as a meta-rule of constitutional construction."[10] In short, the necessity doctrine might underline the signal premise that the Canadian Constitution cannot, in the presence of exceptional circumstances or emergencies, properly or reasonably be viewed as a "death pact," as it were, for the Canadian state and its citizens.[11]

At a strictly constitutional level, therefore, one again has the character and scope of pure Canadian strategic power – in this case, executive potency as manifested in emergencies – most meaningfully defined at the *intersection* of the royal (emergency) prerogative and Charter rights. This dynamic is complicated, though, by the fact that the Charter has nothing explicit to say regarding emergencies per se. It does provide in section 4(2) that, "[i]n time of real or apprehended war, invasion or insurrection, a House of Commons may be continued by Parliament and a legislative assembly may be continued beyond five years if such continuation is not opposed by the votes of more than one-third of the members of the House of Commons or the legislative assembly, as the case may be."[12] Naturally, since there has been no "apprehended war, invasion or insurrection" in Canada since well before the advent of the Charter, this provision has neither been invoked by the executive nor treated in the jurisprudence. But it does provide, if necessary, for legitimate constitutional extension of executive power in times of strategic consequence. To be sure, this speaks to strategic power as *capacity*, not exercise, for such a move would doubtless prove politically contentious and, as with declarations of emergency under the *Emergencies Act*, could well be subject to judicial action after the fact.[13]

As mentioned in Chapter 1, the Charter also has a powerful notwithstanding clause (section 33) providing for the operation of laws by either Parliament or provincial legislatures notwithstanding certain sections of the Charter. This clause has not been invoked to date by any federal government and would not be operative on the "democratic rights" in sections 3, 4, and 5, as well as the mobility rights in section 6, which I discuss in Chapter 8. However, in the event of an emergency, an issue of national security, or a military event, the federal government would have available to it, under the notwithstanding clause, the capacity to override the Charter "legal rights" in sections 7 to 14 as well as the equality provision in section 15. (No justification for such an override would have to be provided under section 1, for that section would also be overridden by section 33.) It is similarly conceivable, depending on the gravity of the circumstances, that a government, confronted with a "real or apprehended war, invasion or insurrection," could invoke both the notwithstanding clause and section 4(2), which would be tantamount to a fairly potent cocktail of executive override of most of the Charter's key rights provisions.[14]

I should note, furthermore, that the POGG power has, outside the emergency branch, at least one additional dimension of strategic moment: the "national concern" branch.[15] It is seldom used by Parliament and still not clearly or persuasively defined in the jurisprudence. It is also approached by the courts with considerable reticence, preoccupied as Canadian jurisprudence has been over most of the country's constitutional history with the POGG power either as a residual or an emergency power. Still, one can credibly presume the emergence of certain new *strategic* matters – not emergencies – characterized by "a singleness, distinctiveness and indivisibility."[16] These matters would not have existed or been anticipated at the time of Confederation, or over time would have become a national concern (and therefore fall under federal jurisdiction), even if originally under provincial jurisdiction. Such new strategic matters could eventually expand the strategic jurisdiction of Parliament and therefore the strategic power of the federal government. Ostensibly strategic matters such as nuclear energy have been justified, in the not too distant past, on account of falling under federal jurisdiction on the basis of this national concern branch.[17] Indeed, the strategic import of uranium was recognized by the federal government immediately after the explosion of the first atomic bombs toward the end of the Second World War: the Government of Canada availed itself of the highly potent yet little known *declaratory power* in section 92(10)(c) of the 1867 Act, which provides that Parliament may declare certain local works, though wholly situated within or otherwise falling under the jurisdiction of a province, as for the *"general advantage of Canada."* Such a declaration would mean that the declared "work" (that is, the work declared in legislation) would immediately fall under federal jurisdiction.

This declaratory power has been used nearly 500 times[18] since Confederation, in particular in the transportation industry and especially in respect of the once highly strategic – and still arguably somewhat strategic – rail sector. (Consider, even today, the intense use of the rail sector to transport oil and natural gas across Canada.) It has also been used in the telecommunications sector and for labour strikes of national significance. A declaration by Parliament is dispositive, meaning that the courts will not enquire into whether the "work" in question – say a uranium mine – is *actually* for the general advantage of Canada, provided that it relates to something physical, material, or tangible.[19] Signally, when Parliament declared atomic energy for the general advantage of Canada in 1946, it also enacted the *Atomic Energy Control Act*.[20] This legislation was contested because of traditional provincial dominance in the area of natural resources, and immediate use of the declaratory power by Parliament effectively eliminated any uncertainty about the legitimacy of the legislation and federal jurisdiction until such time as the Supreme Court could, many years later, in the 1993 *Ontario Hydro* case,[21] confirm the statute on the basis of the national concern branch of the POGG power.[22]

Finally, and critically, Canadian strategic potency is doubtless buttressed by the fact that the criminal law power lies conspicuously with Parliament. Section 91(27) of the 1867 Act states that Parliament has responsibility for "[t]he Criminal Law, except the Constitution of Courts of Criminal Jurisdiction, but including the Procedure in Criminal Matters." (The administration and enforcement of justice, for its part, including the establishment and maintenance of provincial police forces and courts, lie with the provinces under section 91(14) of the 1867 Act.) This federal criminal law power has generally been interpreted broadly by the courts, which have distilled three baseline factors that must generally underpin legitimate criminal laws: a prohibition on a given activity must exist, an associated penalty must exist, and the legislation in question must serve a relevant public purpose, such as "peace, order, security, health, morality."[23] (Contrast this with Australian and American constitutional treatment of criminal law, in which criminal law resides largely with the states, requiring considerable coordination of criminal law-making across the jurisdictions in the former case and resulting in significant inconsistencies in substantive criminal law across the jurisdictions in the latter case – in both cases arguably to the detriment of national strategic efficacy.) Indeed, the criminal law power can ostensibly be used by Parliament to enact legislation relating to a large number of activities – especially economic activities – that would typically have fallen under the provincial property and civil rights power when weighed against federal powers such as the POGG and trade and commerce powers.

For my purposes here, it is instructive that the broad federal criminal law power has strategic consequence in the context of Canadian national security, explored in detail in Case Study D. As a strategic concept, national security refers to the protection of critical Canadian assets and interests (and Canadian people) against a variety of threats, domestic and international, human and natural, deliberate and accidental – a state of affairs that lies somewhere between the spheres of personal safety and international security.[24] On this conceptualization, national security can be said to be material to national strategy to the extent that it involves protection of critical Canadian assets and interests specifically against foreign or foreign-related threats, whether manifested in Canada or abroad. Protection against these threats can be provided in part by the diplomatic and military instruments of the state, but in general terms the provision of this national security, as a function of the executive potency factor, should be seen as a "supporting" – in some cases "defensive" – condition for proper functioning of these two strategic instruments.

At the federal level, the term "national security" or one of its cognates appears in at least thirty statutes, with fewer than a third of them attempting, with considerable difficulty, to define the term.[25] Taken together, statutes such as the *Emergencies Act, Emergency Management Act*,[26] *CSIS Act*,[27] *Royal Canadian Mounted Police (RCMP) Act*,[28] *Security of Information Act* (formerly *Official Secrets Act*),[29] *Canada Evidence Act*,[30] *Citizenship Act*,[31] *Immigration and Refugee Protection Act*[32] *Aeronautics Act*,[33] *Canada Transportation Act*,[34] and, *inter alia*, *National Defence Act* make up the nucleus of Canada's national security legislative framework. For all practical intents and purposes, the leading strategic assets or agencies of the Canadian state in the national security sphere are the Royal Canadian Mounted Police (RCMP), Canadian Security Intelligence Service (CSIS), and Communications Security Establishment (CSE). The RCMP is regulated by the *RCMP Act*, while CSIS is regulated by the *CSIS Act*. The

CSE is regulated by the *National Defence Act*. Nevertheless, national security, especially given its troubled susceptibility to precise legal definition,[35] is in many important respects given constitutional salience and expression by federal criminal law. As such, a number of provisions of the Canadian *Criminal Code*[36] are highly strategic. For instance, the *Anti-Terrorism Act*[37] of 2001 amended the *Criminal Code* to define terrorism and created several offences related to terrorism (with significant extraterritorial effect), including terrorism financing and participation in, facilitation of, and execution of terrorist acts.[38] The act also provided, among other things, for the seizure and forfeiture of property within Canada belonging to terrorist groups.

Provisions related to two of the pivotal criminal law processes enacted in the *Anti-Terrorism Act* – so-called investigative hearings and recognizance with conditions, including preventative arrests in the context of potential terrorist acts – sunsetted in 2006. The federal government attempted to reinstate these provisions, without substantial amendment, in 2007 via Bill S-3.[39] This bill was passed by the Senate but was at second reading in the House of Commons when it recessed in June 2008. A general election was called in September 2008, and the bill was subsequently reintroduced by the government in the House of Commons – this time as Bill C-19.[40] The House was then prorogued. The bill was again tabled in March 2010 as Bill C-17.[41] A federal general election was called for May 2011. The provisions were finally successfully reinstated in April 2013 in Bill S-7,[42] which also included *Criminal Code* amendments creating offences in respect of, *inter alia*, people who leave or attempt to leave the country to commit a terrorist act outside Canada as well as those who harbour or conceal a person involved in terrorist activity to facilitate such activity.

I have already discussed the blunt and powerful executive expropriation power, for military purposes, in section 117 of the 1867 Act. I discuss general federal expropriation powers, in the context of natural resources, in the next chapter.

Natural Resources (and Food)   5

There is an intimate strategic relationship between the express geographic factor of power – not explored per se in this book because excessively abstract – and the less abstract natural resources factor.[1] Canada's physical geography not only provides a physical or spatial – and, indeed, psychological – barrier and buffer against conventional military or national security threats (so-called strategic depth), as well as, *arguendo*, a secure base for the prosecution of military campaigns abroad, but it is also a source of the many natural resources or raw materials that drive the country's industrial capacity. In addition, this land mass informs Canada's human *holding capacity*, which in turn feeds national industrial capacity and provides direct manpower or talent for the diplomatic and military instruments that directly project Canadian strategic power. I discuss industrial capacity and population as factors of power, as reflected in the Constitution, in Chapters 6 and 8, respectively. For now, I should repeat that what is most salient in analyzing the constitutional treatment of these factors of power, as well as the natural resource factor, is not only the raw potential magnitude of the factor in question (bearing in mind the distinction between theoretical constitutional potential and policy-political praxis) but also the extent to which this factor can be mobilized for strategic purposes or, more readily, in the service of one or both of the state's diplomatic and military instruments.

Natural resources, in respect of which Canada has been called a "superpower,"[2] are important for Canadian strategic power in at least three key respects. First and foremost, there is the need for adequate and secure supply of such resources for the Canadian population and state, particularly for its military and diplomatic instruments. Secure access to non-renewable resources such as oil and gas, coal, and uranium is essential for energy production and consumption (and export), while access to renewable resources such as forestry products is critical to construction, both for the general economy (a factor of strategic power) and for military ends. Note the intervention by Hans Morgenthau in this respect, writing at the height of the Cold War:

> With the increasing mechanization of warfare, which since the industrial revolution has proceeded at a faster pace than in all preceding history, national power has become more and more dependent upon the control of raw materials in peace and war. It is not by accident that the two most powerful nations today, the United States and the Soviet Union, come closest to being self-sufficient in the raw materials necessary for modern industrial production, and control at least the access to the sources of those raw materials which they do not themselves produce.[3]

Similarly, food supply is strategically relevant in the basic sense that an adequate, secure supply is critical to the survival of the population and the associated viability of the state's basic strategic instruments. (The army, to take the crudest example, must be fed!) Second, natural resources, if properly – some might say ruthlessly – levered, can be used in certain strategic scenarios as a national "carrot" or "stick" to advance Canadian interests. Targeted or earmarked export of certain resources, such as oil and gas, can arguably be exchanged for, or, in the diplomatic parlance, "linked" to, the receipt by Canada of strategic advantages from another country or group of countries. Conversely, economic sanctions or natural resource export restrictions or prohibitions against targeted countries can be used by Canada to influence the behaviour of these countries. And third, there is the aforementioned vector connecting natural resources, renewable and non-renewable alike, with the overall economic capacity of Canada, which in turn informs the potency of the state's military and diplomatic instruments. I touch briefly on some of this economic dimension at the end of this chapter and leave for the next chapter the primary treatment of the constitutional connection between strategy and economy.

Questions of natural resource jurisdiction in Canada are complicated by the constitutional dichotomy between ownership of, and legislative power over, natural resources. As a general rule in Canadian constitutionalism, ownership of resources coincides with ownership of public lands. Regarding section 109 of the 1867 Act, which vests in the provinces all "lands, mines, minerals and royalties,"[4] Professor (and later Supreme Court Justice) Gérard V. La Forest once remarked that the term "lands" means public lands, while the term "public lands" "also includes the ordinary incidents to land. Thus it is clear that the word [*lands*] would be sufficient to include such mines and minerals as are ordinarily incident to land."[5] Section 109, in jurisprudential terms, is typically regarded as a residuary or default section in relation to ownership of public lands and natural resources, with the dominant presumption (buttressed by section 117) being that each province (or provincial Crown) owns the lands and resources within its territorial limits unless they are captured by section 108, which enumerates, in a schedule to the 1867 Act, specific "public works" and "property" in each province that are to be the property of Canada (or the federal Crown). (They include public harbours, lighthouses, rivers and lake improvements, and, as noted, strategic assets such as military roads, so-called ordnance property, and armouries.) In the simplest terms, this means that the provinces, rather than the federal government, are in principle, if they so desire, able to capture the lion's share of economic rents (royalties, mining taxes, or bids on exploration) coming from the exploration and exploitation of resources on their lands.[6] A notable exception here is offshore resources and, even more importantly, resources in Canada's three federal territories, all of which are owned by the federal government.[7] Another notable exception, of course, is land occupied and exploited by Aboriginal people according to land claims agreements or treaties – depending on the terms of the agreements or treaties and barring justifiable infringements by federal or provincial laws, per *Sparrow*.[8]

The general presumption of provincial ownership of lands and resources is matched by general provincial legislative dominance in respect of natural resources. A number of subsections of section 92 have historically been at play here, but the critical section for strategic purposes over the past score of years has been section 92A – also known as the natural resource amendment – enshrined in the 1867 Act by the 1982 Act.[9] Section 92A states that each province, *within* its territorial boundaries, has legislative responsibility for natural resources in respect of (a) intraprovincial exploration for non-renewable natural resources; (b) intraprovincial development, conservation, and management (and marketing) of non-renewable resources and forestry resources; as well as (c) development, conservation, and management of intraprovincial sites and facilities for the generation and production of electrical energy; moreover, (d) each province can levy direct or indirect taxes relating to its natural resources. In practice, these significant intraprovincial powers are materially restricted when it comes to export of resources out of province (given federal paramountcy) or out of Canada (given exclusive federal jurisdiction over international trade). Provinces can also regulate pipelines, mines, and other facilities via section 92(10), provided, again, that they do not extend beyond provincial boundaries. In the simplest terms, provincial legislative dominance means that provinces, as a general rule, will regulate in their own individual interests. And it stands to reason that a scenario in which each province maximizes its own legislative interests (or, say, welfare) is hardly conducive to the maximization of pan-Canadian or federal interests (or welfare or, ultimately, strategic power). A presumption to the contrary would be a patent fallacy of composition – that is, a false presumption that something that is true of the part is necessarily true of the whole.[10]

Strictly speaking, therefore, vesting ownership and legislative power over natural resources in the provinces is antithetical to ensuring constant (standing) and adequate supply of key natural resources for the country *as a whole* and, in purely strategic terms, in the ultimate service of the military and diplomatic instruments. Writes La Forest in this respect:

> The raising of a revenue is not the sole reason that public property is of fundamental importance to the provinces. It also provides them

with a powerful instrument for the control of their economic and political destinies. By requiring that resources from public property be processed within its boundaries, a province can materially contribute towards the establishment of secondary industries there, and prevent the export of raw material to other countries [or indeed, per section 92A, to other provinces, provided that this prohibition is for all provinces and provided that there is no repugnancy with federal law].[11]

Having established that, in terms of a national planning function, provincial dominance over natural resources is astrategic, if not outright anti-strategic, I can further posit that, in the absence of an emergency, the Canadian constitutional framework does not strictly vest in the federal government the capacity to ensure or require – rather than fiscally incentivize – that there is continuous and adequate supply of needed natural resources.[12] (The federal government can, in the event of a long-term dearth of, say, energy resources, acquire legislative and regulatory responsibility for energy imports and offshore exploration, but it must for the most part, notwithstanding the prospect of federal-provincial cooperative agreements, defer to the legislative and regulatory lead of the provinces in most traditional scenarios of energy exploration.)[13]

Short of an emergency, therefore, if the federal government, to ensure an ongoing minimal national supply of energy (including for the military and diplomatic instruments of the state), wanted to create, say, a national strategic energy (more specifically a petroleum) reserve, it would likely have to purchase such energy from the provinces and private suppliers at market rates. This means that a national strategic energy reserve is constitutionally possible – through the federal spending power, which I take up in Chapter 6 – but otherwise strategically awkward and suboptimal (and not inexpensive). In other words, Canada's constitutional framework is strategically inefficient in respect of ensuring adequacy of natural resources on a national scale. (For their part, the provinces could, of course, legislate with relative ease under section 92A to ensure adequacy of provincial supply, policy-political praxis notwithstanding.)

Nevertheless, the federal government has at its disposal a number of powerful constitutional and quasi-constitutional tools to mobilize, on an *ad hoc* and/or emergency basis, strategic or essential natural resources where they are in short supply, poorly distributed, or otherwise needed. The most powerful of these tools is the aforementioned *Emergencies Act*. As established, it derives from the federal government's rather sweeping emergency powers under the emergency branch of the POGG power in the 1867 Act. Under each of the four types of national emergency in the act, there are exceptional provisions – all still unlitigated – that empower the government to ensure that scarce supplies and essential resources or services are provided. In a public welfare emergency, for instance, section 8(c) provides for federal requisition, use, or disposition of property; section 8(d) provides for authorization of or direction to any person, or any person of a class of persons, to render essential services provided that there is reasonable compensation for services so rendered; and section 8(e) provides for regulation of the distribution and availability of essential goods, services, and resources. Or, in the event of an international emergency, the act provides at section 30(e) for the same power as in section 8(e), as well as for the control or regulation of any specified industry or service, including the use of equipment, facilities, and inventory (section 30(a)); the appropriation, control, forfeiture, use, and disposition of property or services (section 30(b)); and, more specific to the military instrument, the authorization and conduct of inquiries in relation to defence contracts or defence proper or to hoarding, overcharging, black-marketing, or fraudulent operations in respect of scarce commodities. The *Emergencies Act* coexists with the older *Energy Supplies Emergency Act*,[14] also rooted in the federal emergency power, which states at section 15(1), specifically in relation to petroleum resources, that, when

> the Governor in Council is of the opinion that a national emergency exists by reason of actual or anticipated shortages of petroleum or disturbances in the petroleum markets that affect or will affect the national security and welfare and the economic stability of Canada, and that it is necessary in the national interest to conserve the supplies of petroleum products within Canada, the Governor in Council may, by order, so declare and by that order authorize the establishment of a program for the mandatory allocation of petroleum products within Canada in accordance with this Act.

Of course, as discussed previously, both the *Emergencies Act* and the *Energy Supplies Emergency Act* do not displace the entirety of the royal prerogative of the government in respect of national security or emergencies. Indeed, this prerogative also hovers over the controversial "proportionality clause" (Article 605) in the *North American Free Trade Agreement* (*NAFTA*), which repeats the prohibition in the *Canada-US Free Trade Agreement* on Canadian restrictions of energy exports to the United States (in the *NAFTA* case, to Mexico also) for reasons of national conservation, supply shortages, and price stabilization, provided that the share of total energy supply available for export purchase by the United States (or Mexico) from Canada falls below the average level of the previous thirty-six months.[15] Although not yet litigated, the only apparent legislative exceptions to this clause are found in Article 107 of the *NAFTA*, which states that energy imports and exports may be restricted for reasons of national security – that is, as defined in the article, to the extent necessary for Canada to (a) supply a military establishment or enable fulfillment of a critical defence contract; (b) respond to a situation of armed conflict; (c) implement national policies or international agreements relating to the non-proliferation of nuclear weapons or other explosive devices; or (d) respond to direct threats of disruption in the supply of nuclear materials for defence purposes. If these conditions are not met, Canada could still, in strict constitutional terms, defer to the emergency prerogative (or, *in extremis*, the doctrine of constitutional necessity) to assure its domestic supply, even if this were in breach of the *NAFTA*, and, in the likeliest of scenarios, bring about political and strategic retaliation by the United States. (In practice, Canada would almost certainly far sooner do this or, more readily still, legally attempt to justify or litigate its actions as being in accordance with Article 107 than rescind the treaty outright.)[16] Moreover, as discussed above, if necessary – say in the event of a national energy shortage – the federal government could arguably use its spending power to purchase exported oil from the provinces on the free market, within the terms of the *NAFTA*. To be sure, this would require the federal government to effectively *outbid* potential American and Mexican buyers; that is, on volumes of oil above those that would have to be made available to them, based on historical sales over a representative period – a high price indeed for the imperfect strategic efficiency of the Constitution of Canada.

The declaratory power in section 92(10)(c) of the 1867 Act is also available to the federal government, via legislation, insofar as it may deem certain local "works" related to certain natural resources (or indeed food) to be for the general advantage of Canada. As discussed above, the declaratory power was famously used by the federal government in respect of Canada's uranium mines after the Second World War. Indeed, the constitutional possibility, politically realistic or not, of the declaratory power being used by Parliament to invoke federal legislative control over oil and natural gas during the 1970s OPEC oil embargo was a key driver for the western provinces in the negotiations that led to the enactment of section 92A, the natural resource amendment, in 1982 – even if this section does not, in its final form, address the declaratory power.[17] This seems to reaffirm a matter that has been intimated at several points in this book – that is, that the strategic efficacy or potency of a given strategic section of the Constitution might lie not only in the very existence of that section but also from the very *threat* of its use in practice.

To be sure, one can make an ambitious theoretical argument that the declaratory power, unlike the emergency instruments just discussed, could also be levered by the federal government in its general regulation of a given essential natural resource to ensure an *ongoing* or *standing* country-wide supply of that resource, including through legislation relating to *intraprovincial* exploration, development, and transportation of the resource in question. One might envision such a scenario in the event that, say, a given industry or sector (or group of companies) were obstructionist, dilatory or incompetent in exploiting or distributing energy from a prominent source regulated by a particular province. Were that energy seen by the federal state as peculiarly critical to adequate national supply, Parliament could threaten to use or actually use the declaratory power to assume regulatory control of the intraprovincial energy sector in question, which could in turn lead to legislation to compel that sector to accelerate the exploitation or distribution of energy – in the presumptive national interest.[18]

Quaere: could the federal government purchase, for reasons strategic, some or all of the obstructionist private company in question and assert, via Parliament, legislative jurisdiction thereover under section 91(1A) of the 1867 Act? Section 91(1A) states that Parliament has legislative responsibility for its federal public debt and property. (Of course, federal power over such debt and property would flow from the fact of federal ownership, as with a private party, rather than from the royal prerogative.) Such a scenario is not meaningfully explored in the constitutional literature and hardly addressed in the case law – again, perhaps, a measure of the absence of strategic tradition and, *a fortiori*, strategic thinking (even counterfactual strategic thinking) in Canadian constitutional culture. However, were the federal government to purchase a proprietary interest in, say, a private energy concern to advance national strategic interests, there would seem to be an uncontroversial *prima facie* basis for federal laws and regulations – including requirements for specific rates or quanta of energy production – to apply to these energy concerns. The holding in *British Columbia v. Lafarge Canada Inc.* affirms that "public property ha[s] to encompass *some* element of ownership by Canada [the Government of Canada] in order to receive constitutional immunity" from provincial laws (provincial land use laws in the *Lafarge* case) relating to that property.[19]

Provided that the federal statute or regulation in question relating to the acquired property legitimately falls, in pith and substance, under a federal head of power (section 91(1A) or other), there is little to suggest, other things being equal, that the federal government would need to buy anything but a minor or even nominal stake in a private company to assert legislative jurisdiction thereover. Justice Bastarache implies as much in his concurring judgment in *Lafarge*, writing at paragraph 123:

> [T]he relevant test is whether there is evidence of a sufficient proprietary interest in the lands on the part of the federal Crown. [I]t is clear that Crown ownership of land generally coincides with its prima facie classification as s. 91(1A) public property ... [E]ven a partial proprietary interest of the federal Crown in land will help establish a sufficient basis for classifying the land as public property under s. 91(1A).[20]

The considerable fiscal (revenue-collecting) capacity of the federal government, both in absolute terms and relative to the provincial governments, seems to give the federal government disproportionate strategic opportunity – allowing for policy-political considerations – to make, or *threaten* to make, targeted purchases of private or even provincial property across the country to assert federal legislative jurisdiction for strategic purposes.[21] Yet, while federal legislative jurisdiction over such property could be somewhat inured from relevant provincial laws of general application by virtue of the doctrine of interjurisdictional immunity,[22] it would be unconstitutional for the federal government to acquire a proprietary interest in a given concern only to proceed to legislate (colourably), in pith and substance, in an area of provincial competence – such as natural resources [under section 92A]. However, if the said legislation does relate in pith and substance to a federal proprietary interest, and if there is a coinciding provincial proprietary interest (with or without the existence of private proprietary interests), then federal legislation, through the doctrine of federal paramountcy, would trump provincial legislation in respect of that property.

The declaratory power itself could also be used by Parliament to accomplish – perhaps less "elegantly," in strategic terms – what could otherwise be done simply by acquiring a proprietary interest in a concern of national strategic interest. Moreover, if pressed, the federal government has considerable expropriation powers. It can expropriate, for all intents and purposes, only to achieve ends falling within its legislative jurisdiction. So, in respect of an obstructionist, unproductive, or incompetent group of companies or private concerns providing critical services or products to, say, the Canadian defence industry, it seems to follow that the federal government, for legislative purposes falling under the federal militia power in section 91(7) of the 1867 Act, could legitimately expropriate the companies or concerns in question. (This suggests that the federal government has greater war-planning economic capabilities, constitutionally speaking, than meet the eye through a mere survey of relevant "quasi-constitutional" statutes under the militia power. I touch on some of these statutes in Chapter 6 and treat the federal state's war-planning economic capabilities in detail in Case Study B.) Wrote Gérard V. La Forest:

> The power of expropriation of privately owned lands would appear to be inherent in most heads of power under section 91 of the [1867]

Act,[23] as well as expropriation consequent upon a declaration of a work to be for the general advantage of Canada under section 92(10)(c) of that Act. This might possibly include power to expropriate land by virtue of section 91(1A) for the more convenient use of public property, but this would be narrowly construed; the head could not be used as a colourable device for appropriating land for purposes falling outside Dominion legislative power. The federal power of expropriation is by no means limited to purposes coming under enumerated heads of power; expropriation by virtue of the general power to legislate concerning peace, order and good government is also valid ... Finally, there seems [to be] no constitutional impediment to the federal parliament expropriating private property without compensation, however undesirable this may be [in practice].[24]

The federal government would also be well within its constitutional rights, *in extremis*, to expropriate *provincial* lands without compensation to execute purposes falling squarely under a federal head of legislative power. An example of such a strategic purpose would be the building of interprovincial or international pipelines,[25] railways, or bridges – all key to effective mobilization of natural resources. It stands to reason, therefore, that these federal expropriation powers would – even in times short of emergency – materially increase to the extent that there is jurisprudential expansion of strategic federal powers such as POGG (in particular, expansion of the national concern branch or even of a fourth branch dealing with matters of interprovincial significance) and trade and commerce (discussed at length in the next chapter).[26]

The other dimension of supply is the actual physical security of a particular natural resource (or indeed, parenthetically, of agriculture and foodstuffs) as well as that of the infrastructure – so-called critical infrastructure – supporting its production and distribution.[27] The declaratory power and the section 91 general power (POGG under the national concern branch), affirmed in the *Ontario Hydro* case,[28] were primarily concerned with such physical security in the Canadian nuclear sector. (*Ontario Hydro* is arguably the only decision of any strategic import involving section 92A since its inception in 1982.) In that decision, Justice La Forest wrote for the majority at paragraph 83 that he "cannot believe that [section 92A] was meant to interfere with the paramount power vested in Parliament by virtue of the declaratory power (or, for that matter, Parliament's general power to legislate for the peace, order and good government of Canada) over [a]ll works and undertakings constructed for the production, use and application of atomic energy." It follows that, in respect of critical infrastructure of presumptive national importance such as pipelines, electricity-generating facilities or grids, as well as certain transport modes, even if they have an *intraprovincial* character, Parliament, if it so wishes, has at least one "in" or entrée through the declaratory power for regulating the physical security of these assets – again, where they are deemed to be of national strategic value. Evidently, interprovincial critical infrastructure, such as certain pipelines (under the *National Energy Board Act*[29]) and railways (which I discuss in Chapters 6 and 7), is already regulated by the federal government for safety and security.[30]

Can the federal government restrict export of essential, needed, or otherwise valued natural resources to other countries or groups of countries the behaviour of which it seeks to influence? Alternatively, can it use Canadian natural resource (or food) exports or imports as a diplomatic tool to incentivize or reward another country or group of countries? (In diplomatic terms, such transactions are part and parcel of "linkage" strategies, whereby country A links certain benefits or punishments for country B in a given policy area X – say natural resources – to the state of the A-B relationship in policy area Y – say military affairs.) Both courses of action seem uncontroversial under the Canadian Constitution. The royal prerogative, in combination with the POGG residual branch and the trade and commerce power (section 91(2)), as legislative heads of power, give the federal government all the constitutional authority that it needs to play such diplomatic "hardball," as it were, should it so wish. (Of course, this constitutional capacity should be seen in light of the associated federal constitutional incapacity to easily assure constant adequate domestic supply of key natural resources in non-emergency situations.) In practice, the *Special Economic Measures Act* and the *Export and Import Permits Act*[31] provide the legislative backing for such action.[32] Although constitutionally permissible, such action is manifestly subject to the various restrictions of relevant trade deals and frameworks. In the

NAFTA, for instance, Article 103(1) stipulates that, subject to certain exceptions (not relevant here), there are to be no restrictions on imports or exports of goods among the three contracting countries (Canada, the United States, and Mexico). Yet Article 103(3) stipulates, in almost the same breath, that, should import or export restrictions be adopted by a given country, reprisals in the form of countervailing restrictions are permitted. So, in addition to being constitutionally undisputed, the policy option of restricting natural resource exports or imports within the *NAFTA* context (and certainly outside it), while practically available to Canada, would evidently come with costs. (Beyond countervailing duties, to the extent that Canadian diplomatic "linkage" is applied to a strategically more powerful or capable trading partner, such as the United States or, say, the European Union, one can presume that such expected costs might prove to be prohibitive to the imposition of such restrictions. Against a strategically less powerful or less capable partner, such as Mexico, however, such expected costs could, in certain circumstances, well be outweighed by the presumptive benefits of the strategic imposition of restrictions by Canada.[33])

Finally, natural resources in Canada, and perhaps energy resources in particular, are and historically have always been a highly significant driver of the national economy. In fact, until the 1970s, when many Canadian governments – federal and provincial – began to see high oil prices as a rationale for privileging rent capture as a distinct policy objective, Canada's natural resources were seen, largely on the basis of the staple theory of economic development, as a primary driver of aggregate economic growth. For my purposes here, other things being equal, it stands to reason that, the larger the standing economic or industrial might of a country, the greater its aggregate strategic strength. This is true in terms of both constitutional capacity and, manifestly, policy-political praxis. I expand on this logic in the next chapter.

National Economic Might   6

National economic might or capacity is connected, in the most obvious sense, to the state's military instrument by dint of the national capacity, in both peacetime and wartime emergencies, for pure military production. By this I mean military assets such as ships (shipbuilding classically being a major economic industry), planes, helicopters, tanks, vehicles, and munitions, among others – all expensive goods necessarily underpinned by a certain national economic mass. The federal *Defence Production Act*,[1] constitutionally authorized by the federal militia and defence power (section 91(7) of the 1867 Act), gives the minister of public works and government services the presumptive lead in organizing national defence production or supplies required to meet the needs of the Department of National Defence – in short, the military needs of Canada. The act suggests at section 12 that

> The Minister shall examine into, organize, mobilize and conserve the resources of Canada contributory to, and the sources of supply of, defence supplies and the agencies and facilities available for the supply thereof and for the construction of defence projects and shall explore, estimate and provide for the fulfilment of the needs, present and prospective, of the Government and the community with respect

thereto and generally shall take steps to mobilize, conserve and coordinate all economic and industrial facilities in respect of defence supplies and defence projects and the supply or construction thereof.

However, because this section, like the rest of the act, has not been litigated in any strategically meaningful sense, I do not know at the time of writing the precise parameters of the federal government's power to substantially organize or mobilize Canada's defence industry (or indeed the overall national economy), at least in peacetime or on a standing basis. In the event of a declared war emergency, of course, the *Defence Production Act* is supplemented by the *Emergencies Act*, well treated above, which grants the federal government, once the emergency has been declared, expansive powers of economic mobilization and organization in support of the country's military efforts. (Evidently, the larger the economic capacity of the country, other things being equal, the greater its ability to support the military campaign and related industries and production in the event of actual war, and to deter a potential enemy in the event of threatened war, given that the enemy would infer to some extent the war-fighting capability of the country from its economic mass. Conversely, the smaller a country's economic capacity, other things being equal, the smaller its capacity to discourage strategic confrontation or, *in extremis*, military attack by another country.)

In addition to direct defence production, there is a country's capacity to purchase or import from other countries the assets necessary for war preparation (or deterrence) and war-fighting or to purchase assets internationally so as to deny the enemy access to such assets. The larger the economy, other things being equal, the greater a country's purchasing power for such assets. That said, excessive importation of strategic military assets (as with natural resources or food, discussed in the previous chapter) also poses a significant strategic risk for a country, given its dependence on foreign supply, as well as supply or distribution routes that could be disrupted at critical strategic moments. Still, strictly speaking, the balance between indigenous defence-related production and imported production is very much a policy choice rather than a strict constitutional concern, and the core strategic observation stands: the larger the economic capacity of the state, the greater the potency of its military instrument, other things being equal. (Of course, to repeat what has been mentioned a few times in this book, it is not just the magnitude of the factor of power – in this case the national economy – that matters for purposes of determining aggregate strategic power but also, critically, the capacity of the state to mobilize the factor, directly or indirectly, in support of the cardinal strategic instruments, the military and diplomatic instruments.)

The aggregate capacity of the Canadian economy also clearly informs Canada's diplomatic instrument. For instance, a strong economy generally bolsters a country's negotiating position as well as its attractiveness to potential partners for purposes of international trade and investment. A strong economy increases the national capacity to reward other countries with diplomatic assets such as aid, food, intelligence or information, and, to be sure, natural resources sold or exported on favourable terms. The capacity to punish – for example, through economic sanctions or trade or investment diversions to other countries – is similarly commensurate with the strength of the national economy. In addition, economic capacity correlates directly with the sheer potential size of national diplomatic and military forces – that is, in terms of total potential personnel and associated funding.

Naturally, the aggregate economic capacity of the Canadian state is a function of an extremely complicated cocktail of variables. The same is true of the economy's capacity for strategic mobilization (and resistance to disruption). I cannot tease out all of these variables in this book, but I will attempt to survey some of those that presumptively provide the essential economic backbone of Canadian strategic power. They include the macroeconomic capacity to resist strategic shocks, the general strength of the national economic union, the capacity to protect or lever strategic industries or sectors in international trade and investment agreements, the constitutional character of the national strategic transportation infrastructure, as well as the constitutional character of national strategic communications.

The federal government controls considerable national macroeconomic instruments. It does so uncontroversially. In the event, therefore, of strategic shocks directly related to the economy or bearing economic consequences or manifestations – for instance a foreign oil embargo à la OPEC 1973, a run on the Canadian dollar by foreign parties, an international banking crisis, as exists at the time of writing, or even a bona fide war – the presumptive macroeconomic lead is federal in nature. In terms of the division of powers, Parliament not only has legislative responsibility for banks under sections 91(15) (banking, incorporation of banks, and issue of paper money) and 91(16) (savings banks) of the 1867 Act but also, more importantly, constitutional monopoly on monetary policy, writ large, under several sections of the 1867 Act: to wit, section 91(14) on currency and coinage; the said sections 91(15) and 91(16); section 91(18) on bills of exchange and promissory notes; section 91(19) on interest; section 91(20) on legal tender; and perhaps even the federal trade and commerce power in section 91(2), which I take up below.[2] The Bank of Canada, which did not exist at Confederation, among other things, regulates the national money supply, regulates inflation by setting the key interest rate (or key policy rate), and has massive capacity to inject into, or withdraw from, the banking system liquidity in support of national economic goals such as price stability, protection or promotion of the national currency, and even aggregate economic product or national employment levels. The bank operates at arm's length from the federal government but is still clearly a creature of federal power.[3]

In addition to its instruments of monetary policy, Parliament enjoys, under sections 91(1A) and 91(3) of the 1867 Act, expansive taxation and spending (that is, fiscal) powers relating respectively to public debt and property and the raising of money by any mode or system of taxation.[4] In particular, section 91(1A) authorizes Parliament to borrow significant amounts of money, from both Canadian and international sources, to drive national economic goals, bearing in mind policy-political considerations.[5] In other words, beyond monetary policy, the federal state, in the event of a negative strategic shock, can lever the far more powerful fiscal policy instrument to stimulate, propel, or stabilize the economy through deficit spending[6] or, via section 91(3), play with tax rates and incentives for the same purpose.

British historian Niall Ferguson is perfectly direct in his recognition of the strategic import of national debt (fiscal policy) and central banks (monetary policy) over the ages. He posits the evolution, by the eighteenth century, of four peculiar national institutions – a so-called "square of power" – designed to finance wars by states. The first two institutions are a national parliament and a tax-gathering bureaucracy. He goes on to write:

> Third, a system of national debt allowed a state to anticipate tax revenues in the event of a sudden increase in expenditure, such as that caused by a war [or some other strategic event, shock, or crisis]. The benefit of borrowing was that it allowed the costs of wars to be spread over time, thus "smoothing" the necessary taxation. Finally, a central bank was required not only to manage debt issuance but also to exact seigniorage of paper money, which the bank monopolized.[7]

One of the great and interesting strategic complications that comes with the federal fiscal instrument, however, is that – constitutional division of powers oblige – the provincial governments also have a constitutional capacity to borrow,[8] from intraprovincial, national, and international sources, on top of the provincial legislatures' own expansive spending powers based on section 92(5) (management and sale of the public lands belonging to the province and of the timber and wood thereon) in the 1867 Act, the historically important property and civil rights power in section 92(13), as well as section 92(2), which relates to direct intraprovincial taxation to raise revenue "for provincial purposes."[9] Note that this phrase has, for all intents and purposes, become constitutionally nugatory; that is, according to Hogg, quoting Chief Justice Duff in the *Unemployment Insurance Reference*,[10] it means only that "revenue is raised 'for the exclusive disposition of the legislature.'"[11] Hogg also notes the following: "In fact, the provinces have never recognized any limits on their spending power and have often spent money for purposes outside their legislative competence, for example, by running a commuter train service on interprovincial trackage, by acquiring an airline, by giving international aid, or by paying casino profits to Indian communities."[12]

This means that, while the federal spending power is constitutionally expansive (in theory limited only to how much money the federal government can raise), and is nowhere necessarily displaced by provincial spending power (itself also, in theory, a function of the provincial capacity to raise money), its strategic potency – that is, its capacity to advance national strategic ends – can be mitigated or obstructed should one or more provinces use their spending power for ends incommensurable or at direct cross-purposes with such national strategic ends. (In contradistinction to legislative powers, there is no doctrine of federal paramountcy when it comes to spending money by the different levels of government for various purposes.) Conversely, the federal spending power can be amplified if provincial spending powers are used in strategic alignment with the federal power. Indeed, given the political drama that unfolded in Ottawa in the fall of 2008, when the government of Prime Minister Stephen Harper, but for prorogation of Parliament, would have faced an apparently unwinnable vote of confidence on a December fiscal update that seemed exceedingly meek in using the federal fiscal instrument to stimulate a recessionary economy, it could well be submitted that the federal government was in fact waiting to coordinate its fiscal stimulus package with those portended by the provinces – hence its apparently dilatory action. This view is supported by the fact that, prior to the release of the stimulatory federal budget at the end of January 2009, an important first ministers' meeting or conference was convened between the prime minister and the provincial premiers to discuss the economy and coordinate fiscal policy. And, of course, such strategic coordination between federal and provincial spending (or more general economic) powers would have been influential in determining the extent to which Canada's economic and other factors of power could be mobilized in aid of the state's principal strategic instruments.

Still, the critical economic mass or motor that drives the country and informs federal spending or fiscal capacity, including in respect of the military and diplomatic instruments, consists largely of the Canadian economic union. Having treated the federal government's direct macroeconomic tools, I therefore turn now to its microeconomic capacity in respect of this economic union. In particular, I want to understand the federal state's capacity, in constitutional terms, to directly influence the "tightness" or cohesion of the Canadian economic union (a microeconomic concern), with the indirect objective of maximizing its national growth or total product or output (a macroeconomic concern).

In respect of the domestic economic union in Canada, Michael Trebilcock has suggested that it is already "tight" or cohesive:

> Canadians share a common currency, a closely harmonized tax system, a developed rail and highway transportation infrastructure, and all provincial governments are constrained by section 121 of the Constitution Act [1867], which guarantees that all goods must be permitted to move within Canada without being made subject to provincial tariffs. Since the addition of the *Charter* ... in 1982, Canadians have also benefited from section 6, which guarantees personal mobility rights and the right to pursue a livelihood in any province of Canada. Furthermore ..., Canadians have also benefited from relatively unhindered capital flows and freedom of investment within Canada.[13]

Several studies have suggested that the welfare gain to be had from perfect economic union in Canada – that is, from a union denuded of internal economic barriers – would be in the realm of 1 to 1.5 percent.[14] (This would presumably include the much vaunted creation of a national securities commission or the elimination of barriers thereto – a matter largely settled, on jurisdictional grounds, against the federal government in the 2011 *Reference re Securities Act*.[15]) On a static model, this seems to suggest the maximum magnitude of possible improvement of Canadian economic capacity in the event that the federal government had the requisite constitutional capacity to remove all such barriers. However, on a dynamic model – like the Strategic Constitution – in which the economic factor of power is mixed and cross-pollinates with other factors of power, such as natural resources, communications, or population (or even the "pure executive," diplomatic, and military factors), this maximum could increase substantially and along with it its potential impact on overall Canadian strategic capacity.

The federal trade and commerce power in section 91(2) of the 1867 Act – *prima facie* the key constitutional head of power for direct federal microeconomic intervention or, indeed, legislation-led planning – has been largely confined to international and interprovincial trade by dint of restrictive jurisprudence initiated by the Judicial Committee of the Privy Council. (Contrast this with the expansive interpretation given by the courts in Australia to the so-called corporations power in section 51(xx) of the *Commonwealth of Australia Constitution Act, 1900* and the commerce clause in Article 1, section 8, of the US Constitution, both of which have greatly facilitated the erection of more cohesive economic unions within the Australian and American federations.) Exclusive federal jurisdiction over international and interprovincial trade is the so-called first branch of the trade and commerce power, conditioned by expansive jurisprudence by the Privy Council in respect of the provincial property and civil rights power in section 92(13) of the 1867 Act; that is, in respect of most *intraprovincial* microeconomic transactions.[16] The second branch of the trade and commerce power, relating to the federal capacity to regulate general trade for the entire country, was revived by the Supreme Court of Canada in the 1989 *General Motors v. City National Leasing* case, in which Justice Dickson established a five-part test for determining whether Parliament had constitutional authority for the regulation of general trade.[17] That holding reignited speculation – at least for a time – that the federal general trade regulatory power would be strengthened over time, in particular as the Canadian economic union and global economic dynamics become ever more complex. What's more, the logic of the Dickson test, in at least its fourth and fifth parts, is distinctly similar to the logic underpinning the national concern branch of the POGG power, also generally considered to be of potentially expansive consequence for federal constitutional jurisdiction. As Monahan suggests, "the crucial question in applying the fourth and fifth criteria under the general regulation of trade test is the need to ensure that Parliament is able to respond effectively to national economic problems."[18] The possible embryonic fourth branch of the POGG power – that of matters of interprovincial significance – could also be at play here, over time, in strengthening, through jurisprudential channels, federal powers over the national economic union.[19]

An effective economic union requires not only centralized legislative capacity to remove barriers to economic flows but also direct and meaningful circumscription of provincial capacity to erect barriers to such economic flows. On this front, section 121 of the 1867 Act, which reads that "[a]ll Articles of the Growth, Produce, or Manufacture of any one of the Provinces Shall, from and after the Union, be admitted free into each of the other Provinces," having been interpreted by the courts in the narrow sense of prohibitions on strict interprovincial customs duties, has proven to be remarkably inadequate in removing barriers to internal trade.[20] In other words, section 121 has proven to be an insufficient bar to provincial laws and regulations deliberately or inadvertently inconsistent with a maximally efficient national economic union.[21] On top of this, the jurisprudence on what has been called "negative [economic] integration," the removal of such barriers to the economic union, has been less than definitive in removing barriers to the maximum efficiency of the union.[22] I discuss section 6 Charter mobility rights in Chapter 8 on national population.

Beyond the cohesion or force of the domestic economic union, the economic capacity of Canada is doubtless also a function of its capacity to effectively negotiate international trade and investment agreements that serve to buttress national strategic power, including by increasing the magnitude (and "mobilizability," as it were) of the economic factor of power. (Strictly speaking, of course, trade and investment agreements can also yield negative economic results; that is, they can reduce the size of the economic factor of power. However, governments evidently negotiate them with the intent and general presumption that they will enhance this economic factor and thus assume that, policy mistakes aside, such trade and investment agreements typically lead to an increase in the magnitude of the national economy.) Indeed, a pivotal aspect of this negotiating capacity is the ability of the federal government to protect or lever "strategic sectors" of the economy in aid of national aggregate power.

In Canada, negotiation of international commercial agreements, strictly speaking, is a federal constitutional responsibility. Implementation, however, given *Labour Conventions*, is divided between Parliament and the provincial legislatures insofar as the agreement in question deals with matters that fall into their respective jurisdictions. As established above, this compromises in practice not only the aggregate Canadian capacity for meaningful implementation of complex, cross-jurisdictional "deliverables" negotiated in international agreements but often, just as signally, the capacity of the federal government to effectively or decisively assume certain negotiating positions in the first place, given the frequent uncertainty about implementation at the provincial level.

Although international treaties and agreements are a diminishing dimension of modern diplomacy (and strategy), these agreements continue to have material impacts on the economic factor of power. As such, the strategic stakes of proper negotiating capacity for the state are not inconsiderable. I should therefore note the existence of a non-negligible *fin de (20ᵉ) siècle* body of scholarship[23] suggesting that the Supreme Court, building on a stream of *dicta* in a number of cases, and heeding the changing international economic environment, could one day see it fit to qualify or substantially soften – though likely not outright reverse – the categorical bifurcation of treaty implementation powers from *Labour Conventions*. Such a qualification or softening, on this line of argument, would be rooted in either the national concern branch of the POGG power or the second (or general) branch of Parliament's trade and commerce power in section 91(2) of the 1867 Act. Notes Stephen McBride in this respect: "Trade agreements are now based on deep integration, are no longer confined to goods and are inextricably linked to investment. In these circumstances, the reach of the federal Trade and Commerce power might be interpreted as a much more substantial foundation for federal jurisdiction than formerly."[24]

Whether such a retreat will actually happen at the Supreme Court is not evident at this time – indeed far from it. An outright reversal of *Labour Conventions* seems highly improbable in the foreseeable future, given the long-standing incumbency of this decision, the apparent "acceptance" in policy-political praxis of the international negotiating and interprovincial consultative algorithm implied by the decision, and the anticipated political implications, particularly in Quebec, of such a drastic shift in the jurisprudence.[25] Moreover, the Supreme Court's unfavourable ruling in respect of the *Reference re Securities Act* suggests that the time is manifestly not ripe for the *Labour Conventions* regime to be upended. Still, were there anything approaching such a shift, particularly given growing international competition for trade and investment advantage (consider the exceedingly long amount of time that the federal government spent negotiating a free-trade agreement with the European Union), this would clearly be a non-negligible fillip to Canadian economic (and ultimately strategic) capacity.

Of particular strategic relevance to international trade and investment, as mentioned, is the historically important capacity of the federal government to protect or lever for Canadian strategic advantage or interest – in the service of one or more of the factors of power or one or both of the diplomatic and military instruments of power – key "strategic" industries or sectors of the Canadian economy. Because of the potential number of such strategic industries or sectors, it is impossible to give this aspect of Canadian strategic capacity proper treatment here, though I do so in respect of natural resources – in particular, Canadian energy resources – and, by limited proxy, food in Chapter 5. Other strategic sectors that need to be constitutionally canvassed to determine the aggregate federal strategic capacity along the same logic might include the finance sector, communications (which I treat in Chapter 7), certain manufacturing sub-sectors, and, indeed, transportation – to which I now turn, albeit not to examine the international trade and investment dimensions of the national transportation infrastructure.

Transportation infrastructure, of the various species of infrastructure, has been singularly salient in Canada's economic narrative. (Just as saliently, for my purposes here, transportation infrastructure is an aspect of Canada's economy that can be mobilized in direct, conspicuous support of at least one of the two key strategic instruments of Canadian power – the military instrument.[26]) Canadian *strategic* transportation infrastructure, despite the relative constitutional weakness of Canada's economic union, is largely regulated by the federal government. (As a strict policy-political matter, much of this infrastructure, across the various transport modes, as with certain natural resource-related infrastructure discussed in the previous chapter, is owned and operated by the private sector.) Railways, historically and indeed currently, still strategically critical to Canadian power – especially in relation to the economy and the military instrument – are principally regulated by the federal government. This regulation exists primarily on the strength of section 92(10)(a) of the 1867 Act, which places under federal jurisdiction – or, more precisely, exempts from provincial jurisdiction – lines of steam or other ships, *railways*, canals, telegraphs, and other *works and undertakings* connecting a province with any other province or extending beyond the limits of a province, including internationally. (Notably, the interpretation by the courts of "works and undertakings" as a rule has been expansive – that is, taken to include both physical and organizational elements and to be undivided in jurisdictional scope, with federal jurisdiction over interprovincial works or undertakings extending even to local aspects of the work or undertaking in question – in other words, with a relatively low intensity of interprovincial activity required.) As for non-interprovincial or local railways, as discussed previously, in the past they were often declared by Parliament to be for the general advantage of Canada and as such were transferred from provincial to federal jurisdiction. (This is to say nothing of the broad federal expropriation powers outlined in Chapter 4 as well as the federal executive expropriation power for military purposes in section 117.) Interprovincial and international shipping also falls under federal jurisdiction under sections 92(10)(b) and 91(10) of the 1867 Act. In comparison, the trade and commerce power in section 92(2), because historically it has been interpreted so narrowly by the courts, has had little direct impact on the rail sector or on any of the other transport modes in Canada.

The other "heavy lift" transport mode is air travel. Like the rail mode, its regulation is dominated by the federal government under the *Canada Transportation Act* (exclusive federal responsibility for air services in Canada) and the *Aeronautics Act* (exclusive federal responsibility for safety and security of passengers, aircraft, and airports). The Supreme Court famously determined that aeronautics is an indubitable national concern under the federal POGG power in the 1952 *Johannesson v. West St. Paul* case,[27] noting "the rapid growth of passenger and freight traffic by air, the use of aircraft for the carriage of mails especially to the more remote northern parts of the country, and the necessity for the development of air services to be controlled by a national government responsive to the needs of the nation as a whole."[28] (Pedantry requires adding that diplomats usually fly!)

Finally, strategic communications also evidently inform the strength of the economic factor of power, just as they inform the military and diplomatic instruments unmediated by any of the subordinate factors of power. East-west and north-south communications across Canada – in the "macro" modes of phone (telecommunications), broadcast radio, and television – are, for the most part, uncontroversially regulated by Parliament. The Internet, granted, is a more complicated beast.

Communications   7

As established in Chapter 6, national communications capabilities have dual strategic import: first, as a key sinew of the economy factor of power;[1] second, as a direct support of the national diplomatic and military instruments of strategic power.[2] Communications, as understood here, are to be differentiated from the historically broad Canadian constitutional or jurisprudential conception of "communications" – one that, of necessity, included transportation capabilities. That broad conception of communications suffused the Canadian constitutional vernacular until the advent of radio and television.[3] Although my interest here is in the constitutional conception of strategic communications capabilities, the strict definition of communications should be a strategic one (befitting the categories in the Strategic Constitution construct) – to wit, the mediated flow of information in its various forms or modalities. These forms or modalities include radio, telephone, television, signals, and, *inter alia*, cyber – recognizing, naturally, the increasing technical convergence and overlap among many of them. This definition is illustrative and non-exhaustive, such that I do not treat – economy oblige – more "prosaic" or "pedestrian" (less strategic?) forms of communication such as theatre and film, though I do touch on certain exceptional cases in respect of printed literature – particularly newspapers.[4] Regarding strategic communications capabilities and the diplomatic or military instruments of the state, the French strategic analyst Jacques Baud writes:

> La maîtrise de l'information [comprend, entre autres] la maîtrise de la communication entre les forces armées et le monde politique et civil et la gestion de la perception du conflit. Il s'agit non seulement de maîtriser le contenu de l'information diffusée, mais également la manière dont l'information est partagée ... La maîtrise des vecteurs d'information implique a) la possibilité de les employer en permanence avec un minimum de restrictions, et b) la capacité d'en prévenir la neutralisation. Elle suppose donc, non seulement la capacité de résister à des agressions (mesures de protection physique d'installations), mais également la capacité d'agir contre des vecteurs adverses dans le cyberspace.[5]

In short, both form and content – specifically control or degree of control of content – are relevant aspects of strategic communications from the standpoint of the state. Let me posit that a *de minimis* standard of democratic (Canadian federal) control of communications consists of (a) control of the message in strategically important moments (that is, not always) and (b) control of the means of communications (or prevention of disruption of such means).[6] I will treat (b) first and then (a). I am ultimately interested in the effective magnitude of the communications factor of power for the Canadian state as well as the degree to which this factor can be mobilized, in policy-political praxis, in support of the two cardinal strategic instruments – diplomatic and military – of the state.

In the Canadian Constitution, federal regulatory dominance over the principal means of conventional strategic communications – telephony, radio and television broadcasting, and signals communications – is compelling. (The Internet, which I treat below, *qua* communications medium, is not strictly under federal regulation except, in strategic terms, in a segmented way via, say, the *Criminal Code* for discrete types of cyber activity or transactions that can have varying degrees of strategic import. As established below, *Criminal Code* and intelligence interception of electronic communications via the Internet can often relate to communications of strategic consequence.[7]) Telecommunications – in both the technical and content dimensions – are unexceptionally under federal jurisdiction, per section 92(10)(a) of the 1867 Act, based on key cases such as *Toronto v. Bell Telephone Co.*,[8] *Alberta Government Telephones v. CRTC*,[9] and even *Téléphone Guèvremont v. Quebec*.[10] Radio broadcasting and television broadcasting – again both technically and in terms of content[11] – are also under federal jurisdiction, likely under the same section, 92(10)(a), of the 1867 Act, as well as the residual branch of POGG, based on cases such as the *Radio Reference*,[12] *Re CFRB*,[13] *Public Service Board v. Dionne*,[14] and *Capital Cities Communications v. CRTC*.[15] Recall that section 92(10)(a) grants Parliament competence over putatively exceptional local works and undertakings – which would otherwise fall under provincial jurisdiction – such as lines of steam or other ships, railways, canals, telegraphs, and other works and undertakings "connecting [a] Province with any other or others of the Provinces, or extending beyond the Limits of the Province." (Note again the easy interchange in the constitutional vernacular of what is typically called "transportation" and what is typically called "communications.")[16] (In Case Study D, I briefly explain how, in transportation and, by frequent identification or extension, communications, the Canadian courts, *contra* their treatment of the federal trade and commerce power, have taken a "non-segmented" approach to assigning jurisdiction between the federal and provincial governments – usually in favour of the federal government.) Finally, as established in Chapter 2, the Communications Security Establishment (CSE), which leads on signals intelligence in Ottawa, has a clear statutory mandate in the *National Defence Act* – a mandate underpinned by section 91(7) of the 1867 Act.

Canadian jurisprudence on the various communications modes, for all intents and purposes, nowhere invokes "strategy" (or, say, *raison d'état*) or Canadian strategic performance or purposes in the world as a constitutional lever – even under any of the branches of POGG – through which federal legislative dominance can be affirmed. This is in keeping with the "astrategic" constitutional jurisprudential tradition posited in this book.[17] Consider, for example, the complete absence of strategic vernacular – or "strategic imagination" – in the reasoning concerning communications in the important 2009 transportation holding *Consolidated Fastfrate Inc. v. Western Canada Council of Teamsters et al.*[18]

Writing in dissent, Justice Binnie, though eloquent and persuasive in defence of an expansive ("purposive" or "functional") interpretation of section 92(10)(a) in respect of transportation and expanded federal competence for works and undertakings that are increasingly interprovincial in the context of an increasingly complex, modern economy, is patently silent on strategy. Instead, a purely *economic* narrative, discourse, logic, or rationality prevails in his analysis. Refusing to accept differential jurisprudential interpretation of transportation and communications cases under section 92(10)(a), he writes at paragraph 89:

> Canadian courts have never accepted the sort of "originalism" implicit in my colleague's [Justice Rothstein's] historical description of the thinking of 1867. The persistent feebleness of the federal power over trade and commerce and the eclipse of the federal authority related to peace, order and good government bear witness to the ascendance of the "living tree" approach. As our Court recently stated in relation to the division of legislative authority in *Canadian Western Bank v. Alberta*, 2007 S.C.C. 2, [2007] 2 S.C.R. 3, "the interpretation of these powers and of how they interrelate must evolve and must be tailored to the changing political and cultural realities of Canadian society" (para. 23). This is not to say that the passage of time alters the division of powers. It is to say that the arrangement of legislative and executive powers entrenched in the Constitution Act, 1867 must now be applied in light of the *business realities of 2009* and not frozen in 1867.[19]

As with a number of other factors of power, however, astrategic jurisprudence here still yields a strategic outcome – the federal government possesses muscular capabilities, in constitutional terms, to regulate different communications modes and content – satisfying the *de minimis* strategic standard discussed above.

Evidently, a substantial portion of communications assets in Canada is owned by the private sector – for the most part (still), *Canadian* private interests, as dictated by section 7(d) of the *Telecommunications Act*.[20] The degree of such private ownership is largely contingent on the policy-political predilections of government, other things being equal. The same holds true, for all intents and purposes, for the degree of foreign versus Canadian ownership (or control) of such assets. In other words, the ideal strategic mix is a function of government policy-political disposition, and the actual mix is not necessarily a reflection of Canadian strategic power as conceptualized here.

Regarding private versus public ownership, on a standing, non-emergency basis, where it fancies direct ownership necessary – for, say, more direct control (or security) of the medium or content – the federal government can easily purchase communications assets from the private sector, thereby allowing Parliament to acquire, via section 91(1A) of the 1867 Act, legislative competence therefor. Parliament can also, as discussed at length in Chapter 4, use the declaratory power to acquire legislative competence over a particular communications "work." (The vast majority of historical uses of the federal declaratory power have related to intraprovincial or local railways – entities that, as discussed above, have been constitutionally viewed as "communications.") In the strict domain of communications, as defined in this chapter, communications works have been declared for the general advantage of Canada on a number of occasions, including in the incorporation of Bell Canada (1882) and the British Columbia Telephone Company (1923) as well as the reorganization and divestiture of Teleglobe Canada (1987) – the most recent use of the declaratory power. *In extremis*, also available is a federal capacity for outright expropriation of communications assets, such as radio stations.[21] (In emergency situations, similar expropriation powers, including in respect of communications assets, are available under the *Emergencies Act* or, beyond that, via the national security or emergency prerogative supervening on the act.) Regarding foreign ownership or control, specific statutes such as the *Broadcasting Act*[22] and, until recently, the *Telecommunications Act* have prohibited foreign ownership or control of broadcasting and telecommunications assets, respectively, in Canada.[23] However, the 2010 federal speech from the throne and the 2010 budget committed the federal government to increasing foreign investment limits in the telecommunications sector and removing foreign ownership barriers on Canadian satellites. There was a federal general election in May 2011. In 2012, the federal government amended the

Telecommunications Act to waive foreign ownership restrictions on telecommunications common carriers if the carrier earns annual telecommunications revenues not exceeding 10 percent of the aggregate revenues of the Canadian telecommunications industry.

There is also the *Investment Canada Act*,[24] which provides at section 2 for "the review of significant [inward] investments in Canada by non-Canadians in a manner that encourages investment, economic growth and employment opportunities in Canada and ... for the review of investments in Canada by non-Canadians that could be injurious to national security." More specifically, section 25.2(1) of the act reads thus: "If the Minister has reasonable grounds to believe that an investment by a non-Canadian could be injurious to national security, the Minister may, within the prescribed period, send to the non-Canadian a notice that an order for the review of the investment may be made." This national security test (instituted in March 2009) supplements the "net benefit to Canada" test in sections 16(1), 20,[25] and 21(1) for foreign, non-World Trade Organization (WTO) member direct investments exceeding $5 million or, in the case of investment in a company that controls another company in Canada (that is, indirect investment), $50 million – a test that gives the federal government considerable discretion in determining the compatibility of such investments with national policies and circumstances and, presumably, overall Canadian strategy. (Thresholds for review under the *Investment Canada Act* of foreign investments by WTO members are higher. These thresholds are issued annually through ministerial regulation.) Under section 15 of the act, the government also has discretion to review, notwithstanding the aforementioned thresholds, any investment deemed to relate to "Canada's culture or national identity." In practical policy-political terms, the *Investment Canada Act*, at the time of writing, has been used to block or effectively block a proposed investment only twice since 1985 (when it replaced the *Foreign Investment Review Act*[26]) for non-cultural sector reviews and only thrice for cultural sector reviews.[27] Nevertheless, the discretion to prohibit foreign investments in Canada that might be contrary to Canadian strategic interests – or, say, Canadian interests in economic sectors identified as strategic, as discussed in Chapter 6 – is implicit in, and permitted by, the terms in sections 20 and 25.2(1) of the *Investment Canada Act* –

quasi-constitutionally, as it were, on my conception. Policy-political praxis, once again, is a separate matter. (In 2011, the federal government dropped a lawsuit against US Steel Corporation for alleged breach of its production and employment undertakings to the government for the "net benefit" of Canada, following its 2007 purchase of Stelco Steel of Hamilton. The government settled with the American company after it made specific, remedial operational and capital investment commitments.[28])

What about control over content? One *de minimis* manifestation of control, in strategic terms, is the state's capacity to intercept (prevent? destroy?) certain communications that are part of activity that threatens the state (national security) or otherwise strategically relevant to state interests – for example, communications that affect interstate competition or are otherwise important in determining strategic advantage or disadvantage in international affairs. There are different criteria for such interception in Canada of private communications – interception that might bump up against section 8 of the Charter, which deals with security against unreasonable search and seizure.[29] Section 8 typically kicks in to protect a reasonable expectation of privacy – usually through the requirement of a judicial warrant[30] – by those whose communication – telephonic or electronic[31] – is to be intercepted or placed under surveillance by the state. Such interception can be for purposes of criminal prosecution or intelligence. Regarding strict criminal evidence in the form of communication – for, say, a terrorism offence under the *Criminal Code* – as opposed to communications intercepted for *intelligence* purposes, where there is a breach of section 8, one looks to section 24(2) of the Charter to determine whether admission of the intercepted communication brings the administration of justice into disrepute.[32] If the intercepted communication does bring the administration of justice into disrepute, then the evidence is not admissible in court, and there is no obvious case to suggest that unreasonable search and seizure could otherwise be saved under section 1.[33] If the administration of justice is not brought into disrepute, then the evidence clearly is admissible in court. As already established, the Charter, per *Hape*, applies abroad in international search and seizure cases only to the extent that there is agreement by the subject state to its jurisdiction (for agents of the

Canadian state) – with the proviso, naturally, as per the *Khadr* line of cases, that Canadian agents or officials do not engage in processes that contravene Canada's international legal obligations, with all the practical complications, well treated above, that this somewhat overinclusive formulation carries.

However, security agencies such as CSIS and the CSE can also intercept private communications on the basis of warrants that require national security (rather than criminal-investigative) justifications before the Federal Court.[34] Section 21 of the *CSIS Act* states:

> Where the Director or any employee designated by the Minister for the purpose believes, on reasonable grounds, that a warrant under this section is required to enable the Service to investigate a threat to the security of Canada or to perform its duties and functions under section 16 [relating to the role of CSIS in collecting information or intelligence, for the defence of Canada or its international relations, on the capabilities, intentions, and activities of Canadian citizens, foreign citizens, and, *inter alia*, foreign states], the Director or employee may, after having obtained the approval of the Minister, make an application in accordance with subsection (2) to a judge for a warrant under this section.

These CSIS warrants – lasting up to sixty days each and renewable – are powerful, authorizing the service at section 21(3) of the act, for purposes of interception of any communication or obtainment of any information, record, or document, (a) to enter any place or open or obtain access to any thing; (b) to search for, remove or return, examine, take extracts from or make copies of, or record in any other manner the information, document, or thing; or (c) to install, maintain, or remove any thing.

The CSE can autonomously intercept truly foreign communications (relying on the constitutional militia and defence power), without statutory oversight in Canada, via renewable one-year ministerial authorizations, insofar as these communications are not defined as "private communications" by both the *Criminal Code* and the *National Defence Act*.[35] According to section 273.65(1) of the *National Defence Act*, CSE intercepts of private communications can also take place, on authorization of the Minister of National Defence,[36] to obtain foreign intelligence but cannot target Canadian citizens and permanent residents wherever located or indeed any person – Canadian and non-Canadian alike – located inside Canada.[37] More intricately, the CSE can assist CSIS in intercepting foreign communications (thereby overcoming part of the extraterritorial handicap of CSIS as well as the handicap of the CSE in respect of targeting Canadians), provided that such interception takes place and is read within Canada and is authorized by a section 21 CSIS warrant. This dynamic was confirmed in 2009 by the Federal Court in *Re CSIS Act*,[38] with Justice Mosley stating at paragraphs 75 and 76 of the decision that

> Canada has given CSE a mandate to collect foreign intelligence including information from communications and information technology systems and networks abroad. It is restricted as a matter of legislative policy from directing its activities against Canadians or at any person within Canada, but is not constrained from providing assistance to security and law enforcement agencies acting under lawful authority such as a judicial warrant. CSIS is authorized to collect threat-related information about Canadian persons and others and ... is not subject to a territorial limitation. Where the statutory prerequisites of a warrant are met, including prior judicial review, reasonable grounds and particularization of the targets, the collection of the information by CSIS with CSE assistance, as proposed, falls within the legislative scheme approved by Parliament and does not offend the *Charter*.

The 2010 Supreme Court judgment in *R. v. National Post*[39] also noted that the federal executive, in the interest of collecting criminal evidence – including, by simple implication, national security-related matters – is not necessarily blocked, on a case-by-case basis, in intercepting or seizing relevant media communications even by journalist-source privilege (rooted in common law) and that such interception or seizure would not necessarily be in breach of section 2(b) of the Charter[40] or section 8, for that matter, if so-called Wigmore criteria (four conditions) are not met by the parties claiming the said privilege. The *Supreme Court Reports* summary of the majority decision represented the ratio as follows:

> A promise of confidentiality [between journalist and secret source] will be respected if: the communication originates in a confidence that the identity of the informant will not be disclosed; the confidence is essential to the relationship in which the communication arises; the relationship is one which should be sedulously fostered in the public good; and the public interest in protecting the identity of the informant [the source] from disclosure outweighs the public interest in getting at the truth [for instance, for purposes of obtaining criminal evidence]. This approach properly reflects *Charter* values and balances the competing interests [the ability of the executive to collect evidence and prosecute crimes versus the public interest in having freedom of expression and for journalistic sources not to be dried up] in a context-specific manner.

While the *National Post* holding deals principally with the question of criminal evidence and journalist-secret source privilege, deference of the court to the Wigmore criteria confirms the constitutional right of the federal government to intercept or seize certain "privileged" communications (whatever the mode) even from media concerns if the national security interest (the "getting at the truth" interest of the public, per the Wigmore vernacular) is not shown – per the fourth Wigmore criterion and assuming that the first three criteria are proven – by the media concern in question to be outweighed by the public interest in protecting the identity of a particular informant to the media (such as an informant who has provided the media with material information regarding Canadian national security). Justice Binnie says as much in *obiter* at paragraph 58 of this decision: "Having established the value to the public of the relationship in question [that is, the relationship between journalist and secret source], the court must weigh against its protection any countervailing public interest such as the investigation of a particular crime (or *national security*, or *public safety* or some other public good)."[41]

What about the constitutional capacity of the federal government to *direct*, as it wishes or sees fit, messages through the various communication modes or media – particularly in crisis or emergency situations? In other words, what are the federal government's crisis communication capabilities, constitutionally speaking?[42] Such communications might variously serve to protect the "home front" or Canadian interests from, say, terrorist attack, motivate troop conscription or mobilization in the event of war (or domestic insurrection), or, more fundamentally, project governmental order and legitimacy – "constitutional-strategic legitimacy," as it were – across the Canadian population in the context of a national emergency, including war.

To this end, one can presume that what Viscount Haldane said in 1923, in delivering the Privy Council's judgment, in *Fort Frances Pulp and Paper Co. v. Manitoba Free Press Co.*,[43] at paragraph 20, remains largely apposite in the early twenty-first century:

> When war has broken out it may be requisite to make special provision to ensure the maintenance of law and order in a country, even when it is in no immediate danger of invasion. Public opinion may become excitable, and one of the causes of this may conceivably be want of uninterrupted information in newspapers [or indeed in other forms of communication, such as radio and television broadcasting]. Steps may be taken to ensure supplies of these and to avoid shortage.

Viscount Haldane was interpreting the old *War Measures Act* of 1914 (now rescinded and replaced by the modern *Emergencies Act*) and held that constitutional jurisdiction for managing emergencies lay, in an implied way (and only for the period of time necessary for dealing with the emergency), with the federal government – a centralizing necessity that he called "statesmanship."

Of course, the modern *Emergencies Act* has not to date been litigated. It might therefore be difficult to appreciate some of the exact statutory limits of the powers of the federal government under each of the four categories of emergency in the act, including in relation to the direction of specific types of communication from different media (whether one speaks of privately held media or state-owned media, such as the Canadian Broadcasting Corporation, the CBC). In the latter case, the *Broadcasting Act*, which articulates in statute – in very broad terms – Canada's national broadcasting policy, is silent on emergencies and crises per se. This is true both in section 3(d), which speaks explicitly to the broadcasting policy framework, and in section 3(m), which explains the mandate of the CBC. This silence, while *prima facie* unhelpful in strategic terms (like many similar silences on strategy in Canada's constitutional and quasi-constitutional framework[44]), can nevertheless be remedied through new or additional legislative language in this act addressing federal executive rights and responsibilities for specific communications (type, quality, length or frequency, reach, and so on) to the public in the event of national crisis or emergency. This language would be underpinned, constitutionally, by the federal interprovincial communications power in section 92(10)(a) of the 1867 Act or the federal residual power in POGG or, as intimated above, the emergency branch of the general power. The same simple legislative change approach could be applied to other federally regulated communications media, such as radio. The Charter would evidently apply to all of the statutes (and amended statutes) in question.

The same federal regulatory authority, rooted in the same constitutional powers, would exist for the federal government in relation to privately held media, such as private broadcasters or radio stations; that is, the government could explicitly address, in statute, the issue of federal government rights and responsibilities in crisis communications. Indeed, for private media concerns, the more extreme or outer limits of the capacity of the federal executive to communicate what it needs and wishes in crisis or emergency situations would be conditioned by the existence of clear federal expropriation powers, temporary or permanent, corresponding to most of its heads of power (in the event, interprovincial communications). In short, the federal government, in the absence of cooperation or even adequate standards from a private media concern, could expropriate that concern, emergency oblige, to meet its particular strategic objectives in communications.

As for the Internet, including so-called Web 2.0, as a communications medium[45] or, more precisely, as part of the "new media," it is not, at the time of writing, regulated per se in its entirety or "holistically" by either the federal government or the provincial governments in Canada. In an important ruling in 1999,[46] the CRTC decided, *contra* telecommunications and broadcasting, that it would exempt, without terms or conditions, the Internet and other new media from its regulatory scope. That ruling is being challenged by growing pressures for some species of federal regulation of the Internet *qua* medium – *de maximis*, regulation that mirrors that of the broadcasting medium, particularly in respect of Canadian content requirements.[47] One can rightly ask, therefore, what is the federal constitutional capacity to use or control the Internet as a communications medium in the context of national crisis or emergency?

Evidently, the lowest hanging fruit for the federal government in Internet emergency communications is to (a) ensure that government Internet sites and service providers are electronically secure, under the leadership of the CSE, charged – quasi-constitutionally, as it were – with securing "electronic information and information infrastructures of importance,"[48] and (b) use its own websites (the number of which is a function only of the spending power that the federal government is willing to put behind the purchase of Internet sites or domain names) to communicate whatever it fancies. More ambitiously, leaving aside again the "softer" arts of persuasion and even convention, could the federal government condition or control what non-government Canadian websites – defined by the owner rather than the identity of the service provider – communicate in emergency situations? Leaving aside the heavy practical burden of enforcement or implementation, this is evidently uncharted legal and regulatory territory and bumps up rather abruptly against section 2(b) Charter freedoms of expression for individual website owners, both private and commercial – all of whom one can safely presume to be multitudinous. Indeed, this is to a large extent where the current regulatory debate in respect of the Internet – not for emergency situations but for everyday life – finds itself.

Of course, in the emergency context, section 1 of the Charter could theoretically prove to be a saving clause for such federal control, though it would likely encounter possibly insurmountable difficulties in overcoming the third branch of the *Oakes* test – that of minimal impairment of individual rights.

Population   8

As postulated earlier, the exclusive constitutional capacity of the provinces, in section 93 of the 1867 Act, to legislate on education is a patent strategic weakness in the Canadian federation, other things being equal – in spite of, say, the cultural benefits of localized public education. This strategic weakness is particularly glaring regarding development of the "talent pool" necessary to populate and animate the state's diplomatic and military instruments; that is, the strategic centre of the Canadian state is unable to directly and systematically assure development of the talent that it needs to meet Canada's strategic objectives. This is not to say that such talent will not necessarily issue, in some cases, from the provincially led educational systems, only that such successful outcomes, however rare or common, will typically not have been intentionally in the service of strategic performance by the state. This strategic weakness exists notwithstanding the considerable federal spending power on education and "human capital" training or formation, a theme typically falling, in legislative terms, under the broad provincial property and civil rights power in section 92(13).[1] The power to directly tailor curricula to meet national objectives, strategic and otherwise, is clearly an advantage from which only unitary countries such as New Zealand, France, Singapore, Poland, and even Ukraine[2] can profit and which, in strategic terms, is the envy of complex federations such as Canada.[3]

For purposes of economy, I have decided not to belabour the idea of education – in its many dimensions – as a material contributor to the population element or factor of power. This decision is perhaps best explained by the proposition that, assuming a generally high level of country-wide education (as exists and will arguably typically exist in Canada), the greater strategic advantage in "population" terms comes from sheer numbers or sheer manageable numbers. In short, other things being equal, a better or more "strategically" educated population of 35 million – Canada's present population – is of substantially smaller strategic benefit to Canada than a population of, say, 60 or 70 million educated at today's standards, even if the pedagogy is "astrategic" or largely controlled by the provinces.[4] To put it crudely, at 60 million people Canada would have the demographic mass of today's France or United Kingdom but with greater geography and natural resources. Writes John Mearsheimer:

> [T]he size of a state's population and its wealth are the two most important components for generating military might. Population size matters a lot, because great powers require big armies, which can be raised only in countries with large populations. States with small populations cannot be great powers ... Population size also has important economic consequences, because only large populations can produce great wealth, the other building block of military power.[5]

More exotically, though, for my purposes, if Canada could also properly or effectively distribute such an increased population across its land mass – that is, in accordance with national strategic objectives – to create more and bigger cities and economic centres or to assert sovereignty in the North – the strategic impact would be all the greater: the national economy would be larger (not least given the economic synergies created by big, complex cities), natural resources more potently exploited, and the diplomatic force and army larger, since the pool of talent to populate these instruments would be far more substantial.

Granted, immigration aside, the federal government has certain key constitutional tools at its disposal to attempt to increase the national population (namely, the tax and spending power in sections 91(1A) and

91(3), *inter alia*, of the 1867 Act) – to create reproductive tax incentives or baby bonuses to increase the indigenous birth rate. At the same time, however, many equally critical constitutional powers – many microeconomic powers, education, and many aspects of health care – relevant to family planning are at the provincial level. In addition to, or in place of, incentivizing an increased national birth rate, the other essential constitutional power for increasing national population is that of immigration, which in Canada is a joint federal-provincial power under section 95 of the 1867 Act, with federal paramountcy.[6]

The federal government sets national immigration targets annually under the *Immigration and Refugee Protection Act*. It is required by the act to consult with provinces in setting these national targets. However, the act notes clearly that one of its many – often contradictory – goals is to enable the federal government to determine the demographic or population structure of the country. Quebec, more than the other provinces, has its own immigration regime, in legislative terms, stemming from this act and based on an agreed division of labour with the federal government in which Quebec City is responsible for selection of immigrants to the province (for example, for enrichment of the sociocultural heritage of Quebec, economic benefit, and consistency with its demographic goals), while the federal government preserves overall responsibility for national standards of admission of immigrants into Canada, including in respect of screening for national security purposes. Let me suppose, per my nomenclature, that this agreed division of labour between the federal government and Quebec on immigration, being little susceptible to change (in general terms), has effective quasi-constitutional status.[7]

Even with the *sui generis* Quebec immigration arrangement, the federal government has uncontroversial constitutional capacity to determine the aggregate number of immigrants entering Canada as well as the rate of such entry. As a consequence, it is the federal government that, for all intents and purposes, determines the rate of net growth of the Canadian population resulting from immigration. That the federal government may choose to grow the total Canadian population to reach a certain threshold of strategic moment is therefore beyond constitutional reproach.

Evidently, in practical terms, mass increases to immigration levels do not come without concrete *policy-political* costs, including significant additional upstream costs related to security and quality screening as well as downstream costs related to integration and other social services. In particular, any increase in aggregate immigration to the country would likely have to be largely in keeping with the *Canada-Quebec Accord* of 1991 on immigration. Two notable objectives of the accord, as stated in section 2, are to preserve the demographic weight of Quebec within Canada and to integrate immigrants into Quebec in a manner that respects the province's distinct identity. To the extent that one sees this accord as quasi-constitutional, one can see it as materially complicating the otherwise uncontroversial constitutional capacity of the federal government to increase Canada's overall population, regardless of whether such demographic increase is conscientiously aimed at bolstering national strategic power. Although the wording in the accord is not tantamount to a guarantee, it seems reasonable to expect that the annual growth in Canadian immigration in practice would be capped less by the global supply of immigrants than by the global supply of immigrants susceptible to integration into Quebec society. (Section 12(c) of the accord states that Canada shall not admit any immigrant into Quebec who does not meet Quebec's selection criteria.)

What of the "quality" of the immigrants that Canada might select – that is, the ability or "talent" of immigrants, over time and even through offspring, to directly increase the potency of the strategic instruments of the state or the underlying factors of strategic power? *Prima facie*, there is nothing barring the federal government, in constitutional terms, from determining the quality of immigrants entering Canada, which the government currently does through the various classes of immigration in the *Immigration and Refugee Protection Act*. It follows that, if the federal government were interested in a particular immigrant or immigrant group – say for strategic reasons – there would be no constitutional bar to that particular immigrant or group being specifically targeted and recruited by the government, even if, of course, this meant the alteration of existing classes of immigration in statute or the creation in statute of new classes of immigration. To be sure, such recruitment of talent by the federal government would need to be consistent with the *Canada-Quebec Accord*.

One additional key, constitutionally relevant driver of strategic power in respect of the population factor is that of demographic distribution. Massively increased numbers of immigrants would arguably bring greater strategic – and indeed social – benefit to the country if properly and deliberately distributed across its physical territory.[8] Such distribution could serve at minimum to create critical economic masses in cities – and, to be sure, in *more* and *new* cities – and assert sovereignty, including through the military instrument, in underpopulated parts of Canada's huge geography, such as the North, the Maritimes, and the Prairies. Manifestly, such talk raises the vexed question of whether the federal government could meaningfully control or regulate the distribution of immigrants across the territory of the country – as a shorthand for strategically controlling, over time, the distribution of its aggregate population.

A federal *requirement* for immigrants to live in area X (as opposed to area Y) of the country for a period of time (t > 0) could well be a *prima facie* affront to the mobility rights in section 6 of the Charter, which are inured against the notwithstanding clause in section 33. Indeed, there has been no jurisprudence to date on this fact pattern, and precious few section 6 cases at the Supreme Court,[9] so the analysis here has to be largely counterfactual. Section 6(2) states that every citizen and permanent resident of Canada has the right (a) to move to and take up residence in any province and (b) to pursue a livelihood in any province. Furthermore, the rights in section 6(2) are subject to the limitations in section 6(3): that is, (a) any laws or practices of general application in force in a province other than those that discriminate among persons primarily on the basis of province of present or previous residence and (b) any laws providing for reasonable residency requirements as a qualification for the receipt of publicly provided social services. Finally, section 6(4) provides that none of the above precludes any law, program, or activity that has as its object the amelioration of conditions of individuals in a particular province who are socially or economically disadvantaged if the rate of employment in that province is below the rate of employment in Canada.

Would the (re)distribution requirement in respect of immigrants be constitutional? As discussed, were the required distribution or redistribution in question strictly intraprovincial – from, say, big city A to smaller city B – rather than interprovincial, then there would clearly be no breach of section 6 rights. The question of constitutionality, instead, would turn on whether the enacting government was justified on the basis of the division of powers scheme in the 1867 Act. In the event, were the federal government the enacting party, which head of power would be available to it? The 1867 Act is silent on the question of "strategy" per se. The federal government could not therefore credibly argue before the courts that it is interested in redistributing masses of people – immigrants – for purposes of growing its strategic power. (This brings us to a crucial point woven throughout this book: could the courts ever fathom recognizing "strategy" as a proper end of the state?) A possible alternative is use of the federal POGG power – in particular the residual branch as it relates to national security or, more precisely, say, sovereignty. Still, this rationale is unlikely to be credible before the courts – at least not at the time of writing. A far more likely scenario, subconstitutionally, is that the federal government would have to strike an agreement with a province – the proper enacting party for matters within the province – to require such intraprovincial distribution of immigrants. (The federal government, of course, could arguably go it alone if there were a question of distributing immigrants within or indeed between any of the three federal territories.)

Naturally, talk of strict intraprovincial or intraterritorial distribution of population – especially for immigrants – must reckon with the possibility that immigrants may simply, *proprio motu*, jump from province to province or territory, or from territory to province, as is their *prima facie* constitutional right, at least insofar as the taking up of residence or the pursuit of a livelihood is concerned.[10] In this case, one might observe that section 6(2) refers only to citizens and permanent residents and not to aspiring immigrants who are not yet permanent residents – technically foreign nationals. Thus, it is conceivable and constitutionally permissible that the federal government, should it wish to do so, could impose certain residency conditions on foreign nationals pending their receipt of permanent resident status to populate areas of strategic interest to the state. (Of course, on the current practice, leaving aside policy-political costs, this does not leave much time – a few years on average – for the foreign national to reside in his or her designated location before possibly acceding to permanent resident status, though, to be sure, the period preceding accession to permanent resident status could well be increased in statute or regulation.) Moreover, per the ruling in *Canadian Egg Marketing Agency v. Richardson*,[11] the designated residency requirement could theoretically be applied to even permanent residents and citizens if, as per section 6(3), mobility discrimination against the individual in question is not *primarily* on the basis of residence. The *Supreme Court Reports* summary of the case states that the majority of the Supreme Court in *Canadian Egg Marketing Agency* held that sections 6(2) and 6(3)(a) should be read as a single right:

> Section 6 of the Charter guarantees the mobility of persons, not as a feature of the economic unity of the country, but in order to further a human rights purpose. It is centred on the individual. Section 6 relates to an essential attribute of personhood that mobility in the pursuit of a livelihood will not be prevented through unequal treatment based on residence by the laws in force in the jurisdiction in which that livelihood is pursued. Given this purpose, the focus of the analysis in s. 6 is not the type of economic activity involved, but rather the purpose and effect of the particular legislation, and whether that purpose and effect infringe the right to be free from discrimination on the basis of residence in the pursuit of a livelihood.

The court, building on this logic, determined that, to the extent that the mobility discrimination in question is legitimately – indeed primarily – premised on a constitutional head of power, and not on residence, a limitation on mobility would be constitutional. Of course, this begs the same question as that above: could the federal government credibly argue that *strategy* is a legitimate purpose of the Canadian state, in constitutional terms? Or could it, more or less "colourably," offer cognate justifications rooted in, say, a national security or even economic premise?

The "pure strategy" justification or line of constitutional defence, on section 6 grounds, for such a distributive scheme seems rather improbable, given the general and indeed wholly explicable domestic orbit within which Canadian constitutional jurisprudence and scholarship have developed. (That said, perhaps an ostensibly colourable national security or economic line of argument might work: the North needs more people to secure the Arctic against foreign encroachments, given the ever-accelerating melting of polar ice – to take but one example that might be "low-hanging fruit.") This leaves one with only section 1 of the Charter as a possible "saving clause" for the apparent breach of section 6 rights caused by any forced or required (re)distribution of Canadian citizens or permanent residents for primarily strategic reasons. Section 1, of course, "guarantees the rights and freedoms set out in it subject only to such reasonable limits prescribed by law as can be demonstrably justified in a free and democratic society." This provision was famously adjudicated by the *Oakes* test,[12] in which Chief Justice Dickson set out a four-part test for determining what in fact were these *soi-disant* "reasonable limits." Dickson said that an impugned provision could be saved under section 1 if there were proof of a pressing and substantial objective; a rational connection between the provision and the objective; minimal impairment of an individual's rights and freedoms; and a predominance of benefits from the said provision vis-à-vis the negative impact on the associated rights. These considerations are patently domestic in their concerns. They ignore strategy as a legitimate end of the Canadian state, even in the context of (the values of) a "free and democratic society." Yet the jurisprudential record in respect of *Oakes*, while inconsistent and non-uniform, suggests that a limitation on mobility rights, even for strategic purposes, if reasonably presented, could well be justified as pressing and substantial (first branch of the *Oakes* test) – a standard on which the courts are usually very deferential to the government. The limitation might also pass the second branch – that of rational connection – even if a domestically focused court would be hard pressed to be persuaded of the rational connection in policy between population distribution and strategic weight.[13] However, the limitation would likely falter at the third branch of the test – that of minimal impairment, upgraded in later jurisprudence to an impairment that is "as little as is reasonably possible."[14] It stands to reason that the courts would strike down the limitation as not being the best among more reasonable alternatives for growing the strategic might of the state – constitutionally legitimate alternatives the permutations of which are distilled and discussed throughout this book. Of course, some of these alternatives, depending on the factor of power to which they relate, are more strategic than others – as it were. This line of reasoning suggests that the courts, despite the absence of any such tradition, would be somewhat knowledgeable in respect of, or "culturally" attuned to, considerations of strategy or at least more knowledgeable than the executive branch in this respect. Alas, any presumption of superior judicial ken in Canada on matters strategic must, at the time of writing, be made in error.[15]

The Strategic Constitution as Conceptual and Analytical Framework

9

Canada has a *Strategic Constitution*. The Canadian Constitution, despite its manifestly astrategic conception, and despite a correspondingly weak tradition of strategically sensitive constitutional jurisprudence, can be employed with great flexibility by the federal government – should the requisite strategic policy acumen and political will be there – to project considerable power to advance various national strategic ends and purposes. Of course, these ends and purposes stand to be defined by different governments according to their preferences and the demands of the times. Some of these strategic ends and purposes are discussed in Part II of this book.

The Canadian state can project its power directly through its cardinal instruments – the diplomatic and military instruments – or through the mediation of a number of elements or factors of strategic power: national diplomacy, the military, the "pure" federal executive (or executive potency), natural resources (and food), the national economy, strategic communications, and finally the national population. In and of themselves, Canada's diplomacy and military – as both factors and instruments of power, primarily rooted in the royal prerogative – are, with only a few exceptions, largely untrammelled, in constitutional terms. Each of the seven factors of power, for its part, has its particular constitutional limitations, in most cases related to the federal division of powers (textual, statutory, and jurisprudential) and in a few cases occurring as a result of Charter stricture. In the aggregate, however, the picture painted in this book is of a Canadian Constitution that, while silent on strategy proper, in principle does not inhibit various species of meaningful strategic action by the federal state, even if it does not allow for every given action – at least not through unmediated federal delivery (the optimal manifestation of strategic efficacy). That so much strategic activity is enabled by the Canadian constitutional framework when such activity was nary envisioned by the Fathers of Confederation and subsequent constitutional draftspersons, and though such activity is little explored or even understood in Canada's constitutional jurisprudence (and scholarship), is a remarkable paradox.

Post-*Operation Dismantle* and, in the United Kingdom context, post-*Council of Civil Service Unions*, Canadian decisions like those in the *Khadr* line of cases, and even the lesser-known *Smith* case, are non-negligibly clipping at the prerogative and the federal executive's *marge de manoeuvre* – perhaps even more than statute. (The role of Aboriginal rights decisions in constricting this *marge de manoeuvre* and overall Canadian strategic power is still greatly underappreciated and merits further study.) Nonetheless, the federal state's *marge de manoeuvre*, while far from total, remains significant and broad, and the common law constitutional limits on strategic executive action – including in national emergencies or bona fide war – fairly elastic. Ultimately, this debate will crystallize around the ever complex intersection of royal prerogative and Charter rights – the apparent field or "sweet spot" of strategically relevant jurisprudence in Canada. I return to this sweet spot and other points of strategic contestation in the Canadian Constitution – what the Canadian state can and cannot do, in practice, given the Constitution – in the conclusion of the book.

Part II looks at four highly topical policy cases and seeks to apply the conceptual framework established in Part I – the Strategic Constitution – to understand, through what one might term "constitutional statics," the interaction between the Canadian Constitution and "real-life," applied strategic scenarios – all with a view to distilling a practical picture of Canadian strategic power, as underwritten by the Constitution. These case studies have been selected because of their prominence in recent

Canadian national policy-political debates and because together they cover a fairly broad, if not representative, spectrum of the types of international activity in which the Canadian state engages or might wish to engage at the strategic level. The cases are

- Canadian strategic leadership in the Americas region;
- bona fide war (as in the recent war in Afghanistan);
- Arctic sovereignty; and
- the post-9/11 national security environment, particularly in relation to counterterrorism.

PART II
Applying the Conceptual Framework:
Four Policy Case Studies

Case Study A
Canadian Strategic Leadership in the Americas

In 2007, Prime Minister Stephen Harper announced that Canada intended to become a major player, if not a strategic leader outright, in Central and South America as well as the Caribbean region (or the Caribbean Basin, at a minimum, as a subset of this large geographic space). One might call this Canada's "Americas pivot." The federal Americas strategy has yet to be defined – let alone carried out – in detail, but at the time of writing it is aimed at positioning Canada to advance three strategic goals or interests in the Americas: economic prosperity, security, and democratic governance, all broadly conceived.[1] It is noteworthy that this strategy is arguably inspired in part by the growing strategic footprint of Australia, a highly comparable federation, in its own region, the South Pacific, and, to a far lesser extent, Southeast Asia.[2]

For my purposes, the relevant line of enquiry is to determine whether, or the extent to which, the Canadian Constitution – in particular, the Strategic Constitution as defined in Part I – allows Canada to position itself, should the requisite policy-political chutzpah and skill be there, as a regional leader to achieve the ends articulated by the prime minister. As per the conceptual framework in Part I, this is first and foremost a question of *means* – that is, a question of the constitutionally grounded national capabilities underlying various policy-political choices that, in praxis, can enable the Canadian federal state to promote the said objectives or *ends* in the Americas.

Perhaps the "lowest-hanging fruit" in any analysis of Canada's constitutional capacity relating to strategic leadership in the Americas consists in the rather plain observation that meaningful diplomatic (or strategic) engagement in the region indubitably requires – "downstream," as it were – a critical mass of Canadians who are fluent in Spanish (and/or Portuguese), who are deeply familiar with the cultures and histories of the different peoples and countries of the region, and who are trained in, or have a strong understanding of, the civil law tradition.[3] Although education was not strictly identified in the Part I framework as a factor of strategic power, it is treated in sections 93 and 93A of the 1867 Act and is a provincial legislative competence under the Canadian Constitution. It stands to reason, therefore, that the provinces have the (strategic) lead in determining which languages are studied by students in their educational systems (in particular, at the preschool, elementary, and secondary school levels but also, to some extent, at the university level), the degree of their immersion in the history and geography of the Americas, as well as the availability and intensity of civilian pedagogy in the faculties of law.[4] (As a practical matter, at this juncture, French or English is the second language of choice in virtually all Canadian primary and secondary schools, though not necessarily among universities; Latin American and Caribbean geography are nary privileged; and only one law school outside Quebec – a bona fide civil law jurisdiction – offers extensive civilian training: the University of Ottawa Faculty of Law.[5]) The natural implication is that the federal government, while *prima facie* offering a strategy for national leadership in the region, has precious little direct control over, and is far from the key player in respect of developing, the "talent," at least in pedagogical terms, of the Canadians who will be charged with advancing this Americas strategy. In short, the federal division of constitutional powers, particularly in its treatment of education, militates astrategically, in a rather brutal way, against a professed national strategy for leadership in the Americas.[6]

There are, to be sure, indirect avenues or levers available to the federal government to either persuade or incentivize provinces to create pedagogical regimes consistent with the national strategic goal of leading in the Americas. They include federal-provincial policy cooperation – for instance in the form of federal-provincial conferences[7] – and use of the federal spending power, underpinned primarily by sections 91(1A) and 91(3) of the 1867 Act.[8] While federal involvement in intergovernmental consultations on education has historically been sporadic, given provincial jealousies in guarding sole legislative jurisdiction over schooling, there has been a history – granted, a controversial history – of federal use of the spending power to advance national objectives for education.[9] (In Australia, national regional leadership in the South Pacific and national effectiveness in Asia as a whole were advanced at least in part by means of a national languages strategy – emphasizing Asia literacy for Australians and in-school learning of Mandarin, Bahasa Indonesia [or Malay], Korean, Japanese, and, in later incarnations, Hindi – led by the federal or Commonwealth government via the Council of Australian Governments, the principal mechanism for high-level national intergovernmental cooperation in Australia.[10]) However, while these levers are available to the federal government, and speak to the general flexibility of Canada's constitutional framework on a number of fronts, they are patently second best, in strategic terms, because they rely extensively on provincial policy moves, the sustainability and consistency of which are difficult to gauge over the long run. Recall that, given the conceptual framework in Part I, the best strategic scenario is one in which the federal government – the federal executive or the strategic centre of the state, as it were – has direct and indeed exclusive constitutional capabilities to act regarding a strategic factor of power to advance whatever strategic end it chooses.

Let me attempt to assess Canadian constitutional capabilities to strategically lead in Latin America by examining three key areas of Canadian strategic engagement in the region: first, the "governance" agenda; second, economic or commercial engagement; and third, military engagement.[11] Each area broadly tracks one of the strategic goals articulated by Prime Minister Harper in his 2007 speech – respectively, democracy, economic prosperity, and security.

Governance

A "governance" agenda for Canada in the Americas would presumably involve some description of sustained or medium- to long-term Canadian leadership in helping to build modern, stable states and societies in the region – one or perhaps two or three countries at a time. This would mean, among other things, training regional leaders, officials, and professionals, from the security services to the judicature to the university. It would require considerable sums of development assistance money. It would demand prodigious diplomatic efforts, over a decade or more, to mobilize, organize, and protect Canadian leadership on the ground both from internal resistance – that is, from within the affected regional state or states – and, just as signally, from competitive, obstructive, hostile, or even incompetent interventions from other interested state or non-state players.[12] In short, for a serious governance agenda, the diplomatic instrument, broadly defined, would be king. (Recall that diplomacy is understood here to include strategic instruments such as, *inter alia*, treaties, development aid, sanctions, intelligence and "information sharing," as well as "plain vanilla" capabilities such as coercion, negotiation, lobbying, important appointments, and international deployment of certain national assets. Canadian "diplomats" are therefore understood to include not just officials in the Department of Foreign Affairs and International Trade but also officials in other federal departments, cabinet ministers, and any other individuals commissioned by the executive branch of the federal state to use the diplomatic instruments and participate in the diplomatic activities just described.)

Leaving aside the education variable, Canada's constitutional capacity to strategically engage in the Americas region, in purely diplomatic terms, is, strictly speaking, largely untrammelled. For starters, the "macro" decision to emphasize or privilege the Americas over another region – or to divert resources, for strategic reasons, to the Americas from another region of Canadian interest (say Africa or Central Asia) – is constitutionally beyond reproach; that is, clearly it is a creature of the royal prerogative, strictly of the executive branch.[13] (Again, I speak here of constitutional capacity; policy-political praxis is an altogether different matter.) The royal prerogative, for all intents and purposes, would justify a great variety of federal government moves, from recognizing or not recognizing different governments in the Americas region to lobbying, advising, and even threatening or attempting to subvert or destabilize such governments. (As repeated below in the section on military engagement, the *Khadr* warning in respect of Canadian external behaviour needing to be consistent with the country's international obligations would not be immaterial if Canada were to actively subvert or destabilize a government in the Americas.) There would be no constitutional bar to federal decisions to create, join, or leave any grouping of regional states or parties (for example, the Organization of American States or a subset or subcommittee thereof). "Interstitial" moves, such as communicating with regional governments and general policy planning regarding the Americas – irrespective of the federal department involved – would also comfortably be covered by the prerogative. Assuming acquiescence from host states (espionage excepted), Canadian embassies, consulates, and federal departmental offices or operations could be established anywhere in the region, just as Canadian diplomats and other federal officials could be sent to the region, according to any given country-by-country distribution, on the strength of the prerogative.[14] Indeed, the prerogative would also legitimate the deployment of human (foreign) intelligence assets to the region, outside the ambit of the *CSIS Act*, in support of a Canadian governance agenda, whatever its details.[15] (As mentioned in Part I, an agency for such pure human foreign intelligence assets does not exist at present in Canada. One could, in constitutional terms, easily be set up simply by dint of the prerogative – that is, strictly speaking, without an enabling statute, just as easily as the federal government could direct such an agency to specialize in, or concentrate on, Latin America.[16]) I leave aside for the moment the notion – discussed below and introduced in Chapter 8 – that certain constitutional strictures on Canada's capacity to effectively grow its population can limit the size of the overall talent pool from which diplomatic personnel are drawn.

Development assistance money, broadly conceived, could easily be directed to, or earmarked for, the region via the prerogative and according to conditions determined exclusively by the federal cabinet – even in the absence of formal development assistance legislation (and certainly without any formal need for provincial support, consultation, or legislation).[17] Of course, the amount of such money, critically, would be a function of the size of the Canadian economy – itself a function at least in part, in strategic terms, of some of the federal government's constitutional powers regarding the natural resources, economy, communications, and population factors of power that make up the Strategic Constitution.[18] As established in Part I, the provinces could still play a non-negligible role in international development, for their spending powers are not required to be strictly intraprovincial in character – that is, there is no constitutional capacity, strictly speaking, for the federal government or Parliament to bar provincial *spending* for international purposes. Indeed, provinces have spent money on international development in the past.[19] Here a complication arises, evidently, as discussed in Part I, regarding the strategic coherence of development spending by the federal and provincial levels of government.

As argued above, total Canadian population ultimately informs the aggregate talent pool available to populate the diplomatic instrument (as with the military instrument). It also informs the size of the national economy, from which tax revenues are drawn in support of expenditures for initiatives such as strategic leadership in the Americas. As explained in Part I, outside federal and provincial incentives to Canadians to reproduce at greater rates, national capabilities to increase population via immigration appear to be a key aspect of the strategic calculus here for purposes of determining Canada's capacity to increase its population for strategic ends. The same capabilities would presumably inform Canada's capacity, in governance terms (for humanitarian or economic purposes), to resettle citizens of the Americas within Canada. And in this regard, the federal government uncontroversially has the capacity, constitutionally speaking, to select its immigrants and to determine the associated total quantum of immigrants (in aid of a particular national population growth rate). However, this capacity is complicated, *inter alia*, by the quasi-constitutional requirement, articulated in the *Canada-Quebec Accord* on immigration, that total immigration intake into the country take into account the need to preserve the demographic weight of the French-speaking population. (As discussed in Part I, distribution of incoming population, though not necessarily as important as the general capacity to determine the quantum and character of newcomers to Canada, is also constitutionally complicated, particularly in respect of section 6 Charter mobility rights. See Case Study C for a full treatment of this *problématique* in respect of Arctic sovereignty.) And this, on its face, seems to militate against untrammelled growth of the aggregate national population via immigration as well as against complete federal discretion regarding intake of immigrants specifically from the Americas (non-native French speakers, in other words).[20]

Economic Engagement

On the prosperity front, region-wide, sub-regional, or bilateral trade agreements (for example, free-trade agreements or FTAs) and investment agreements (for example, foreign investment protection and promotion agreements or FIPAs) could clearly be negotiated and signed by the federal government by dint of the prerogative.[21] Still, *Labour Conventions* oblige, aspects of such agreements or treaties that fall under provincial legislative jurisdiction, such as education and intraprovincial natural resources, would require provincial legislative concurrence and participation for purposes of implementation – something that, as established in Part I, could significantly complicate the efficacy of federal strategy. Anticipation of such potential difficulties in implementation, including in respect of provincial – or even municipal or other sub-federal – procurement laws and regulations, would also doubtless weaken the negotiating capacity of the federal government, given its likely need to anticipate or incorporate provincial considerations or preferences into its negotiations. Canadian access to foreign markets through such agreements would be increased, through reciprocity, to the extent that provinces would agree, among other things, to "open up" provincial (or municipal) procurement to goods and services of the partner country in question. This was a controversial issue in recent debates on *NAFTA*, for which Canadian provincial procurement has historically excluded goods and services from the United States and Mexico, and is a vexed issue in the context of the *Comprehensive Economic and Trade Agreement* (CETA) currently being negotiated between Canada and the European Union. Because the decision regarding provincial procurement laws is not for the federal government to make, prospects for reciprocal economic benefits from other countries at the sub-federal level (for example, in the *NAFTA* case, procurement of Canadian goods and services by American and Mexican states and cities or, more peculiarly to the Americas, Argentinian provinces and cities or Brazilian states and cities) are at the mercy of decision making at sub-strategic levels – in other words, interests that, being provincial, cannot result in maximization of economic benefit for the Canadian aggregate.[22] Moreover, in the event that there is Canadian provincial buy-in for the liberalization of municipal procurement practices, it is perfectly conceivable that the federal state on occasion should be held liable and penalized at international law for breaches of such undertakings at sub-federal levels – breaches that the federal government, in constitutional terms, would have few direct levers to remedy. (I leave aside the prospect of Aboriginal strategic moves, under section 35(1) of the 1982 Act, blocking implementation of certain trade or commercial agreements or otherwise helping to produce a breach of such agreements.) Once again, then, one can observe in Canada the astrategic tail wagging the strategic dog.

The federal spending power would evidently allow the federal government – the foreign investment laws and regulations of the target state permitting – to independently purchase or invest in various strategic assets or industries in different countries in the Americas. Such purchases or investments would not necessarily have a strict rentier imperative for Canada but might instead be consistent with a strategy of facilitating and ensuring Canadian supply of critical resources, such as oil, natural gas, and even food. The federal spending power would also allow Parliament to incentivize Canadian private investment in resources in the Americas, though here the motive would indeed arguably be more of the rentier ilk than strictly strategic – or perhaps both. Of course, because the provinces themselves possess spending powers, they too could invest directly in concerns or assets in the region and incentivize such foreign investment by provincial concerns or residents. (I have already established that there is no certainty that such provincial purchases, investments, or incentives – more likely rentier than accidentally strategic – would necessarily conduce to any aggregate Canadian strategic interest; that is, coherence or consistency between federal and provincial spending in the Americas could not be guaranteed.)

Both the federal government and the provincial governments could, other things being equal, play with their tax codes (built, constitutionally, on the same bases as the spending power) to incentivize, disincentivize, or deter certain types of investment in Canada from the Americas

– all with the goal of promoting Canadian strategic leadership in the Americas. Leaving aside the complexity or coherence or consistency between the federal and provincial levels, this could involve blocking or frustrating certain competitive or strategically threatening companies or industries from the region – take, for instance, Brazilian aeronautics or banking – to advance Canadian industry in the region, consistent with, say, a vision of Canadian economic leverage in the region. Conversely, this could also involve facilitating the progress of certain companies or industries from the Americas – say regional suppliers of Canadian aeronautics, banking, telecommunications, or mining concerns – deemed conducive to advancing Canadian strategic ends in the region. Companies or industries deemed "strategic" by the Canadian government would be those that are seen as directly propitious to the stated, broad Canadian ends of democracy, economic prosperity, and security or, more generally, propitious to one or more of the basic factors of strategic power that inform the overall potency of the Canadian state's diplomatic and military instruments and therefore the state's overall strategic power in the region. (This means that Canada could advance its purposes in the region directly through achievements articulated through the vector of democracy, economic prosperity, or security or indirectly through moves that enlarge the federal state's factors of power.)

The federal spending power would also be the appropriate vector by which the Canadian government could provide debt relief or forgiveness to countries of strategic interest in the region.[23] To the extent that the external debt held by target countries in the region is multilateral – that is, held by Canada and other countries or international organizations or even held privately by Canadian banking concerns – the Canadian government could use the strength of the royal prerogative to mobilize, persuade, or incentivize multilateral or private lenders to participate in such a debt relief regime.

The federal government could also uncontroversially impose different economic sanctions on regional countries, including in response to, say, the seizure, nationalization, or maltreatment of Canadian-owned assets in a given country. Of course, as established in Part I, the impact of such a capability in large part would be a function of the relative strength or size of the Canadian economy vis-à-vis that of the target state

– in particular, the capacity of the Canadian economy, in relative terms, to withstand the decreased demand for the sanctioned goods and services (relative to the target state's capacity to withstand the embargo on specific imports from Canada). Apart from certain major economies in the Americas, like that of Brazil and perhaps Argentina, other things being equal, there is little question that Canada could comfortably withstand diminished demand from that country because of imposed economic sanctions. And even with Brazil or Argentina, this "hit" to Canadian demand or welfare would be a function of, *inter alia*, existing trade intensities between the two countries (which at present are not enormous) as well as the elasticities of national supply and demand.[24]

Military Engagement

As with diplomacy, the military instrument, leaving aside supporting factors of strategic power, is given great flexibility by the Constitution in respect of promoting a federal strategy for leadership in the Americas. The royal prerogative largely allows the federal executive to deploy Canadian forces and military assets untrammelled in the region, with the size of those assets, on the human side, determined at least in part by the size of Canada's population (discussed above and again below in Case Study B). (Of course, this is leaving aside domestic law in regional countries and, just as significantly, international law. One must also presume that the *de novo Khadr* standard of Canadian officials not being involved in any process contrary to public international law applies here.) (See Case Study B, on full war, as well as Case Study D, on the post-9/11 security environment.) The prerogative, in principle, would cover the extreme scenario of the Canadian government sending military troops into theatres in the Americas region – say to prevent, stanch, or reverse a *coup d'état* or some state failure or emergency or even to protect certain Canadian-owned strategic assets or assets deemed strategically important to Canada – as well as more *de minimis* moves such as training regional military forces, membership in a given military coalition or alliance, sharing intelligence, and erecting military bases.[25] (As with the global choice of the Americas as the region of strategic preference or emphasis for Canada, the choice of country for a military base would be purely a function of the royal prerogative, subject, evidently, to the acquiescence or agreement of the host state. However, as with the *Khadr* line of decisions above, one should also heed the less notorious *Smith* holding[26] treated in Part I as a non-negligible "clip" on the prerogative.)

I discuss the entire upstream-downstream spectrum of Canadian military capabilities, as informed by the Strategic Constitution, next in Case Study B, in the context of bona fide war.

Case Study B
Bona Fide War

Until recently, Canada had been involved, head-first, in its first bona fide war, in Afghanistan, since the 1950-53 war in Korea. The Korean and Afghanistan missions are qualitatively different from intervening "non-full-war" or "non-bona fide-war" military missions – including and especially Canadian peacekeeping missions – such as Suez (1956), Congo (1960), Cyprus (1964), the Middle East (1970s and 1980s), Iran-Iraq (1988), the Persian Gulf (1990), Somalia (1992), the Balkans (1980s), Haiti (1990s), and Kosovo (1999), principally because of the superior degree to which these two missions – wars – engaged the various strategic factors of power of the Canadian state.[1] The stated Canadian goals or objectives – the "definition of victory," as it were – for the war in Afghanistan, with at least half of the total focus being on Kandahar province, were numerous and diverse, ranging from providing security in Kandahar (and, by significant extension, one can infer, for Canada) to providing basic services (for example, water, education, employment) and humanitarian assistance in Kandahar as well as contributing to the stabilization of the Afghanistan-Pakistan border. In addition, the Canadian government stated that it wished to contribute to the creation of nation-wide institutions for Afghanistan and to national reconciliation among competing groups, tribes, and militias.[2]

Strategic engagement in such wars has both upstream and downstream dimensions. Upstream dimensions include national preparation for war, broadly speaking, as well as national declaration of war (and related prewar decision making). Downstream dimensions include strict military operations (such as combat), national support of the war (in particular, material support), wartime decision making, and the declaration, treaty, or agreement that ends the war. I treat each dimension in turn below.

National War Preparation

In general, national preparation for war has material and social aspects. I will focus almost exclusively on "material" aspects of war preparation; that is, the material resources, including manpower, that underpin national efforts to prepare or plan for military missions. Evidently, there exist important social-psychological aspects of war preparation, including development or moulding of the national geist, mentality, spirit, or even culture that disposes, or fails to dispose, a given population to perform in, endure, and otherwise support national war efforts. As per the analysis in Part I, however, I will set aside these more diffuse aspects of strategic power. Needless to say, education – a largely provincial constitutional responsibility that does not strictly figure in the Strategic Constitution construct – is a non-negligible lever in respect of the development of a national psyche, spirit, or mentality that helps a state to win wars.

The strict national planning function for war lies uncontroversially with the federal government, principally via the royal prerogative and, in particular cases, under the aegis of the *National Defence Act* (relying on section 91(7) – the militia power – of the 1867 Act), which provides legislative underpinning for, *inter alia*, the activities of the Department of National Defence and the Canadian Forces. Defence, intelligence (discussed at length in Case Study D[3]), security, and foreign relations planners in various departments of the federal government regularly iterate or "game," and have exclusive constitutional capacity to game, war plans and military contingencies involving a wide variety of enemies (state and non-state), alliances, geographic or spatial theatres, species of conflict, length and intensity of conflict, and a host of other variables and scenarios. Defensive bases might be established anywhere in the country: if not on existing federal land, then either through the purchase of private or provincial land or through outright expropriation of such land – including, as discussed in Part I, Aboriginal title or treaty land the underlying ownership of which lies with the provincial Crown.[4] (Recall that section 117 of the 1867 Act allows for federal expropriation, on the strength of *Human Rights Institute*,[5] of "any Lands or Public Property required for Fortifications or for the Defence of the Country." Clearly, in practice this would seem an extreme or "draconian" move by the government, but it would still be wholly constitutional. One might also presume, consistent with Gérard V. La Forest's assertion,[6] discussed in Part I, that an executive power to expropriate is inherent in federal heads of power such as section 91(7).) Offensive bases – those outside Canadian territory – could be established under federal competence via the militia power, though such a capacity would depend, in the main, on agreement or acquiescence by a host state.[7] Military procurement (spending power), under the *National Defence Act*, is also exclusively a federal capability.[8] Procurement is clearly a function, *inter alia*, of national economic capacity (national purchasing power), though it seems that the critical vector of enquiry for purposes of determining the potency of national preparatory capacity for war is the extent to which the federal state can, constitutionally speaking, properly mobilize national economic capacity for military preparation. Microeconomically, this would involve monitoring or driving industrial performance, efficiency, or output in certain strategic industries (for example, certain natural resource, energy, manufacturing, and heavy industrial sectors, strategic communications, strategic transportation, and even agriculture) as well as assuring the security of these strategic industries or protecting their very existence in Canada. Notes John Kenneth Galbraith in *The New Industrial State* regarding such federal state-led military planning function in the United States:

> With the $60 billion it spends ... each year ... the [US] Department of Defense supports ... the most highly developed planning in the industrial system. It provides contracts of long duration, calling for

a large investment of capital in areas of advanced technology. There is no risk of price fluctuations. There is full protection against any change in requirements, i.e. any change in demand. Should a contract be cancelled the firm is protected on the investment it has made. For no other products can the technostructure plan with such certainty and assurance.[9]

In actual wartime, these capabilities presumably need to be supplemented by a capability to require that the output of these strategic industries be mobilized specifically for war – that is, on top of being simply produced. Of course, there is no strict bar to federal legislation, under section 91(7) of the 1867 Act, creating certain public companies – Crown corporations – or programs to produce, or to incentivize private companies, via the federal spending power, to produce, specific strategically important output (for example, munitions, fortifications, defensive infrastructure, military equipment, and so on). However, such companies or programs would doubtless bump up against non-negligible federalism issues relating to provincial regulation of most industrial concerns under the broad property and civil rights power (section 92(13) of the 1867 Act). Indeed, section 91(7) is arguably just one of a large number of constitutional levers available to the federal government and Parliament – policy praxis notwithstanding – to prepare the country for war.

Part I established that the federal *Defence Production Act*, constitutionally authorized via section 91(7) of the 1867 Act, gives the minister of public works and government services the presumptive lead in organizing national defence production or supplies required to meet the needs of the Department of National Defence – in short the military needs of Canada. The act even suggests in section 12 that

> The Minister shall examine into, organize, mobilize and conserve the resources of Canada contributory to, and the sources of supply of, defence supplies and the agencies and facilities available for the supply thereof and for the construction of defence projects and shall explore, estimate and provide for the fulfilment of the needs, present and prospective, of the Government and the community with respect thereto and generally shall take steps to mobilize, conserve and

coordinate all economic and industrial facilities in respect of defence supplies and defence projects and the supply or construction thereof.

However, because this section, like the rest of the act, has not been litigated in any strategically meaningful sense, at the time of writing the precise parameters of the federal government's power to substantially organize or mobilize Canada's defence industry – or, indeed, its economy at large – remain unclear, at least in peacetime or on a standing basis.[10] More broadly, federal capacity to prepare or plan for war is rooted in the dull lever of Parliament's competence over interprovincial and international trade via section 91(2) of the 1867 Act and in more blunt levers such as the federal spending power, federal declaratory power, federal expropriation powers, and various branches of the general power (residual, emergency, national concern, and even interprovincial significance).

The federal spending (and borrowing) power can be used to incentivize, through the federal tax system, production of, or investment in, specific products of military value. It could also be used, as suggested in Part I, to purchase a federal interest, however large or small, in a given property or concern, to assume federal legislative control over it, per section 91(1A) of the 1867 Act. For instance, the federal government could purchase a minority or majority stake in a given mine, oil refinery, munitions plant, communications concern, or even shipbuilding company – works, constitutionally speaking, not undertakings – to claim for Parliament direct legislative concern over that work (where it would otherwise, in principle, fall within provincial legislative jurisdiction) to assure a specific quality or supply of a given product or service deemed critical to military success in Afghanistan. In addition, even in the absence of any desire to assume legislative control over a given work, the spending power can be used by Parliament to directly purchase for the federal government specific assets of military import that are otherwise not being produced at an acceptable quality or quantum. The argument made in Part I concerning the federal government's capacity to purchase petroleum (provincially regulated) on the market – including at a possible premium in order not to violate *NAFTA* – for the purpose of building a national petroleum reserve readily comes to mind.

One could conceive of similar use of the federal purse to build up, in the context of war preparations, national reserves of iron ore (for shipbuilding, tanks, planes, body armour), nickel (bullets), copper (wiring), and many other raw materials, not to mention food, deemed essential to military equipment and infrastructure. Use of the federal declaratory power over uranium immediately after the Second World War is the obvious instructive precedent here. Note that, as discussed in Part I, threatened use of the declaratory power, while not issuing in federal jurisdiction over specific works and undertakings, in some cases could also have the requisite "energizing" effect on the provincial regulators or the direct owners of the works in question, forcing them to align the operations of the works with the strategic (military) goals of the federal government in its war preparations. Historically, as noted, transportation and communications assets have often been targets of the declaratory power or threats of its use (though the power is certainly not limited to such assets[11]), even if the presumptive reasons behind such use of the power have not always been part of a military planning scheme. And, of course, expropriation for explicit military purposes could also occur under section 117 of the 1867 Act and even, as mentioned, under section 91(7) of that act: consider, for instance, privately held cyber assets that might need to be activated, deactivated, or otherwise manipulated or protected, under the aegis of the Canadian military, to advance the war aims of Canada.

In the event of a declared war emergency, the *Defence Production Act* is supplemented by the *Emergencies Act*, well treated above (rooted in the federal emergency power), which grants the federal government, under the statutory category of war emergency, expansive powers of economic mobilization and organization in support of the country's military efforts.[12] (Evidently, the larger the economic capacity of the country, other things being equal, the greater its ability to support the military campaign and related industries and production in the event of actual war, and the greater its ability to deter a potential enemy in the event of threatened war, given that the enemy might infer the war-fighting capability of the country from its economic mass. In this latter respect, conversely, the smaller a country's economic capacity, other things being equal, the smaller its capacity to discourage strategic confrontation or military attack by another country.) And, as established in Part I, where the provisions of the *Emergencies Act* are inadequate for purposes of realizing a national war or security imperative, the federal government can still rely on its supervening royal prerogative (the emergency or national security prerogative) to achieve its ends.

In addition to direct defence production, there is the federal government's capacity to purchase or import from other countries the assets necessary for war preparation (or deterrence) and war fighting. The larger the national economy, other things being equal, the greater the Canadian government's purchasing power for such assets. That said, excessive importation of strategic military assets (as with natural resources or food) also poses a significant strategic risk for a country, given its dependence on foreign supply or distribution routes that could be disrupted at critical strategic moments. Still, strictly speaking, the balance between indigenous defence-related production and imported production is a policy choice, rather than a constitutional concern, and the core strategic observation stands: other things being equal, the larger the economic capacity of the state, the greater the potency of its military instrument, including as supported by purchases of foreign military assets.

The Canadian state would also need to ensure that the military instrument is adequately populated. The size of the national military, outside political discretion, is a function of national economic capacity and the aggregate national population. Far more directly, and to the extent that economic capacity – or national spending, specifically on recruitment – and national population together fail to yield adequate personnel for the military, one can justly enquire into the national capacity to require, on a standing or *ad hoc* basis, Canadian citizens to populate the military instrument. In other words, constitutionally speaking, what is the federal peacetime conscription capability? Is there a federal peacetime "military training" capability short of conscription? While the second question tends toward the "social" or social-psychological dimensions touched on at the start of this chapter, Parliament could surely, in respect of the first question, legislate under the militia and defence power to effect military conscription in Canada. Charter issues would almost certainly be raised, particularly to the extent that such conscription happens outside a strict wartime context; that is, in preparation for some eventual war. That said, it seems that any violation of, say, section 7 Charter rights by a federal conscription law could be saved under section 1 to the extent that the context is actually intrawar or imminent war rather than peacetime, *interbellum*, or distant *antebellum*. More to the point, would national conscription be considered disproportionate under the third branch of the *Oakes* test? In *Operation Dismantle*, Justice Wilson speaks directly to this counterfactual in her *dicta* at paragraph 65:

> Let us take the case of a person who is being conscripted for service during wartime and has been ordered into battle overseas, all of this pursuant to appropriate legislative and executive authorization. He wishes to challenge his being conscripted and sent overseas as an infringement of his rights under s. 7. It is apparent that his liberty has been constrained and, if he is sent into battle, his security of the person and, indeed, his life are put in jeopardy. It seems to me that it would afford the conscriptee a somewhat illusory protection if the validity of his challenge is to be determined by the executive. On the other hand, it does not follow from these facts that the individual's rights under the *Charter* have been violated. Even if an individual's rights to life and liberty under s. 7 are interpreted at their broadest, it is clear from s. 1 that they are subject to "such reasonable limits prescribed by law as can be demonstrably justified in a free and democratic society." If the Court were of the opinion that conscription during wartime was a "reasonable limit" within the meaning of s. 1, a conscriptee's challenge on the facts as presented would necessarily fail.[13]

Declaration of War and Related Decision Making

Although until fairly recently there might have been at least an embryonic case for suggesting that a declaration of war by Parliament constitutes an emerging constitutional convention in Canada, there is no strict constitutional requirement that Parliament declare or approve a war otherwise declared or initiated by the federal government. (No formal declaration of war was made in either of the full or bona fide war cases of Korea and Afghanistan.[14]) The declaration of war, constitutionally speaking, is the province of the federal executive and a creature of royal prerogative in its purest or highest form – judicially unreviewable, for all intents and purposes, in the absence of Charter claims.[15] Note that, while there was never a formal declaration of war on the Taliban government in Afghanistan in 2001, Parliament *did* vote in 2007 – in a nonbinding vote that was not a matter of confidence – in favour of extending the Afghan mission until 2009 and then again in 2008 to conclude the formal military mission in 2011.[16] Relatedly, the federal executive, via the royal prerogative, uncontroversially has the constitutional competence to stand up any number of decision-making structures to reach the decision to go to war as well as to prosecute the war (that is, for intrawar decision making). These structures can range from formal or *ad hoc* cabinet committees – war cabinets, as it were – to interdepartmental intelligence committees and indeed international watching or briefing groups. For instance, the federal government, following the 2008 Manley report, stood up a formal cabinet committee on Afghanistan, with a supporting secretariat (the Afghanistan Task Force) in the Privy Council Office.[17]

The provinces do not play any constitutional role in any initiation of hostilities or a national declaration of war by Canada. This might seem self-evident but has not always been resolved, constitutionally or in practice, in favour of federal executives; that is, in other federations, past or present. Note the warning by James Madison in *The Federalist No. 19* of the danger of excessive sub-state ("sub-strategic") influence in war preparations: "Military preparations must be preceded by so many tedious discussions, arising from the jealousies, pride, separate views and clashing pretentions, of sovereign bodies; that before the diet can settle the arrangements, the enemy are in the field; and before the federal troops are ready to take it, are retiring into winter quarters."[18]

Military Operations

Military operations are strictly the province of the federal executive, under the royal prerogative. Offensive operations – typically outside Canada, as in Afghanistan – are uncontroversially so. Macro military issues, including determination of the enemy or adversary, appointment of key generals and commanders, overall military doctrine, definition of victory or success, and tactical issues, including determination of how many personnel and how much equipment should be deployed – and where and when – in support of the global objectives, all fall under the prerogative, effectively untrammelled. I should stress, however, as explained in Chapter 3, that the *Khadr* 2008, *Khadr* 2009, and *Khadr* 2010 stipulations that Canadian officials operating abroad are subject to the Charter "to the extent that the conduct of Canadian officials involved [Canada] in a process that violated Canada's international obligations" are, at least theoretically, operative on Canadian troops in the field – that is, to the extent that conduct of the troops is in violation of Canada's international legal obligations. This seems to have complex implications for the behaviour of troops in situations like the one at the centre of the *Amnesty International* case,[19] discussed in Part I, in which Canadian troops transferred Afghan detainees to Afghan authorities, arguably with the attendant possibility that they would be mistreated if not outright tortured. *Amnesty International*, decided prior to the *Khadr* holdings, easily reaffirmed the supremacy of the royal prerogative in military operations. But now, in light of the *Khadr* holdings, that holding is somewhat compromised; *bref*, one of these outcomes surely must give before long. (Of course, there is also in the *Khadr* holdings the implied oddity that the officials in question were Canadian *intelligence* officials, not Canadian *soldiers* or *military personnel*. Were they proper soldiers, the implied impact would have been all the more plain. But the *Khadr* decisions did not seem to differentiate between *types* or *modes* of Canadian officials, so one could well assume, awaiting future litigation of a more precise fact pattern, that it likely applies with equal strength to Canadian intelligence, military, diplomatic, and other officials operating abroad.)

However, military and diplomatic officials, operating as they do in the "anarchical" world of international affairs,[20] particularly in wartime,[21] tend to regularly abut areas of legal "grey" in their operations, meaning that a "hard" reading of the *Khadr* line could well constitute a material fetter on their activities and therefore a material drag on the aggregate capacity of the federal government to achieve its ends in a bona fide war scenario.

I should also note the import of the 2009 *Smith* holding (discussed in Part I and Case Study A) as another possible "clip" – albeit one emanating not quite from the heights of the Supreme Court – on the royal prerogative in respect of foreign affairs or strategy or, indeed, for military operations. That case also seems consistent with the supposition made at the start of this book that Canadian constitutional jurisprudence is patently astrategic; that is, even when it pertains to foreign affairs (the *Smith* case having dealt with the intervention or non-intervention by the Canadian government in *prima facie* non-strategic circumstances, specifically an American death penalty case), there is often little thought given, including in *obiter*, to the precedential import of the holding for more strategic fact patterns. (As suggested in Part I, it is not impossible, though certainly not a foregone conclusion, that a proper foreign relations or military affairs case – that is, the more strategic fact patterns – involving the intersection of administrative law and the royal prerogative should force a serious reconsideration of the *Smith* decision at the Supreme Court level.)

Recall that, in *Smith*, the Federal Court determined that the Government of Canada had breached the right to procedural fairness of Ronald Smith, a death row inmate in Montana, by denying him diplomatic assistance (or clemency support) to commute his death sentence, contrary to the long-standing policy of many past Canadian governments. The court conceded that exercise of the government's prerogative in relation to foreign affairs was generally non-justiciable but that "government decisions of an administrative character which affected the rights, privileges or interests of an individual ... are reviewable and are subject to the principles of procedural fairness."[22] According to the court, the breach of procedural fairness consisted in the government's arbitrary change of approach or policy in relation to clemency support for Canadians facing execution in foreign countries.

At some point in the not too distant future, the *Smith* precedent could take on strategic significance – with potentially absurd consequences – in "high policy" cases, including in respect of bona fide war scenarios. I cited in Part I, for instance, the prospect of a sudden or *prima facie* "arbitrary" change in military alliances or relationships by a given Canadian government – very possible in the context of wartime military operations – as potentially frustrating the "legitimate expectations" of certain Canadians (for example, those who might be commercially or financially invested in the ousted or now "out of favour" foreign country). Such a counterfactual, not considered in the reasoning in the *Smith* decision, not only speaks to potential, non-negligible judicial incursion into erstwhile prerogative-protected military affairs but could also at some point – were this precedent upheld at the Supreme Court level – be assimilated into government strategic decision making, resulting in a more jurisprudentially pedantic, likely more risk-averse, calculus by the federal executive regarding the employ of its military instrument.

Defensive operations – typically within Canada (consider some species of attack in Canada by the Taliban or their allies) – are also under the purview of the prerogative and can also be governed by the provisions of the *Emergencies Act*, specifically the provisions pursuant to declaration of a war emergency by the federal executive. Beyond the act, however, the actions of the executive in the context of war are surely underpinned by the doctrine of necessity (or the emergency and national security prerogatives). Moreover, one can safely presume that domestic deployment of the Canadian Forces under a war emergency would trump the aid of the civil power provisions in Part IV of the *National Defence Act* (in which call-out is requisitioned by the provinces), such that the provinces would play no material or direct strategic role in domestic defence operations.[23]

The *Emergencies Act*, rooted in the emergency branch of the POGG power, like all legislation, is subject to the Charter. Still, as explained in Part I, the Charter's notwithstanding clause (section 33) provides for the operation of laws by the federal Parliament (or provincial legislatures) notwithstanding certain sections of the Charter, for a period of up to five years. This clause has not been invoked to date by any federal government and would not be operative on the democratic rights in sections 3, 4, and 5 as well as the mobility rights in section 6. However, in the context of military operations intrawar, the federal government would have available to it, under the notwithstanding clause, the capacity to override the Charter's "legal rights" in sections 7 to 14 as well as the equality provision in section 15 – again, for a period of up to five years. (No justification for such an override would have to be provided under section 1, as that section would also be overridden by section 33.) It is similarly not inconceivable, depending on the gravity of the circumstances, that a government, confronted with a "real or apprehended war, invasion or insurrection," might invoke both the notwithstanding clause and section 4(2), which would be tantamount to a fairly potent cocktail of executive override of most of the Charter's key rights provisions. Section 4(2) states that, "[i]n time of real or apprehended war, invasion or insurrection, a House of Commons may be continued by Parliament and a legislative assembly may be continued by the legislature *beyond five years* if such continuation is not opposed by the votes of more than one third of the members of the House of Commons or the legislative assembly, as the case may be."[24] The combination of sections 4(2) and 33 – logically independent of each other – means that Parliament and the wartime government could operate for more than five years – arguably for as long as it might take to conclude the war – and that many of its wartime laws could be inured from the Charter (save, again, from sections 2 through 5).

Concluding the War

Just as with the declaration of war or the commencement of military operations, there is no constitutional necessity for Parliament to speak on the cessation of military operations and, for the most part, the terms of such cessation. They are the strict province of the federal executive under the royal prerogative. This would be the case even if the cessation of hostilities were spelled out in a proper peace or ceasefire treaty. The treaty or agreement would be entirely negotiated by the federal executive. Naturally, Parliament would be required to vote on any possible implementing legislation for such a treaty or agreement. *In extremis*, it is also possible that provincial assent would be required to implement certain aspects of the concluding treaty or agreement, where such terms fall into areas of provincial legislative competence. Indeed, in the unlikely event of a treaty of Canadian military *concession* or *surrender* or *defeat*, a victorious adversary might insist on terms that cover, say, education (for example, reform of history or civics curriculum) or industrial policy (for example, prohibitions on production of certain goods) in Canada. (Consider the terms of defeat effectively dictated to Nazi Germany or

Imperial Japan at the end of the Second World War.) The consent of provincial legislatures to implementation of such terms might, as established in Part I, influence negotiation of the concession treaty or agreement – to the extent that Canada would have *marge de manoeuvre* for such negotiation – but would also inform the "implementability" of such a treaty or agreement. This could issue in a strange paradox that arguably proves the "astrategicality" of Canada's *Labour Conventions* treaty implementation regime. This can be called the constitutional paradox of (Canadian) strategic defeat: Canada loses a war, negotiates an end-of-hostilities treaty with the victor, but is not, provincial resistance oblige, able to implement the treaty. This would bring new meaning to Trotsky's famous aphorism of "neither war nor peace." One might "game" the paradox as follows: Canada loses a war. The federal government signs a surrender treaty but is unable to implement parts of it over objections by one or more provinces. Other things being equal, the victor resumes war to force implementation of the agreed treaty. The federal government surrenders again, signs a new treaty, but is again unable to implement it. War resumes. And so on. (In fairness, it is possible that the victor would eventually – perhaps upon witnessing this paradox – cause a new, more unitary constitution to be enshrined in Canada.)

In summary, notwithstanding this paradox of implementation, Canada's constitutional capacities in the context of bona fide war, policy-political choices aside, are significant, with the fewest fetters to executive capacity coming in the context of the war declaration and the concluding stages of war. The scope of federal decision making, prewar and intrawar, is also constitutionally expansive and uncontroversial, with executive prerogative dominance over war cabinet policy deliberations only trammelled – barring the rather extreme use of section 4(2) of the Charter – by the constitutional requirement that each Parliament not exceed five years in length (per section 4(1) of the Charter, with section 56.1(2) of the *Canada Elections Act*[25] now fixing government terms, not quite yet quasi-constitutionally, at four years). Where there is manifest complexity and nuance is in the realm of national preparation for war. Federal strategic potency in leading national preparation for war is heavily invested in the as yet unlitigated and untested section 91(7) of the 1867 Act (supporting statutes such as the *National Defence Act* and *Defence*

Production Act). This lever is clearly significant intrawar, but its strategic scope is not yet firmly established in the *antebellum* period. The federal spending power is also highly material for war planning or preparation, as are coercive capabilities such as the declaratory power or direct expropriation, subject to the requirement of reasonable coherence with provincial spending on dual-purpose assets and contingent on national economic capabilities. Emergency powers come into play hugely in the actual intrawar context (either under the *Emergencies Act* or via the national security or emergency prerogative).[26] On the other hand, distributed microeconomic capabilities among the federal and provincial levels, as well as constitutionally rooted challenges to growing Canada's aggregate population base – notwithstanding a clear federal capacity, *pace* the Charter, to raise an army by conscription in times of war (a capacity less clear in the *antebellum*) – together seem to materially compromise the strategic base from which the diplomatic and military instruments of the state draw their potency. Finally, Canadian constitutional capacity in respect of direct military operations, while still largely untrammelled, for the first time ever has begun to be materially clipped, as it were, by anti-prerogative holdings such as *Khadr* and, to a lesser extent, *Smith*. And while it would be a stretch to posit that military operations at present are materially affected by these two decisions, it is reasonably safe to suggest that military decision making before long might begin to assimilate these decisions, unless reversed, into the national strategic calculus regarding the employ of Canadian forces in bona fide war.

Case Study C
Arctic Sovereignty

Geography – or land, as it were – is among the "purest" theoretical factors of strategic power, even if I do not treat it explicitly in the Strategic Constitution construct. The more land a country has, other things being equal, the more strategically powerful it is: it has "strategic depth" for purposes of defence (consider the difference, in terms of defensibility, between Russia and Singapore), territory to populate with people, and land from which to draw natural resources in support of the other factors of power. The importance of geography logically lends itself to the classical imperative of states to defend their territory (territorial integrity) and, by implication (and where possible), to maximize such territory.

What of the Arctic? For Canada, Arctic sovereignty essentially consists in the assertion, and international recognition, of Canadian sovereignty over a maximum swath of territory in the Canadian North.[1] For purposes of this case study, territorial maximization means the maximization of land territory connected to maritime borders as well as the maximization of maritime "territory" proper.

By virtue of the UN Convention on the Law of the Sea, or UNCLOS, each state has, counting from its maritime borders, twelve nautical miles of territorial waters – meaning that such waters are deemed *de jure* "internal" to that state – and 200 nautical miles of exclusive economic rights (an Exclusive Economic Zone, or EEZ). Of course, where there is potential for a breach, disregard, or indeed non-recognition of international law, including by other states,[2] one cannot safely assume that there is identity between the *de jure* and *de facto* variants of maximized territory (land and maritime). As such, the *de facto* variant is the principal concern of the strategist.[3]

Although international legal recognition of Canadian sovereignty over certain territories or waters in the Arctic would lead to "effective [Canadian] occupation and administration"[4] of such territories and waters, and though Canada might well wish to pursue such international legal recognition, the strategic-constitutional framework developed in this book takes international law (and international geopolitical dynamics) as more or less constant, privileging instead the domestic "constitutional statics" or Canadian constitutional capacity – or, in Part II, policy-political exploitation of such capacity – that drives outcomes in respect of Canadian interests. For purposes of this particular case study, therefore, the "effective [Canadian] occupation and administration" comprise the primary analytical preoccupation; that is, I explore Canadian capabilities, in constitutional terms, to assert such effective control over a maximum swath of territory in the North. In turn, such assertion could conduce to, or benefit from, international legal recognition but is not contingent on such recognition for "strategic success" to be declared.

To push the point further, territorial maximization for Canada as a strategic goal not only reinforces the presumptive geography factor of power of the Canadian state but also, as discussed, creates gains for the Canadian state in a number of the factors of strategic power established in the Strategic Constitution construct. More geography, for example, means greater opportunities for the Canadian state in natural resource exploration – specifically in, say, hydrocarbons.[5] Natural resource exploration would also clearly benefit the economic factor of power, as would the more exotic strategic possibility, raised by Michael Byers in respect of (the admittedly small) Hans Island – disputed by Canada and Denmark – that Canada, were it to become the proprietor of (or, in strategic terms, control) new land, could earn economic rents by leasing such land. Writes Byers:

Whichever country prevails will rightfully control who visits Hans Island and what they do there. That country could also choose to sell the island, like Russia sold Alaska to the United States in 1867. It could give the island away, like Britain did when it assigned the North American Arctic Archipelago (*sans* Greenland) to Canada in 1880. It could lease it out, like Cuba leased Guantanamo Bay to the United States in 1903. It could mine the island, blow it up or leave it alone. It could even declare the island a condominium and share it with another country.[6]

The strategic objective of territorial maximization is situated in the presumptive context of the melting of considerable polar ice (due to climate change) and the concomitant capacity, or the perception of such capacity, by multiple foreign states to navigate Arctic waterways and ultimately control such waterways and various swaths of Arctic or northern land – insular and non-insular – as well as associated onshore and offshore resources.[7] (For his part, Rob Huebert argues that, alongside climate change, resource development capabilities – that is, improved polar transportation and exploration technology – and indeed changes in international law are responsible for growth of the Arctic sovereignty imperative.[8]) In particular, as mentioned, sovereignty should consist of effective Canadian control of its Arctic borders.[9] Notes P. Whitney Lackenbauer regarding the Northwest Passage (NWP), arguably the most contested waterway in the Arctic sovereignty game (and indeed a proxy issue for the entire Arctic sovereignty debate):

> No one disputes that the NWP, running from the Davis Strait to the western Beaufort, is "Canadian" insofar as no foreign country claims that it has stronger rights to the airspace, waters or seabed than Canada. The sovereignty issue in this case is not about rival "ownership" in the sense of possession. The issue relates to how much power Canada has over these waters and the air corridor overhead – in short, the debate is over just how "Canadian" they are, and what this means in practice.[10]

Beyond the NWP, some key issues of dispute are Hans Island (the only Arctic *territorial* dispute involving Canada – as mentioned, with Denmark); the Beaufort Sea (overlapping claims with the United States); the Lincoln Sea (overlapping claims with Denmark);[11] and the Lomonosov Ridge[12] (possible overlapping claims with Russia and Denmark).

Conceding in principle that the land – though not the ocean waters – regarding which sovereignty is at issue or contested falls into one or more of the three federal territories, one must note at once that it is Parliament, through the *Constitution Act, 1871*,[13] that has constitutional competence for broad law-making and administration in the territories. Much of the practical decision making in the territories – typically the constitutional competencies given to the provinces – is delegated today to the governments of the territories. However, the federal government preserves and has final authority over nearly all macro-strategic elements of territorial governance.

And whereas the Constitution is explicit about onshore jurisdiction, Peter Hogg, commenting tangentially on the issue of offshore minerals – where the Supreme Court, in the *B.C. Offshore Reference*,[14] consistent with treatment of this matter in Australia and the United States, had confirmed federal legislative jurisdiction and ownership rights over the territorial sea and federal legislative jurisdiction and exploitation rights over the continental shelf – writes:

> While the *Constitution Act, 1867* ... is not explicit on the status of offshore resources, it is noteworthy that all these powers affecting external *sovereignty* [emphasis added] that are mentioned [in the 1867 Act] are, without exception, confided to the federal Parliament. These include trade and commerce (s. 92(2)), military and naval service and defence (s. 91(7)), beacons, buoys, lighthouses and Sable Island (s. 91(9)), navigation and shipping (s. 91(10)), and other major offshore resources, namely, seacoast fisheries (s. 91(12)). In all these matters, the *Constitution Act, 1867* recognizes that "once the low-water mark is passed, the international domain is reached" [*United States v. Texas* (1950), 399 U.S. 707, 719]. For domestic constitutional purposes, as well as for international law purposes, the actor in that domain is the federal government, not the provinces.[15]

Moreover, where the written Constitution and the courts are otherwise silent on the question of territorial sovereignty, the royal prerogative is in full effect, relating as it does, according to F.A. Mann, to "the whole catalogue of relations [of the Crown] with foreign nations [including] sovereignty over land, sea, and air."[16]

A reasonable policy framework for assessing Canadian constitutional capabilities for achieving the strategic goal of territorial maximization to advance Arctic sovereignty might include five dimensions: domain awareness, defence, actual physical presence, transportation, and resource exploitation.

Domain Awareness

Domain awareness consists in the capacity of the federal government to properly map the Canadian North – broadly conceived and including both land and sea – and, equally importantly, to know who is in, and what is happening in, the Canadian North. These imperatives are hardly trivial: to assert sovereignty or, in the terms set out, to maximize territorial occupation and administration, the state must know what the territory in question is and indeed what is happening in it. On these scores, recalling once again that policy-political praxis is an altogether different matter, the constitutional capabilities of the federal government are significant. First and foremost, because the federal government formally and beneficially owns the land and resources in the Canadian North, it has the general constitutional competence to map that land and audit its resources.[17] Offshore, there is evidently no question about federal constitutional competence to pass and enforce laws – or raw "order," as it were, via military (naval) patrols – and make policy in the 200 nautical mile EEZ associated with all chunks of land in the Canadian North.[18] (Strictly speaking, of course, in terms of strategic power, the reach of the military instrument could easily exceed the 200 nautical mile EEZ, as the Canadian sovereignty imperative might warrant.) And the federal government, not least by virtue of its diplomatic instrument (royal prerogative),[19] uncontroversially leads in the actual mapping or geo-mapping of the continental shelf beyond the EEZ for potential purposes such as demonstrating to the United Nations the extent of legitimate Canadian land claims, per the process under UNCLOS or, more specifically, the UN Commission on the Limits of the Continental Shelf.[20]

This "macro"-constitutional competence ushers in numerous cognate competencies related to the actual execution of mapping and situational awareness in northern territories and waters. Although a number of federal departments[21] would evidently have roles to play, the assets of the Department of Defence or, functionally speaking, "defence" assets would likely be central to the mapping and reconnaissance-cum-surveillance-cum-intelligence activities related to the North. Federal satellite imaging, transport equipment (navy, Coast Guard, others), and human intelligence would help to establish a "synoptic picture" – mapped and fused – of the North. And communications (for example, CSE) and human intelligence, as well as transport assets (for example, offshore patrol), would be essential to the task of determining "what is going on" in the North, as conceived in this "synoptic picture."

Defence

The federal government's constitutional competence regarding the actual defence of the Arctic is uncontroversial. Troop or military asset deployments in Arctic waters, skies, or non-Canadian or otherwise contested Arctic land (for instance, Hans Island) would all be governed by the royal prerogative for the military, largely untrammelled, as well as the royal prerogative in relation to national security and sovereignty. Domestic troop or asset deployments in the North – because it is federal land – would also presumably not require any resort to aid of the civil power (or defence call-out) provisions that exist at the provincial level. *In extremis*, the *Emergencies Act* could be used in the event of an international, war, or some species of declared public order emergency (such as an epidemic or a breakdown in some critical infrastructure relating to the Arctic). Evidently, in the most raw, "realist" sense, the prerogative to declare and fight a war remains unqualifiedly the province of the federal government, and in this sense one could well conceive, in certain future scenarios, small or even substantial clashes between Canadian military forces and foreign forces over Arctic lands or waters.[22]

Of course, one of the complications for Canada and for Canadian troop presence and deployment in the Arctic is the need for non-negligible manpower to populate the state's military instrument – including, say, for a possible military base in the Canadian North, infantry exercises in the North, or navy and air force patrols or power projection in the Arctic. And part of the "populating" challenge hinges on the aggregate population of Canada. (Arguably, this challenge could also be said to inform the capacity of the Canadian state to be meaningfully *aware* of what is happening in the North, as discussed above.) More readily, though, the challenge of developing or maintaining the physical presence of Canadians in the North highlights some of the most interesting "constitutional statics" in the Arctic sovereignty game.

Physical Presence
A key dimension of pressing Canada's Arctic sovereignty claims, in strategic terms, both on land and on water, is the basic need for human presence in the North – or in the Arctic theatre, as it were. How does the Canadian state populate the North? In other words, how does Canada develop a critical mass of Canadians in the North to properly "occupy" it? These Canadians could come from one or more of three sources: first, a significantly increased birth rate in the North; second, relocation of non-northern Canadians to the North from one or more of the ten provinces (including, say, in concert with a possible increased birth rate for the aggregate Canadian population); and third, settlement of immigrants to Canada in the North.[23]

Part I established that, while the federal government has the constitutional capabilities to incentivize – primarily via the federal spending power – increased reproduction and even relocation of Canadians to the North,[24] it has precious few tools to actually *require* or *compel* Canadians to live in the North – in particular, for strategic purposes. This dearth of instruments seems to apply, to a large extent, as much to the federal state's capacity to compel incumbent Canadian immigrants to settle in the North as to new Canadians. I explore these considerations below.[25]

A federal *requirement* for incumbent Canadians or recent immigrants (assuming that they are already citizens or permanent residents) to live in area X (as opposed to area Y) of the country for a period of time ($t > 0$) could well be a *prima facie* affront to the mobility rights in section 6 of the Charter. (Section 6 rights are inured against the notwithstanding clause in section 33.) There has been no jurisprudence to date on this fact pattern to provide guidance and few section 6 cases at the Supreme Court. As such, my analysis will have to be largely counterfactual. Section 6(2) states that every citizen and permanent resident of Canada has the right (a) to move to and take up residence in any province (where territories, in Charter terms, are equivalent to provinces[26]) and (b) to pursue a livelihood in any province. Furthermore, the rights in section 6(2) are subject to the limitations in section 6(3); that is, (a) any laws or practices of general application in force in a province other than those that discriminate among persons primarily on the basis of province of present or previous residence and (b) any laws providing for reasonable residency requirements as a qualification for the receipt of publicly provided social services. Finally, section 6(4) provides that none of the above precludes any law, program, or activity that has as its object the amelioration in a province of conditions of individuals in that province who are socially or economically disadvantaged if the rate of employment in that province is below the rate of employment in Canada.

In the case of provincial distribution or redistribution, were the required distribution or redistribution of Canadians – new and old – in question strictly *intra*provincial – from, say, big city A to smaller city B in the same province – rather than interprovincial, then there would be no breach of section 6 rights. The question of constitutionality would turn instead on whether the enacting government was justified on the basis of the division of powers scheme in the 1867 Act. Were the federal government the enacting party, which head of power could it use? Because the 1867 Act is silent on the question of "strategy," the federal government presumably could not argue before the courts that it is interested in redistributing masses of people – immigrants – for purposes of, say, northern or Arctic sovereignty. (Or could it one day?) A far more likely scenario, sub-constitutionally, is that the federal government would have to strike an agreement with a province – the proper enacting party for matters within the province – to require such intraprovincial distribution of Canadians (via provincial levers, themselves strategically suboptimal – in particular the provincial spending power or the broad provincial property and civil rights competence).

Of course, in the case of the federal territories, as established in Part I, the federal government arguably could go it alone if there were a question of distributing Canadians within or indeed among any of the three federal territories. However, because the territories are sparsely populated to begin with, this federal constitutional capability would not be terribly useful or indeed be strategically nearly moot until the population in the territories were developed up to a certain critical baseline. It would therefore be the movement of Canadians – new and old – into the territories directly or from other parts of Canada that would be the essential "first play" to allow for the buildup of a sufficiently critical population mass to begin to meet a strategic threshold for purposes of projecting or asserting territorial sovereignty in the North.

Section 6(2) of the Charter refers only to citizens and permanent residents and not to aspiring immigrants who are not yet permanent residents – technically foreign nationals. Thus, it is conceivable that Parliament or the federal government, respectively through legislation (under the immigration head of power) or via regulation, should it wish to do so, could easily impose certain residency conditions on foreign nationals pending – or as a condition of – their receipt of permanent resident status to populate areas of strategic interest to the state. (Of course, on the current practice, leaving aside policy-political costs, this does not leave much time – a few years on average – for the foreign national to actually reside in his or her designated location before possibly acceding to permanent resident status. Having said this, the period preceding accession to permanent resident status could be increased in law or regulation.) Moreover, per the ruling in *Canadian Egg Marketing Agency v. Richardson*,[27] the designated residency requirement could theoretically be applied even to permanent residents and citizens if, as per section 6(3), the mobility discrimination against the individual in question is not *primarily* on the basis of residence. In this sense, the majority of the Supreme Court in *Canadian Egg Marketing Agency* held that sections 6(2) and 6(3)(a) should be read as a single right:

> Section 6 of the Charter guarantees the mobility of persons, not as a feature of the economic unity of the country, but in order to further

a human rights purpose. It is centred on the individual. Section 6 relates to an essential attribute of personhood that mobility in the pursuit of a livelihood will not be prevented through unequal treatment based on residence by the laws in force in the jurisdiction in which that livelihood is pursued. Given this purpose, the focus of the analysis in s. 6 is not the type of economic activity involved, but rather the purpose and effect of the particular legislation, and whether that purpose and effect infringe the right to be free from discrimination on the basis of residence in the pursuit of a livelihood.

The court, building on this logic, determined that, to the extent that the mobility discrimination in question is legitimately – indeed primarily – premised on a constitutional head of power, and not on residence, a limitation on mobility is constitutional. Of course, this begs the same question as that above: could the federal state argue that strategy – or sovereignty – is a legitimate purpose, in constitutional terms? Or could it, more or less "colourably," offer more palatable cognate justifications rooted in, say, a national security or even an economic premise, such as the Canadian North needs more people to secure the Arctic against foreign (state and non-state) encroachments, given climate change?

Failing this, one would be left with only section 1 of the Charter as a possible "saving clause" for the apparent breach of section 6 rights caused by any forced or required (re)distribution of Canadian citizens or permanent residents for strategic reasons. Section 1 famously "guarantees the rights and freedoms set out in it subject only to such reasonable limits prescribed by law as can be demonstrably justified in a free and democratic society." This provision is adjudicated – again, famously – by the *Oakes* test,[28] in which Chief Justice Dickson set out a four-part test for determining these "reasonable limits." He said that an impugned provision could be saved under section 1 if there were proof of a pressing and substantial objective; a rational connection between the provision and the objective; minimal impairment of an individual's rights and freedoms; and, finally, a predominance of benefits from the said provision vis-à-vis the negative impact on the associated rights. These considerations are patently domestic in their ambit. They ignore strategy as a legitimate end of the Canadian state, even in the context of (the values of) a "free and democratic society." Yet the jurisprudential record regarding *Oakes*, while inconsistent and non-uniform, suggests that a limitation on mobility rights, even for strategic purposes, if reasonably presented, could well be justified as pressing and substantial (first branch of the *Oakes* test) – a standard on which the courts are usually deferential to the government. The limitation might also pass the second branch – that of rational connection – even if a domestically focused court is skeptical of the rational connection in policy between population distribution and the strategic objective of national sovereignty in the North. Granted, the limitation could falter at the third branch of the test – that of minimal impairment, upgraded in later jurisprudence to an impairment that is as little "as reasonably possible."[29] Although improbable, the courts could see the limitation as not being the best among more reasonable alternatives for securing Canadian northern sovereignty, compared with, say, direct diplomacy with other states.

Transportation

Transportation on Canadian "soil" or offshore and in the various modes – car or truck or snow vehicle, rail, air, and of course water – is clearly critical to the capacity of the federal state to assert and project effective occupation and administration of the North. The vast geography of the North requires efficient displacement capabilities. *In extremis*, the state must have a robust capacity to transport representatives of its two chief instruments of strategic power – military and diplomatic – as well as their accompanying assets or equipment. (Recall that, given the expansive definitions here of the military and diplomatic instruments, intelligence personnel and assets mobilized for northern performance or projection would necessarily be deemed part of the diplomatic instrument. Similarly, one might posit that, in certain cases, police or paramilitary presence in the North, such as the federal Arctic Rangers, insofar as such presence plays a role in sovereignty projection, forms part of the military instrument.)

Because the three territories making up the North are federal territories, there is little doubt that Parliament has general legislative jurisdiction in each of them for transportation issues, across the three modes. On the ground, this jurisdiction is complicated somewhat by existing delegation of province-like powers from the federal government to the three territorial governments.[30] Still, the federal government – leaving, as agreed, international law in respect of territorial limits and travel regulations as an exogenous "given" – has total jurisdiction over transportation issues related to, or otherwise touching on, the international, including border patrol and off-border patrols or projections of sovereignty. In short, should there be, for instance, a question of patrolling (by ship or vessel) the NWP, whether these are ultimately deemed Canadian or foreign waters, there is little constitutional question that this capability is, strategically speaking, in the federal realm. Of course, the air transport mode – ranging from, say, civilian reconnaissance planes to unmanned aerial drones – is also regulated principally by the federal government under the *Canada Transportation Act* (exclusive federal responsibility for air services in Canada) and the *Aeronautics Act* (exclusive federal responsibility for safety and security of passengers, aircraft, and airports) on the famous premise that aeronautics is a national concern under the federal POGG or general power. Evidently, where a certain manifestation of transportation for purposes of sovereignty treads from the civilian to the military, federal legislative jurisdiction asserts itself via the section 91(7) militia power or the POGG power in the 1867 Act, and executive jurisdiction prevails via the royal prerogative.

Just as intraterritorial transportation is indubitably a federal legislative and executive competence, so too jurisdiction over transportation between the provinces and the three territories comprising the North is federal. In other words, rail transport (existing or prospective) between, say, Manitoba and Nunavut, or between Saskatchewan or Alberta and the Northwest Territories, for purposes of projecting sovereignty (say by moving people or equipment of various kinds to the North from the South), would fall under federal legislative jurisdiction via section 92(10)(a) of the 1867 Act. The declaratory power in section 92(10)(c), which would allow federal expropriation, upon dispositive declaration by Parliament that a certain local "work," despite being under presumptive provincial jurisdiction, is for the general advantage of Canada and therefore under federal jurisdiction, would also be available to the federal government. Granted, within the territories, already under federal jurisdiction, this power would largely be moot, except, arguably, to the extent that it could be used to efficiently override any authority delegated to territorial governments by the federal government. More interestingly, however, the declaratory power could be used by Parliament, strategically, to ensure continued functioning of transportation arteries (rail and road for example) between the provinces and the territories. If a particular intraprovincial railway or road in, say, British Columbia, Alberta, Saskatchewan, or Manitoba were deemed critical to the overall transport network that moves people, heavy equipment, or natural resources into the territories and ultimately to the Arctic, but were considered poorly maintained, strategically vulnerable (including to foreign attack or disruption), or otherwise poorly regulated at the provincial level, then Parliament could declare that railway or road to be for the general advantage of Canada under the declaratory power. (This logic is consistent, of course, with my interest not only in the magnitude of a given factor of strategic power but also in the federal state's capacity to mobilize that factor in support of the cardinal strategic instruments.)

As intimated, this declaratory power would also have significant application to natural resources in the North.

Resource Exploitation

Among the great stakes in the Arctic sovereignty game are the significant natural resources, proven and prospective, in the North and offshore in the seabed of the Arctic Ocean. There are at least two principal dimensions of the sovereignty imperative for Canada in respect of these resources: first, the need for Canada to maximize exclusive control, or monopoly, over these resources; second, the ability of the federal state to exploit such resources for economic rent – as a fillip to the economic factor of power – or more directly in aid of the military instrument. A third possible dimension is the ability of the federal state to have these Arctic resources contribute to the overall resource or energy security or stability of Canada. Note the example cited by Shelagh Grant of the first imperative at play:

> [In the 1960s,] foreign companies held the majority of drilling rights and leases for Arctic oil and gas fields. To affirm overall [*de facto*] sovereign control over transportation and development, Canada unilaterally claimed the right of authority over the internal waters of the Archipelago, as well as its air space, land-fast ice and seabed. This and other claims were later validated by the United Nations Law of the Sea Conference upon ratification by a majority of states.[31]

A July 2008 study by the US Geological Survey estimated that total mean undiscovered, conventional oil and gas resources in the Arctic included 90 billion barrels of oil, 1,669 trillion cubic feet of natural gas, and 44 billion barrels of natural gas liquids – all largely offshore.[32] Moreover, the Government of Canada estimates that approximately one-third of Canada's aggregate hydrocarbon potential is at stake in northern resources that remain untapped.[33]

To start, as with the historical example offered by Grant, the federal government can use combinations of its military and diplomatic instruments to directly seize or – via strategic dissuasion, deterrence, or "force projection" – threaten to seize assets,[34] territories, or seas claimed *de facto* and even *de jure* occupied or controlled by a foreign country and therefore force that country (for instance, Denmark, though not necessarily much larger countries such as the United States or Russia[35]) to cede or yield the said assets, territories, or seas to Canada. I have already treated at some length the means by which the federal government can lever or manipulate the various factors of power outlined in the Strategic Constitution to influence the potency of each of these two instruments of Canadian power.

Within the Canadian federation, the federal government, unlike the provinces, still collects non-renewable natural resource revenues from both the Northwest Territories and Nunavut, though not from the Yukon, since the 2003 devolution agreement with that territory. One might even say that this agreement is quasi-constitutional, given the conception of constitutionality discussed in Part I. A similar devolution regime for the Northwest Territories had just been agreed in principle between the federal government and the government of the Northwest Territories when this book went to print. This agreement is reflected in the *Northwest Territories Devolution Act*,[36] tabled in Parliament on December 3, 2013.

In respect of the third, perhaps more speculative or exotic, consideration of resource sovereignty in the Arctic – the notion that the federal government could use Arctic resources to meet national energy needs or, more precisely, to assure national energy supply – both offshore resources and resources in the three territories are owned by the federal Crown. In the former case, to the extent that sovereign control over a given resource – say offshore oil – is assured by Canada, it would not be controversial that the federal government could require, in principle, that a given quantity or rate of oil be extracted – say to meet national needs. However, as established in Part I, such resources would presumably be immediately available for export through *NAFTA*, and federal legislation privileging national consumption (or storage) at the expense of market-priced export would be contrary to the agreement. The federal government might then legitimately consider options – all constitutionally within its purview: alternatively, to breach the trade agreement in favour of increasing domestic energy supply, while incurring the legal or retaliatory costs, or, *in extremis*, to seek to renegotiate or outright pull out of the deal. More elegantly, the federal spending power is there to enable the federal government to purchase oil at market rates to create a national petroleum reserve that would otherwise act to stabilize national energy supply in emergency scenarios.

In the context of regulating energy production within the territories, while the federal government still extracts resource revenues from territorial governments, regulatory devolution means that it might have greater difficulty enforcing production requirements at this level. Leaving aside, however, the basic spending power that the federal government could use to incentivize certain production quotas in the interest of national supply, and naturally assuming that the federal government has strategically secured the territories against any foreign attempts at strategic interference or even annexation (in the context of a melting NWP, for instance), the federal government could still, as a rule, override territorial legislation in the Yukon and Northwest Territories (where there is or, in the case of the Northwest Territories, shortly will be resource management devolution) for purposes of meeting national energy supply needs and indeed legislate directly (or outright) in this regard in the case of Nunavut. Evidently, the *NAFTA* "statics" described in the offshore scenario would also be at play in the context of the three Canadian territories. As with offshore energy, the federal government could, for all intents and purposes, block, via the *Investment Canada Act*, foreign investments in, or purchases of, Canadian energy assets or interests that might be perceived as incompatible with the objective of assuring a basic national aggregate energy supply.

Case Study D
National Security/Counterterrorism since 9/11

National security in Canada has taken on peculiar import since the al-Qaeda attacks on the United States in 2001. As explained in Part I, national security, as a concept, refers to the protection of critical Canadian assets and interests against a variety of threats, domestic and international, human and natural, deliberate and accidental – a state of affairs that lies somewhere between the spheres of personal safety and international or global security. The term "national security" or one of its cognates appears in at least thirty federal statutes, with fewer than a third of them attempting to define the term, the net result of which is that there is no authoritative or dominant definition of national security in Canadian statute.[1]

This reprioritization of security policy in Canada arguably culminated in the release of the 2004 National Security Policy (NSP) under the government of Prime Minister Paul Martin.[2] The definition of national security in the NSP was more holistic or comprehensive than the one typically presumed by those specialized in post-9/11 counterterrorism. The Martin white paper covered six essential areas of security policy: intelligence, transport security, public health emergencies, general emergency management, critical infrastructure protection, and international security. It was premised on the following three policy goals: first, protecting Canada and Canadians at home and abroad; second, ensuring that Canada is not a base for threats to its allies (in particular, the United States); and third, contributing to international security.

Since "international security" (or "offensive" security) has already been treated in Case Studies A and B, this case study focuses on the *prima facie* "domestic" aspects of national security in the presumptive post-9/11 threat environment – specifically in relation to terrorism. So the focus is on all of the first five essential areas of the 2004 NSP (but not the sixth), as well as on the first and second goals of the NSP (but not the third), with greater emphasis on the first than the second. In short, the central line of enquiry is the following: how can the Canadian state, within the framework of the Strategic Constitution, protect Canadians (and ensure that Canada is not a base for threats to Canadian allies) in the face of terrorist threats? Answering this question requires an examination of the first five policy areas outlined in the NSP, with the analysis premised on the understanding or logic that, for all intents and purposes, national security, in relation to counterterrorism, has two phases: a pre-attack phase and a post-attack phase.[3] The pre-attack phase relates to all elements of national preparation to prevent or avoid or foil attacks, while the post-attack phase relates to reaction to, or recovery from, attacks, wholly successful or not. Although the distinction between the two phases is not clean or crisp, policy areas such as intelligence, transport security, and critical infrastructure can be said to effectively fall into the pre-attack phase – though intelligence activities, as is the case with the other two areas, easily spill over into the post-attack stage – and areas such as emergency management and public health emergencies fall into the post-attack phase – even if "mitigation" efforts are pre-attack in character. (In fact, emergency management and public health emergencies could plausibly be combined into a single emergency management section, even if, strictly speaking, the former area might deal predominantly with non-bioterrorism and the latter with bioterrorism.[4])

Intelligence

In this case study, the relevant practical, intelligence-related enquiry is as follows: Does the Canadian federal state have adequate intelligence capacity, *constitutionally speaking*, to prevent or foil terrorist attacks on

Canadian territory or against Canadian interests (in Canada or abroad)? Or, in the *ex-post* scenario (that is, after an attack), does this intelligence capacity exist, *constitutionally speaking*, to prevent future attacks? (Note: the idea of arresting or convicting a terrorist actor, leaving aside the fact that the arresting authorities and the prosecuting Crown[5] are often not strictly involved in the "intelligence" function, is, on the logic here, strategically relevant only insofar as such an arrest or conviction aids in the strategic end of preventing terrorist attacks. "Justice," in this sense, has no intrinsic strategic value; the same is true, as established at the outset, throughout this book.)

There is little constitutional controversy over federal constitutional competence for domestic *security intelligence*, properly defined,[6] across the totality of Canadian territory, within and across provincial and territorial borders. (Provinces' constitutional capacity, strictly speaking, to engage in national – interprovincial – or international intelligence activities is limited by their incapacity to legislate with national or international effect. However, provincial police authorities, by dint of provincial jurisdiction over intraprovincial policing and administration of justice, often do contribute significantly to federal intelligence efforts relating to counterterrorism.) There is similarly little doubt that the federal government may, if it wishes, by dint of the royal prerogative, stand up a proper Canadian human foreign intelligence agency – something that does not exist at present. (More "elegant," as discussed in Part I, would be a statutory change in section 16 of the *CSIS Act* to remove the territorial restriction on CSIS activities in relation to military and foreign relations intelligence.) CSIS, supported by the *CSIS Act*, rooted in the federal militia and POGG powers,[7] is clearly the lead federal agency for security intelligence, and its intelligence activities, including limited ones abroad, are, according to section 12 of the *CSIS Act*, to be strictly in the service of Canadian national security, while its foreign and defence intelligence activities, according to section 16, are restricted to territorial Canada.

CSIS does not see section 12 as restricting its investigative, information collection, and analytical activities to territorial Canada. And though in 2007 Justice Blanchard of the Federal Court, in *Re CSIS Act*,[8] was agnostic on this point, he did rule, relying on *Hape*,[9] that the court could not authorize section 21 CSIS warrants for CSIS security intelligence activities outside Canada for the plain reason that Canadian law, including the Charter, could not operate in foreign countries in the absence of their consent to the operation of Canadian law. Nevertheless, the Blanchard ruling leaves practical room for section 21 warrants on the basis of information obtained by CSIS with the help of Canadian agencies with more muscular extraterritorial tentacles.

In its limited foreign intelligence capacity, CSIS is supported by the CSE,[10] the Chief of Defence Intelligence (CDI),[11] the International Assessment Staff (IAS) in the Privy Council Office (PCO), and indeed, informally, the "information" or "intelligence" capabilities of departments and agencies such as the RCMP, the Department of Foreign Affairs and International Trade (DFAIT),[12] and Citizenship and Immigration Canada (CIC) – the point being that intelligence (domestic and foreign) is more than the strict province of formal agencies but rather consistent with the type of rarefied information or analytical conclusions that support the broader goals of national security or, in this case, counterterrorism.[13] Specifically, such information or analysis is intended to advise the federal government of existing or potential terrorist threats to trigger action by the government to address the threats.

As discussed previously, there are now, based on the *Khadr* line of cases, material – though still somewhat nebulous and, in practical terms, ill-defined – constitutional (Charter) limits on what Canadian intelligence agents or officials can do abroad: they must not breach international legal (human rights) standards to which Canada is subject – a rule that might well turn out to be a significant hindrance to Canadian intelligence capabilities in international counterterrorism situations in which there is dubious clarity regarding the status of international law or in which there is clarity on the illegality of the international "process" (to use the vernacular from *Khadr* 2008) but in which serious Canadian security (counterterrorism) interests are nonetheless engaged. An example of dubious clarity in international law is the case of a "targeted killing" – including, say, by drone – involving Canadian officials or agents in another country, with that country's blessing, relating to a suspected terrorist planning an attack on Canada from that country. Hesitation, if not outright self-deterrence, by Canadian security agencies to seek out intelligence in such situations could well compromise key Canadian security interests (roughly as defined in the NSP).

Intelligence also plays a leading role in relation to the contested national security certificate process in the *Immigration and Refugee Protection Act*.[14] That process provides for (typically preventative) detention and deportation of foreign nationals and permanent residents (but *not* Canadian citizens) deemed to constitute a threat to the security of Canada. The review of security certificates by the Federal Court "differs from other types of court applications in that the security certificate procedure is preventative – the intention being to deal with threats before they manifest themselves. Accordingly, the review of the reasonableness of the certificate is administrative in nature and does not reference the full array of rights and procedural safeguards included in criminal law."[15] A security certificate deemed reasonable by the Federal Court is dispositive in that it is tantamount to a removal order of the individual in question.

These provisions were ruled unconstitutional – variously contrary to sections 7, 9, and 10(c) of the Charter and not saved by section 1 – in *Charkaoui v. Canada*.[16] The declaration nullifying the certificate regime was suspended for one year, though the court required, with immediate effect, that detention reviews take place within the first forty-eight hours and thereafter at intervals of six months. Wrote Justice McLachlin in the *Charkaoui* judgment at paragraph 24:

> In the instant case, the context is the detention, incidental to their removal or an attempt to remove them from the country, of permanent residents and foreign nationals who the ministers conclude pose a threat to national security. This context may impose certain administrative constraints that may be properly considered at the s. 7 stage. Full disclosure of the information relied on may not be possible. The executive branch of government may be required to act quickly, without recourse, at least in the first instance, to the judicial procedures normally required for the deprivation of liberty or security of the person.

At the same time, it is a context that may have important, indeed chilling, consequences for the detainee. The seriousness of the individual interests at stake forms part of the contextual analysis. As this Court stated in *Suresh*, "[t]he greater the effect on the life of the individual by the decision, the greater the need for procedural protections to meet the common law duty of fairness and the requirements of fundamental justice under s. 7 of the *Charter*." Thus, "factual situations which are closer or analogous to criminal proceedings will merit greater vigilance by the courts": *Dehghani v. Canada (Minister of Employment and Immigration)*, [1993] 1 S.C.R. 1053, at p. 1077, *per* Iacobucci J.

In February 2008, Parliament passed Bill C-3 (reintroduced after an identical bill died on the order paper because of a federal election) that met the various concerns of the court in *Charkaoui* regarding the security certificate regime. In particular, the bill included a special advocate (*amicus curiae*) mechanism to represent the interests of the individual named in a given security certificate. Under Bill C-3, the process for detaining and releasing a person subject to a security certificate became the same whether the person in question was a permanent resident or a foreign national. Warrants can be issued by the federal executive if it has reason to believe that a person is, among other things, a danger to national security (section 81). A review of the reasons for detention must take place in the first forty-eight hours and at six-month intervals thereafter until a decision is made by the Federal Court regarding reasonableness of the certificate. A right of appeal to the Federal Court of Appeal exists, under section 79, only if the judge certifies that a serious question of general importance is involved. (The judge must articulate that serious question). Release with conditions considered appropriate by a judge, per section 82(5), is facilitated, in general terms, by the new security certificate regime.

What about detention of Canadian *citizens* in relation to terrorism threats, including for intelligence purposes? Security certificates are clearly inapplicable in such circumstances. In the absence of emergency situations in which the *Emergencies Act* would be invoked by Parliament, or in which the executive would resort to the emergency prerogative (supervening on the *Emergencies Act*), citizens could be detained only in respect of a terrorist threat (or act) if they were in breach of the *Criminal Code*. Of course, short of this higher standard, a security service such as CSIS would have the legal capability to disrupt terrorist threats *sans* detention of the relevant actors by the police.[17] Such disruption, perhaps in simplest form, might involve security agents informing suspects under surveillance that they were in fact under surveillance – thereby effectively undermining the organization or secrecy of the terrorist activity.

Evidently, the size – in terms of people and resourcing – of the intelligence capability of the federal state, as well as the quality of the national talent that goes into intelligence, are functions of a number of variables. As with the military and diplomatic instruments that intelligence might support, the size of the economy and size of the population will impact the size of the intelligence capacity and, arguably, the talent of those populating it. The quality of the intelligence services depends, *inter alia*, on national education and training. Because the provinces are legislatively competent in Canada for education – particularly regarding curricular development – and notwithstanding federal interventions, particularly at the postsecondary level, via the spending power, there is no necessary logical link between the pre-professional *formation*, as it were, of Canadian citizens and the strategic intelligence needs of the Canadian state, especially regarding counterterrorism and especially at the level of human intelligence (both domestic and foreign).[18] Widely held, high-level linguistic competence (say in Middle Eastern and South and Southeast Asian tongues), heavy travel experience (or experience living in foreign societies), analytical competence, intercultural sophistication, and, *inter alia*, what might be termed intelligence "judgment" or "instinct" are arguably the dominant relevant competencies required of excellent intelligence analysts or operational agents. And while the federal government, again via its spending power, might train and recruit broadly among all Canadian citizens (and, for certain situations, among foreign citizens, particularly were it to establish a proper human foreign intelligence agency), it stands to reason that such recruitment and training in almost all cases would take place after the human "raw material" had already been formed – for the most part in societal areas (especially education) that are overwhelmingly under provincial jurisdiction.

Transportation (and Critical Infrastructure Protection)

There are two ways of viewing the transport security imperative regarding the more general national security imperative – or the counterterrorism imperative – at play in this case study: one "defensive" and the other "offensive." (I use transport assets as a proxy for the far larger, less well-defined, category of critical infrastructure, that is, infrastructure that were it compromised, including through an attack, would have important consequences for the strategic vitality of the state or, more precisely, the vitality of the various factors of power and, ultimately, the two cardinal strategic instruments. Such critical infrastructure can include energy infrastructure, financial and banking systems, and, among others, communications assets, including cyber assets.[19]) In the "defensive" optic, I am interested in the capacity, constitutionally speaking, of the federal government to defend strategic transportation assets against various species of terrorist attack or "re-attack."[20] These strategic transportation assets might include key aviation assets, rail links, ports, and certain bridges. (In the pre-attack/post-attack framework, the defensive optic would fall principally into the pre-attack category.) In the "offensive" optic, however, I am interested in the capacity, constitutionally speaking, of the federal state to mobilize strategic transportation assets across the various transport modes in direct aid of the instruments of Canadian strategic power – for instance to mobilize rail or aviation assets to transport military assets across the country or even internationally to deal with strategic terrorist threats. (The offensive optic would be relevant for both the pre-attack and the post-attack phases.)

Canadian strategic transportation infrastructure, despite the relative constitutional weakness of Canada's economic union, is largely regulated by the federal government. The safety and security of the transportation infrastructure are part of this regulatory field. (As a strictly practical matter, much of this infrastructure, across the various transport modes, is owned and operated by the private sector.) International or interprovincial railways, historically and currently strategically critical to Canadian power (especially in relation to the economy and the military instrument), are principally regulated by the federal government on the strength of section 92(10)(a) of the 1867 Act. As for non-interprovincial or local railways, they have often been declared by Parliament to be for the general advantage of Canada and as such have often been transferred from provincial to federal jurisdiction. (This is to say nothing of the broad general federal expropriation powers outlined in Part I as well as the federal executive expropriation power for military purposes in section 117 of the 1867 Act – all tools clearly in play in the context of possible strategic terrorist threats to the Canadian state.) Interprovincial and international shipping also falls under federal jurisdiction under sections 92(10)(b) and 91(10).[21]

Like the rail mode, regulation of the air mode, since the 1952 *Johannesson* case,[22] has been dominated by the federal government – though somewhat incongruously not under section 92(10), but as a national concern (POGG), under the *Canada Transportation Act* (exclusive federal responsibility for air services in Canada) and the *Aeronautics Act* (exclusive federal responsibility for safety and security of passengers, aircraft, and airports).

As a general rule, therefore, there is, in addition to the air mode, little controversy over the capacity of the federal state to regulate protection of assets that it might deem strategically critical in both the rail and road modes, provided that the rail lines or roads or bridges are international or interprovincial in character. A strategic artery of international trade, including for, say, transport of necessary military goods – for instance the cross-border Windsor-Detroit Ambassador Bridge or the Niagara Falls-Buffalo Peace Bridge – would therefore, on the Canadian side of the border, be regulated, for security purposes, by the federal government. Evidently, there are policy-political issues or decisions in play here, such that actual responsibility for securing such assets on the ground (for example, policing assets or "hardening" infrastructure against possible attack) might well be distributed across several jurisdictions, federal, provincial, and municipal. In the Strategic Constitution framework, the degree to which the federal government wishes to impose or not impose security standards XYZ on strategic assets ABC (transport assets or critical infrastructure) that are otherwise under federal jurisdiction is entirely a function of policy discretion.

Of course, neither provincial (or municipal) constitutional responsibility for transport assets nor the dominant private sector ownership position in critical transport infrastructure necessarily poses a material obstacle to federal regulatory governance of such assets for security purposes, with the declaratory power and federal spending power (that is, to purchase even a minor interest in a critical asset[23]) perennially available to the federal government. In emergency situations, the emergency power in POGG (*Emergencies Act*) enables the federal government, upon declaration of certain types of emergency, to dispossess or expropriate transportation assets from private parties for reasons deemed strategic or otherwise essential to national security or counterterrorism. (The same expropriation capacity, in emergency situations relating to national security or counterterrorism, also seems to apply with little controversy to private assets on Aboriginal title or treaty lands.) A clear example of such a key transport asset is an intraprovincial intermodal transport network that is highly vulnerable to attack or otherwise indispensable to the provision of essential goods, including military or "dual-use" (military and non-military) goods. Indeed, it might even be arguable, using as a precedent the *Ontario Hydro* holding in respect of uranium mines, that the invocation of security-like scenarios regarding certain transport modes traditionally under provincial legislative jurisdiction could well justify a federal claim to jurisdiction over such a mode under the national concern branch of POGG. In short, as a purely policy matter, the federal government might well choose to change the balance of public-private ownership of a particular critical (transport) asset or the balance of the federal-provincial division of labour in respect of delivery of security services for such assets. However, as a purely constitutional matter, federal jurisdiction over the security of such infrastructure is quite broad.

Emergency Management and Public Health Emergencies

Counterterrorism emergencies can be pre-attack or post-attack in nature. In the former case, as discussed above, there would be certain intelligence in respect of a planned or apprehended – or even imminent – terrorist attack against Canada or Canadian interests, in response to which the federal government might be inclined to use emergency or emergency-like powers. In the latter case, the more conventional emergency scenario, an attack – presumably a largely successful attack – has already been executed, or is in the process of being executed, against Canada or Canadian interests.

Chapter 4 explored federal power regarding emergencies and discussed the watershed *Anti-Inflation Reference* of 1976,[24] which laid the constitutional jurisprudential basis for modern Canadian treatment and understanding of national emergency powers. In that case, which dealt with the constitutionality of proposed federal legislation to curb national inflation – in the event, national stagflation, deemed a bona fide national emergency – through the "supervision, control and regulation of [national, public, and private sector] prices, profits, wages, salaries, fees and dividends by way of monitoring and limiting increases," the Supreme Court determined that the federal government could rely, even in peacetime, on the general power – specifically the emergencies branch, though not necessarily the national dimension or national concern branch – to deal with real or apprehended national emergencies. Writing for Justices Martland, Ritchie, and Pigeon in support of the plurality decision, Justice Ritchie noted (a) the ability of Parliament, strictly in the context of national emergencies, to intrude into provincial legislative jurisdiction and (b) the necessarily temporary nature of national emergencies, under the general power, including in relation to (a). Ritchie observed:

> In my opinion such conditions exist where there can be said to be an urgent and critical situation adversely affecting all Canadians and being of such proportions as to transcend the authority vested in the Legislatures of the Provinces and thus presenting an emergency which can only be effectively dealt with by Parliament in the exercise of the powers conferred upon it by s. 91 of the British North America Act "to make laws for the peace, order and good government of Canada." The authority of Parliament in this regard is, in my opinion, limited to dealing with critical conditions and the necessity to which they give rise and must perforce be confined to legislation of a temporary character.
>
> I do not consider that the validity of the Act rests upon the constitutional doctrine exemplified in earlier decisions of the Privy Council,

to all of which the Chief Justice has made reference, and generally known as the "national dimension" or "national concern" doctrine. It is not difficult to envisage many different circumstances which could give rise to national concern, but at least since the Japanese Canadians case,[25] I take it to be established that unless such concern is made manifest by circumstances amounting to a national emergency, Parliament is not endowed under the cloak of the "peace, order and good government" clause with the authority to legislate in relation to matters reserved to the Provinces under s. 92 of the British North America Act.

In a *de maximis* sense, the emergency powers of Parliament know very few constitutional limits once Parliament has determined that an emergency exists and that the federal government must act to deal with the emergency in the national interest – or for national survival (as in the case of war or, say, a catastrophic terrorist attack: consider a chemical, biological, radiological, or nuclear, so-called CBRN, attack or one that devastates the national energy supply[26]). This is confirmed by the extant relevance of the emergency prerogative of the federal executive, which supervenes at common law even on legislation such as the *Emergencies Act* to the extent that such legislation has not displaced or ousted it.[27] As discussed in Part I, cases such as *Re Manitoba Language Rights* confirm that the Constitution cannot be a "suicide pact" – the implication being, again, that Parliament and the federal government must do all that is necessary (the doctrine of constitutional necessity), in an emergency situation, to preserve the state and the rule of law. In the *Anti-Inflation Reference*, much the same is said even by Justices Beetz and Grandpré in their dissent from the Supreme Court majority:

> The power of Parliament to make laws in a great crisis knows no limits other than those dictated by the nature of the crisis. But one of the limits is the temporary nature of the crisis. The extraordinary nature and the constitutional features of the emergency power of Parliament dictate the manner and form in which it should be invoked and exercised. In cases where the existence of an emergency may be a matter of controversy, it is imperative that Parliament should not

have recourse to its emergency power except in the most explicit terms indicating that it is acting on the basis of that power; and while such an indication is not conclusive to support the legitimacy of the action of Parliament, its absence is fatal.[28]

On the side of the decisive plurality, Chief Justice Laskin observes for the court:

> It is my view that a similar approach of caution is demanded even today, both against a loose and unrestricted scope of the general power and against a fixity of its scope that would preclude resort to it in circumstances now unforeseen. Indeed, I do not see how this Court can, consistently with its supervisory function in respect of the distribution of legislative power, preclude in advance and irrespective of any supervening situations a resort to the general power or, for that matter, to any other head of legislative authority. This is not to say that clear situations are to be unsettled, but only that a Constitution designed to serve this country [Canada] in years ahead ought to be regarded as a resilient instrument capable of adaptation to changing circumstances.[29]

In the event of a planned or apprehended terrorist attack, about which the federal government – say via CSIS, the RCMP, or the CSE – has material intelligence, depending on the suspected intent or expected consequences of the attack, the government can declare a state of emergency, according to the *Emergencies Act*.[30] Of the four types of emergency described in the act, the most probable types to be declared by the executive would be a public order emergency (thirty days), an international emergency (sixty days), or, if the suspected or known terrorist actor is a foreign state, a war emergency (ninety days). (Many of the specific parameters of each emergency, including the nature and extent of the controlling role of Parliament, are well treated in Chapters 4 and 5.) In the case of a public order emergency, the terrorist threat would have to be consistent with the definition of "threats to the security of Canada" as defined in section 2 of the *CSIS Act*. Indeed, the most plausible consistency would exist in respect of sections 2(c) ("activities within or relating to Canada directed toward or in support of the threat or use of acts of serious violence against persons or property for the purpose of achieving a political, religious or ideological objective within Canada or a foreign state")[31] and 2(d) ("activities directed toward undermining by covert unlawful acts, or directed toward or intended ultimately to lead to the destruction or overthrow by violence of, the constitutionally established system of government in Canada"). *Mutatis mutandis*, the orders and regulations availed to the federal executive for dealing with a public order (terrorism) emergency include the regulation or prohibition of certain public assemblies, travel to and from specified areas, and use of specified property; the designation and securing of protected places; the assumption of control, restoration, and maintenance of public utilities and services; and the authorization of, or direction to, any person or persons to render essential services. In the case of an international emergency, the terrorist threat at issue would, under section 27 of the act, "involv[e] Canada and one or more other countries" and result "from acts of intimidation or coercion or the real or imminent use of serious force or violence and that is so serious as to be a national emergency." Independently of the *Emergencies Act*, such an emergency would doubtless come, as with a war emergency, with the clear possibility of a declaration of war and the various bona fide war scenarios (and constitutional statics) described in Case Study B. Under the *Emergencies Act*, however, a declaration by the federal executive of an international emergency would include orders and regulations permitting, *inter alia*, control or regulation of any specific industry or service (including in respect of inventory); appropriation, control, and forfeiture of property and services; authorization of specific people to provide essential services; designation and securing of public places; regulation or prohibition of travel outside Canada by Canadian citizens or permanent residents (but not within Canada, contrary to section 6 of the Charter); and authorization of emergency expenditures for the executive. Finally, in the case of a war emergency (meaning "war or other armed conflict, real or imminent, involving Canada or any of its allies that is so serious as to be a national emergency"), the federal executive would have maximum latitude under the *Emergencies Act* to make such orders and regulations (presumably including *at least* all those availed in other emergencies) as it believes, on reasonable grounds, necessary or advisable for dealing with the war emergency (section 40(1)). (Note the laconicity of this section and the deliberate absence of the explicit orders and regulations concomitant to the other types of emergency. This economy of language in the most extreme terrorism scenario – the war scenario – largely mirrors an untrammelled royal prerogative, with ultimate executive comportment largely conditioned in the realm of common law, rather than the more restrictive "straitjacket" of statute.) However, these orders and regulations do not, per section 40(2), include the right of the federal executive to compel Canadians or permanent residents to serve in the Canadian Forces. (Recall that this scenario was raised in Case Study B and by Justice Wilson in *Operation Dismantle*. It follows that, while the war emergency declaration could not provide the legal basis for conscription into military service, such conscription could still be effected through separate legislation and, according to Wilson, would likely be saved under section 1 of the Charter, even if it might breach the section 7 rights of conscripts.)

To the extent that the *Emergencies Act* does not allow the executive to do certain things deemed necessary to deal with the emergency – that is, to prevent or meaningfully mitigate the attack – Parliament may amend the act accordingly. However, as mentioned, the *Emergencies Act* arguably does not exhaust the entirety of the emergency prerogative of the executive at common law, so, on the doctrine of constitutional necessity, extreme measures not otherwise expressly forbidden by or ousted in the *Emergencies Act* would certainly be available to the executive to address the terrorist emergency independently of the parameters of the act – if Parliament were, for whatever reason, unwilling to amend the act. Of course, recalling the *constat* in Part I to the effect that key post-*Operation Dismantle* "strategic" jurisprudence generally occurs today at the intersection of prerogative powers and Charter rights, this emergency prerogative (or, more precisely, executive actions taken under this prerogative) is also subject to the Charter, though it is highly probable that the courts would be exceptionally deferential to the executive in reasonably argued and evidenced emergency situations (as suggested in the *Anti-Inflation Reference* ratio) – thereby allowing any breaches of specific Charter rights to be saved under section 1. Measures that would be justifiable under the emergency prerogative might include certain military activities on Canadian soil – that is, those not otherwise covered by the *National Defence Act*, such as aid of the civil power.

As established in Part I, the Charter also has a powerful notwithstanding clause (section 33) providing for the operation of laws by either the federal Parliament or the provincial legislatures notwithstanding certain sections of the Charter. This clause has not been invoked to date by any federal government and would not be operative on the "democratic rights" in sections 3, 4, and 5 as well as the mobility rights in section 6. However, in a terrorism emergency, the federal government would have available to it, under the notwithstanding clause, the capacity to override the Charter's "legal rights" in sections 7 to 14 as well as the equality provision in section 15. (No justification for such an override would have to be provided under section 1, for that section would also be overridden by section 33.) It is similarly conceivable, depending on the gravity of the circumstances, that a government, confronted with a "real or apprehended war, invasion or insurrection" – in concert or identified with, say, terrorist threats – could invoke both the notwithstanding clause and section 4(2), which would be tantamount to a fairly potent cocktail of executive override of most of the Charter's key rights provisions.[32]

Finally, what about the constitutional capacity of the federal government to direct or even choreograph communications in the context of terrorism emergencies (pre- or post-attack)? Such crisis communications might variously serve to protect the "home front" or Canadian interests from, say, an imminent terrorist attack (or a repeat terrorist attack in the aftermath of a first successful one), direct national recovery efforts (including in the context of significant public health consequences after a successful attack), or, more fundamentally and generally, project governmental order and legitimacy across the Canadian population in the possible aftermath of a successful terrorist strike.

Since the modern *Emergencies Act* has not been litigated to date, it might be difficult to appreciate some of the exact statutory limits of the regulatory powers of the federal government under each of the four categories of emergency in the act (or under the three categories relevant for counterterrorism), including in relation to the direction of specific types of communication[33] from different media – that is, privately held media or state-owned media, such as the CBC, a Crown corporation. In the latter case, the *Broadcasting Act*, which articulates in statute, in broad terms, Canada's national broadcasting policy (where broadcasting is uncontroversially under federal legislative jurisdiction), is silent on emergencies and crises per se; this is true both in section 3(d), which speaks explicitly to the broadcasting policy framework, and in section 3(m), which explains the mandate of the CBC. Parliament could evidently change the language in the *Broadcasting Act* to address federal executive rights and responsibilities for specific communications (type, quality, length, frequency, reach, and so on) to the public in the event of national crisis or emergency or specifically in terrorism situations. To be sure, this language would be underpinned, constitutionally, by the federal interprovincial communications power in section 92(10)(a) or the federal residual power in POGG or, as intimated above, the emergency branch of the general power. Of course, this legislative change mechanism could also be applied to other federally regulated communications media, such as radio.

The same federal regulatory authority, rooted in the same constitutional powers, would exist for the federal government in relation to privately held media, such as private broadcasters or radio stations – that is, the government could explicitly address, through national statute and regulation, the issue of rights and responsibilities of the federal government in crisis communications. Indeed, for private media concerns, the outer limits of the capacity of the federal executive to communicate what it needs and wishes in crises or emergency situations would be conditioned by the existence of clear federal expropriation powers – temporary or permanent, threatened or actually used – corresponding to each of its heads of power (in the event, interprovincial communications); in short, the federal government could, in the absence of cooperation or even adequate standards from a private media concern, expropriate, or threaten to expropriate, that concern in an emergency situation to meet its strategic objectives in relation to crisis communications. The declaratory power, or threatened use thereof, would also be there and serve a similar purpose by advancing national emergency communications needs in the immediate prelude to, or aftermath of, a terrorist strike.

As for the Internet, which today, as discussed in Chapter 7, is not *as a system* regulated by either the federal government or the provincial governments in Canada, the former could, in the context of communications regarding a terrorist threat or strike, use its own websites to communicate whatever it wishes. There is no limit in practice, other than that of the federal purse, to the number of sites (or domain names) that the government could purchase from other interests – domestic and foreign – to distribute or diffuse its message. Of course, all this talk of emergency communications capabilities presumes that the federal government is able to defend or otherwise have communications infrastructure that is essentially resilient, *inter se* (physically, technically), against terrorist attacks, including cyber-attacks. I dealt with the constitutional statics underlying such resilience for communications assets in Chapter 7 and, for all intents and purposes, treated them by proxy in the discussion on transportation assets and critical infrastructure protection earlier in this case study.[34]

Conclusion

Having introduced and developed the Strategic Constitution construct in Part I and done the various "constitutional statics" on it to distill a picture of effective Canadian strategic power, and having tested in Part II the Strategic Constitution construct in four policy case studies, there is now a picture of a national constitutional framework in Canada that is, in strategic terms, highly flexible. Although it is not designed – and in many cases not jurisprudentially interpreted – for meaningful performance in international affairs, this framework can be applied to such matters should the proper policy-political chutzpah and competence of the federal executive – the "strategic centre," as it were – be there. In short, Canada's Constitution, while not originally designed for strategic performance by the national government, is remarkably plastic – though manifestly imperfect and in many cases inefficient – in allowing the federal government to perform strategically in various scenarios, either directly through the diplomatic or military instruments or indirectly through the various factors of power underpinning these instruments: the machinery of the federal executive, natural resources, the economy, communications, and the national population. In other words still, the Strategic Constitution (or Canada's Strategic Constitution), while operating against the spirit and intent of the original constitutional architecture of Canada, is remarkably potent; policy-political choices aside, the strategic capacity of the Canadian state, as explained by the Constitution, is significant. *Bref*, the Constitution of Canada is pregnant with immense strategic potential.

This is the basic conclusion of this book, which has sought to interpret the Constitution in a new idiom (strategy), one that departs from the traditional and dominant idioms of federalism and Charter rights. Without belabouring or repeating the many scenarios and permutations explored in the book, I can add a little colour to this conclusion by asking a negative question: what, given the plasticity suggested by the Strategic Constitution construct, can the federal government, in constitutional terms, *not* do strategically or *not* do with great efficacy? There are nine such areas of strategic inefficacy.

First, at perhaps a "sub-strategic level," the patent incoherence between the development, upstream, under provincial jurisdiction – arguably not just in the area of education but also in cognate policy areas covered under "property and civil rights" – of the "raw (human) material" that eventually populates the strategic instruments of the state (the diplomatic and military instruments) yields the astrategic paradox of the federal executive articulating, downstream, a desired strategic end or objective, but not being able to independently or self-sufficiently field a necessarily competent "team" to be able to execute it. This paradox was demonstrated starkly in Case Study A, with the federal government articulating a national strategic intent to lead in (or pivot to) the Americas region but otherwise being unable, in constitutional terms, to efficiently assure an adequate supply of the Spanish and Portuguese speakers needed to make this posture credible. For all intents and purposes, such a national supply of linguists could only be assured with first-order efficacy by the provinces, the variegated interests of which might well not be consistent with, or supportive of, the strategic prioritization of the Americas region.

Second, given the 1937 decision of the Privy Council in *Labour Conventions* (a decision little susceptible to near-term softening or reversal in the Canadian courts), the federal government is often (though not always) ineffectual, inefficient, or otherwise powerless in negotiating international treaties or agreements the implementation of which has many important elements falling under provincial legislative jurisdiction.

The federal government might therefore sign an international agreement only to find itself in the embarrassing strategic position of not being able to meet its commitments at international law because of provincial resistance to implementation of particular sections of the agreement. More probably, the federal government, anticipating such complications, would have to negotiate extensively with provincial governments to obtain their accord to eventual implementation of a unified national position. This dynamic, in principle, compromises federal efficacy in concluding international trade and investment agreements: witness the slowness of Canadian negotiations with the European Union on a *Comprehensive Economic and Trade Agreement*.

The astrategic character of Canada's treaty power as it stands today is perhaps best illustrated by the paradox of Canadian strategic (military) defeat, which consists in the inability of the federal government, in the event of Canadian defeat in military conflict, to implement the terms of defeat or surrender over the potential objections of provinces protective of their legislative jurisdiction (say, in education or other matters of local import). To be sure, the quite recent Federal Court holding in *Turp v. Canada*[1] proves that there remains no doubt that the federal executive can easily, on the untrammelled strength of the royal prerogative, withdraw from a treaty, even if parts of that treaty have been implemented in law by the federal government and one or more provinces. However, as established in this book, provincial delinquence regarding parts of a treaty can cause the federal government to be liable for the breach at international law. Provincial delinquence in the counterfactual context of Canadian strategic defeat (no one wishes this, naturally!) could well issue in additional pain in the form of continued war until the terms of defeat were comprehensively implemented. (True, one could argue that this distributed power of implementation would make total Canadian acceptance of defeat a drawn-out process indeed.)

Third, there are growing, albeit still embryonic and not at all clear, limits to what the federal government can authorize its various agents of power – starting with intelligence agents or officials but also, potentially, military or diplomatic personnel – to do under the royal prerogative without bumping up against the *Khadr* prohibition against Canadian official participation internationally in processes contrary to Canada's international obligations. (The outer limits of this prohibition are bound to be tested in practice until more precise fact patterns – for instance, ones relating specifically to the Canadian Forces in a foreign theatre – are brought before the Supreme Court. And most such future cases will be decided in the context of what seems to be the agreed principal field of "high strategic" jurisprudence in Canada: the intersection between the royal prerogative and certain Charter rights.)

The *Smith* precedent, for its part, though not a Supreme Court-level precedent, suggests a possible creeping encumbrance on the royal prerogative in strategic cases not through Charter jurisprudence but through administrative law as it relates to procedural fairness. This precedent, too, will be tested in practice and will need to be clarified (or corrected) at the Supreme Court before long so that the federal executive has more clarity in respect of its strategic *marge de manoeuvre*.

Fourth, there are clear limits, in the absence of national emergencies, and leaving aside the federal spending power (which would allow the federal government to create, say, a national petroleum reserve), to the federal constitutional capacity to *require* or *compel* provinces (*contra* the three federal territories) to meet national supply requirements and to distribute energy nationally to meet national energy needs – or, say, the needs of the military – or otherwise remedy energy imbalances in different regions of the country.

Fifth, because, strictly speaking, there is no practical federal paramountcy regarding uses of the spending power at the federal level or the provincial level (that is, both spending powers are constitutionally untrammelled), federal uses of the fiscal instrument for purposes of stimulating the national economy (or, in other words, increasing the economic factor of power) on occasion can be contradicted, mitigated, or otherwise undermined by certain fiscal moves at provincial levels.

Sixth, federal regulatory presence on the Internet – and indeed in related "new media" – is undeveloped and unsophisticated. The same is true of the provinces. *Bref*, the Internet, from both technical and content perspectives, remains, *as a system*, largely unregulated in Canada, *pace* nascent moves by the CRTC to change this fact. In strategic terms, this basic reality manifests itself most prominently in emergency scenarios, in which federal capacity to control communications content – say, to communicate basic threat information or project legitimacy across the national territory and population – is limited largely to the federal capacity (via the spending power) for provision of relevant information to the public on its own websites (or social media accounts) or to its capacity to establish new sites (via the purchase of new domain names) or purchase sites from other parties – including, say, parties with inaccurate or otherwise counterproductive messaging for purposes of meeting government objectives in addressing a given emergency.

Seventh, there can be a quasi-constitutional – perhaps still only conventional, and likely a "soft" rather than "hard" – limit to the aggregate quantum of immigrants that the Canadian state can allow into the country, given the stipulation in section 2 of the 1991 *Canada-Quebec Accord* on immigration regarding the need to preserve the demographic weight of Quebec in the federation. Again, to the extent that this accord is quasi-constitutional, one can see it as materially complicating the otherwise uncontroversial constitutional capacity of the federal government to increase Canada's overall population through immigration – including, *arguendo*, for purposes of increasing national strategic power. Although the wording in the accord is not tantamount to a guarantee, it seems reasonable to expect that the annual growth in Canadian immigration would be capped in practice less by the global supply of immigrants than by the global supply of immigrants susceptible to integration into Quebec society as a proportion of the total global supply of immigrants. Of course, it is not yet clear how this stipulation plays – quasi-constitutionally, as it were – in the context of a Québécois population that is diminishing (through diminished birth rates or emigration from the province), but it seems to posit a non-negligible complication in the federal government's constitutional capacity to increase the magnitude of a key factor of strategic power: national population (holding the mobilization of that factor constant). Indeed, in my numerous public volleys over the past several years to make the case for a Canada of 100 million people by the end of this century, it has struck me that the most compelling critique or complicating factor deals not with the environmental impacts of such increased demographic weight but with the future of the Quebec question – in part because of this quasi-constitutional dynamic that I adduce herein.

Eighth, and not unrelated to my 100 million Canadians conjecture, there are limits to the federal government's ability to forcibly distribute the national population across the territory of Canada. Among citizens and permanent residents, forced or required distribution – say, to create bigger cities or strategic centres, or to assert sovereign control over a given part of Canadian territory – is likely, in the absence of national emergencies, contrary to section 6 of the Charter. There seems, *prima facie*, to be little prospect of such a move being saved under section 1 of the Charter – especially under a "strategy" line of argument. Yet foreign nationals immigrating to Canada could be required, under the Canadian Constitution, to be resident in a given part of Canada for the period of time before they become permanent residents. And, in principle, there is no constitutional bar to the federal government increasing the length of this pre-conversion period through statutory or regulatory change – to promote more enduring distribution of newcomers to Canada.

Ninth and lastly, as acknowledged from the outset, this book could not give, and has not given, the relationship between Canadian strategy and Aboriginal peoples comprehensive treatment (this is doubtless for future books on Canadian strategy). Nevertheless, it is increasingly clear that, while most strategically consequential federal laws, programs, and moves will be "compelling and substantial" (to meet the first stage of the justificatory part of the *Sparrow* test in respect of the infringement of Aboriginal rights, including title), the second stage, relating to Crown fiduciary duty, supplemented later by the *Haida* decision (indeed by the entire "consultation trilogy") and by a line of recent cases speaking to the importance of the honour of the Crown, will tend to blunt the capability, constitutionally speaking, of the federal government to move directly and independently (and decisively) on a host of strategic fronts. Algorithms for dispatching the consultation and accommodation imperatives with Aboriginal parties – sub-strategic but clearly strategically relevant players – will need to be refined and iterated and, to be sure, calibrated against the importance of the various strategic interests and ends being advanced by Canada – from Arctic sovereignty to peace and war. This delicate interplay among ends, means, and process will make for a very interesting Canadian twenty-first century.

Notes

Introduction

1 It is noteworthy that many definitions of "strategy" privilege the military aspect of power, as in Colin S. Gray, *Modern Strategy* (New York: Oxford University Press, 1999), 17: "Strategy is the bridge that relates military power to political purpose." See also Hervé Coutau-Bégarie, *Traité de stratégie* (Paris: Economica, 2002), 27, or Book II, Chapter 1, of Carl von Clausewitz, *Vom Kriege* (Berlin: Die Deutsche Bibliothek, 2010). The US Department of Defense, for its part, defines "national strategy" more expansively as the "art and science of developing and using the political, economic and psychological powers of a nation-state, together with its armed forces during peace and war, to serve national objectives." Joint Chiefs of Staff, *D.O.D. Dictionary of Military and Associated Terms*, JCS Joint Pub 1-02 (Washington, DC: GPO, 23 March 1994), 255. In this book, I understand "strategy" as encompassing both the military and the diplomatic instruments (undergirded by what I will call "factors of strategic power") that serve Canadian national strategic interests or objectives, however defined.

2 *Constitution Act, 1867* (U.K.), 30 & 31 Vict., c. 3.

3 Writes Jack Granatstein, *Canada's Army: Waging War and Keeping the Peace* (Toronto: University of Toronto Press, 2002), 10: "Strategy was the province of the imperial masters, not the Canadians, whether French- or English-speaking ... Strategy was not for Canadians to decide; tactics, perhaps, but strategy, never." Surely, one might offer, this means that Canada's Constitution, in international relations terms, is at most *tactical* in character.

4 *Constitution Act, 1982*, enacted as Schedule B to the *Canada Act, 1982* (U.K.), 1982, c. 11.

5 Consider the excellent list of Canadian foreign policy books in John Kirton, "The 10 Most Important Books on Canadian Foreign Policy" (2009) 64, 2 International Journal 553. Of them, only one book – *Canada Looks Abroad*, by R.A. MacKay and E.B. Rogers (Toronto: Oxford University Press, 1938) – gives more than cursory treatment to the constitutional framework supporting Canadian performance (or non-performance) in international affairs. Still, the treatment of the Constitution in that book reduces quickly and simplistically to the question of international treaties. No other aspect of Canadian constitutionalism is connected to Canadian strategic power – and, of course, vice versa. See the discussion of international treaties and their relative import in Canadian strategy in Chapter 2.
6 Michael Howard, in his preface to Philip Bobbitt, *The Shield of Achilles: War, Peace and the Course of History* (New York: Anchor Books, 2002) xvi. Bobbitt himself writes in his prologue, xxv-xxvi, that "[t]he modern state came into existence when it proved necessary to organize a constitutional order that could wage war more effectively than the feudal or mercantile orders it replaced ... The process takes place in the fusing of the inner and outer dominions of authority: law and strategy."
7 Henry Kissinger, *Does America Need a Foreign Policy? Toward a Diplomacy for the 21st Century* (New York: Simon and Schuster, 2001), 20.
8 *Statute of Westminster*, 22 & 23 Geo. V, c. 4. The *Balfour Declaration* of 1926, issuing from the imperial conference that year, evidently anticipated the *Statute of Westminster*, which gave the declaration legislative effect. Jurisprudentially, it was the holding in *Croft v. Dunphy*, [1933] A.C. 156, that asserted, for the first time, that Canada's Parliament could legislate with *extraterritorial* effect, thereby buttressing s. 3 of the *Statute of Westminster, 1931*, which provided for the same thing. See note 10 below.
9 F.R. Scott, "Expanding Concepts of Human Rights," in *Essays on the Constitution* (Toronto: University of Toronto Press, 1977), 358.
10 The *Statute of Westminster, 1931* is part of Canada's constitutional framework, the definition of which I discuss below. Its s. 3 provides that the Canadian Parliament may legislate with extraterritorial effect. (See note 8 above.) This extraterritorial legislative capacity cannot be properly identified, however, with a foreign affairs legislative power per se, for it refers to *all* federal legislative heads of power, and they are evidently quite different, in functional terms, from foreign affairs properly understood. The *Letters Patent Constituting the Office of the Governor-General of Canada, 1947*, R.S.C. 1985, Appendix II, No. 31, Art. II, a prerogative instrument of the queen and arguably a part of the Constitution, on my definition (even if not, strictly speaking, according to the definition provided in s. 52(1) of the *Constitution Act, 1982*), consecrate at s. 14 the right of the governor general of Canada to accept foreign diplomats on behalf of Canada. This evidently speaks directly, at least in part, to the federal government and foreign affairs – if only for the executive, not the legislative, branch.

11 Section 51(xxix) of the *Commonwealth of Australia Constitution Act, 1900*, 63 & 64 Vict., states that the Commonwealth (federal) government has legislative responsibility for foreign affairs.
12 Bora Laskin, *Canadian Constitutional Law*, 4th ed. (Toronto: Carswell, 1975), 199.
13 Noting the Clausewitzian logic of war being politics by other means, I quote from Michael Cotey Morgan, "Between War and Peace" (May 2009) Global Brief 42, on the interchangeability of the diplomatic and military instruments of the state: "The twentieth century's catalogue of horrors tells us that diplomacy has limits. This is not to say that diplomacy has achieved no success – quite the contrary – but it is essential to understand what it can and cannot do. It cannot solve all problems ... This means that, in some circumstances, paradoxically, it makes sense [in the short run] to choose war over peace, and to fight to bring a more just and stable peace within reach."

Chapter 1: Framing Some Key Concepts
1 See, for instance, Joseph Nye Jr., *Soft Power: The Means to Success in World Politics* (New York: Perseus, 2004), as well as Joseph Nye Jr., *The Paradox of American Power: Why the World's Only Superpower Can't Go It Alone* (Oxford: Oxford University Press, 2002).
2 Strictly speaking, in Canadian constitutional law, executive power follows the grant of legislative power, as affirmed in cases such as *Liquidators of the Maritime Bank v. Receiver General of New Brunswick*, [1892] A.C. 437, as well as *Mowat v. Casgrain* (1897), 6 Que. Q.B. 12, with Parliament, in turn, strictly speaking, constraining or conditioning executive power. Moreover, the association of strategic power with federal constitutional powers in certain key areas (the factors of strategic power) does not preclude the possibility of federal-provincial cooperation in these areas or in the promotion of Canadian strategic interests. (Such intergovernmental cooperation, in constitutional terms, can be understood by the constitutional principle that legislative powers are *exhaustively* distributed between Parliament and the provincial legislatures.) Nor, of course, does it preclude the possibility of federal-provincial competition or conflict in certain areas. (Notwithstanding my observation at the end of this chapter about certain Aboriginal parties becoming strategically relevant actors in Canadian constitutionalism, First Nations do not figure as legislative actors in the exhaustive distribution of legislative powers. They are therefore far less strategically relevant than provinces for purposes of understanding Canadian strategic power in constitutional terms.)
3 Alexander Hamilton, "Federalist No. 70," in *The Federalist Papers* (New York: Bantam Dell, 1982), 426, famously wrote of the superior "energy" of the executive branch in relation to the other branches of government. At 427, he wrote that "[t]he ingredients, which constitute energy in the executive, are first unity, secondly duration, thirdly an adequate provision for its support, fourthly competent powers."

4 The definition of the Constitution in s. 52(2) of the 1982 Act was ruled non-exhaustive in *New Brunswick Broadcasting Co. v. Nova Scotia (Speaker of the House of Assembly)*, [1993] 1 S.C.R. 319.
5 Patrick Monahan, *Constitutional Law*, 3d ed. (Toronto: Irwin Law, 2006), 178. See the somewhat more pedantic definition of the Constitution given by Gil Rémillard in *Le Fédéralisme canadien – Tome I: La Loi constitutionnelle de 1867* (Montréal: Québec/Amérique, 1983), 143: "La constitution matérielle canadienne, c'est-à-dire l'ensemble des règles qui prévoient l'organisation et le fonctionnement de l'État canadien, est formée des éléments suivants: 1. la Loi constitutionnelle de 1867 (A.A.N.B.); 2. les amendements qui y ont été apportés; 3. des lois britanniques et canadiennes d'importance constitutionnelle [y compris la Loi constitutionnelle de 1982]; 4. l'interprétation judiciaire; 5. les conventions et coutumes; 6. la *common law* et les grands textes constitutionnels britanniques." *Quaere* whether Monahan, *contra* Rémillard, goes too far in including the entire catalogue of pre-Confederation imperial ("constitutional") statutes.
6 John A. Macdonald, the key figure in authoring the *British North America Act, 1867* (in particular the Quebec Resolutions of 1864), wanted a strong central government, meaning a preponderance of aggregate federal power over aggregate provincial power. Yet he cared little for military affairs and never fancied Canada professionalizing the military, let alone being able to independently project strategic power beyond its borders. *Quaere*: did this strong central (parochial or colonial) state contain the seeds of the eventual strategically sound state described in this book?
7 See Case Study C in Part II on Arctic sovereignty.
8 *A.G. Can. v. A.G. Ont. et al.*, [1937] 1 D.L.R. 673.
9 The Supreme Court persuasively tied ss. 9 and 15 of the 1867 Act to the royal prerogative in *Re Resolution to Amend the Constitution*, [1981] 1 S.C.R. 753. In its majority holding, the court stated: "A substantial part of the rules of the Canadian constitution are written. They are contained not in a single document called a constitution but in a great variety of statutes some of which have been enacted by the Parliament at Westminster ... Another part of the Constitution of Canada consists of the rules of the common law. These are rules which the courts have developed over the centuries in the discharge of their judicial duties. An important portion of these rules concerns the prerogative of the Crown. Sections 9 and 15 of the B.N.A. Act provide ... But the Act does not otherwise say very much with respect to the elements of 'Executive Government and Authority' and one must look at the common law to find out what they are, apart from authority delegated to the executive by statute."
10 Book 1, Chapter 7, of Sir William Blackstone's *Commentaries on the Laws of England* (Oxford: Clarendon Press, 1765-69), http://www.lonang.com/exlibris/blackstone/bla-107.htm.

11 The true relative influence of each factor or element of strategic power on the state's aggregate strategic power is a function, in constitutional terms, of both the potential raw magnitude or scope of the factor or element and, just as importantly, the extent to which that factor or element can be mobilized to inform one or both of the state's diplomatic and military instruments. I am interested here in the case law for each of the strategic *sections* falling under a given category or factor of strategic power and not, strictly speaking, the case law relating to the specific power categories or factors or elements taken as a whole, mindful as I am of the warning of Justice Beetz in the *Reference re Anti-Inflation Act, 1975*, [1976] 2 S.C.R. 373, that excessively diffuse subject matters should not be seen as a legitimate basis for exclusive legislative power for either the federal or a provincial government.
12 See Case Study A in Part II on Canadian strategic leadership in the Americas.
13 H. Scott Fairley, *Canada, External Affairs and the Constitution: A Theory of Judicial Review* (S.J.D. diss., Harvard Law School, 1987) [unpublished], 6. Note also the instructive *obiter* from Chief Justice Laskin in the *Anti-Inflation Reference*, *supra* note 11, in respect of the 1867 Act: "The *Russell* case was decided in an era when ... the Privy Council viewed the British North America Act as an *ordinary* statute to be construed on the same basis as other statutes" (emphasis added).
14 *Ibid.*, 46; emphasis added.
15 *Quebec Act, 1774* (U.K.), R.S.C. 1985, Appendix II, No. 2.
16 The *Canada-Quebec Accord* on immigration, the non-negligible strategic consequences of which are discussed in Chapter 8, can be said to have quasi-constitutional status.
17 In *John A., the Man Who Made Us – Volume 1* (Toronto: Random House, 2007), Richard Gwyn observes that, though the division of powers has been a perennial topic of political and jurisprudential debate for Canada, it was scarcely debated in the rapid drafting of the Quebec Resolutions at the Quebec Conference in 1864. (See *supra* note 6.) Yet one can argue that many of the s. 92 (and s. 93) heads of provincial power, starting with s. 92(13) on property and civil rights, were strongly anticipated by earlier imperial acts in British North America, such as the *Quebec Act, 1774*. One might also humbly wager that Fathers of Confederation such as G.E. Cartier and E.P. Taché, both avowed French Canadian *autonomistes*, would have made plain their preferences for certain s. 92 powers to Macdonald as he prepared the consolidated position of the United Province of Canada in the period prefatory to the Quebec Conference.
18 In the pivotal case of *Citizens' Insurance v. Parsons*, [1881] 7 A.C. 96, the Judicial Committee of the Privy Council used the logic of s. 94 of the 1867 Act in respect of uniformity of laws relating to "property and civil rights" among three of the four original provinces (Quebec excluded) to deduce that the laws in question referred to the equivalent of the body of laws covered exceptionally by the *Quebec Civil Code* – at the time the *Code civil du Bas-Canada*, predicated on the *Coutume*

de Paris – for the province of Quebec. As such, the property and civil rights section – 91(13) – of the 1867 Act became a *de facto* residuary clause in the jurisprudence for all "civil law" (non-criminal law) questions, including, *inter alia*, contractual rights, labour relations, securities regulation, and agricultural products. (Compare the "police power" of the states in the American federation, rooted in the 10th Amendment to the US Constitution, which states: "The powers not delegated to the United States by the Constitution, nor prohibited by it to the States, are reserved to the States respectively, or to the people." The police power authorizes states to make laws in regard to "safety, health, welfare, and morals.") For the record, s. 94 of the 1867 Act reads as follows: "Notwithstanding anything in this Act, the Parliament of Canada may make Provision for the Uniformity of all or any of the Laws relative to Property and Civil Rights in Ontario, Nova Scotia, and New Brunswick, and of the Procedure of all or any of the Courts in those Three Provinces, and from and after the passing of any Act in that Behalf the Power of the Parliament of Canada to make Laws in relation to any Matter comprised in any such Act shall, notwithstanding anything in this Act, be unrestricted; but any Act of the Parliament of Canada making Provision for such Uniformity shall not have effect in any Province unless and until it is adopted and enacted as Law by the Legislature thereof."

19 Pierre Elliott Trudeau, *Federalism and the French Canadians* (Toronto: Macmillan, 1968), 198. One might note, in support of Trudeau's insight, that in the *Labour Conventions* case, *supra* note 8, Lord Atkin, in asserting provincial legislative jurisdiction under s. 92(13) of the 1867 Act over certain aspects of international treaties, states: "If the position of Lower Canada, now Quebec, alone were considered, the existence of her separate jurisprudence as to both property and civil rights might be said to depend upon loyal adherence to her constitutional right to the exclusive competence of her own Legislature in these matters." Of course, Trudeau's might be a slightly tendentious view – one that neglects the obvious role of Ontario, especially under the rule of Oliver Mowatt, in driving a number of the Privy Council challenges in the late nineteenth century and early twentieth century. Still, even in consulting today what is arguably one of the two leading constitutional treatises in Quebec, *Droit constitutionnel*, 4e éd. (Québec: Éditions Yvon Blais, 2002), by Henri Brun and Guy Tremblay, one quickly observes that the decentralist imperative is a clear leitmotif. Granted, perhaps an equally influential text, the late Gérald-A. Beaudoin's *La Constitution du Canada: Institutions, partage des pouvoirs, Charte canadienne des droits et libertés* (Montréal: Wilson and Lafleur, 2004), does not have conspicuous evidence of such a leitmotif.

20 *Calder v. British Columbia*, [1973] S.C.R. 313.

21 *Indian Act*, R.S.C. 1985, c. I-5. To a lesser extent, the royal prerogative still played and continues to play a residual role in Aboriginal governance, for the prerogative in regard to the creation of Aboriginal reserves by Ottawa has perhaps been limited, but certainly not completely ousted, by the *Indian Act* and the *Territorial Lands*

Act, R.S.C. 1985, c. T-7. See *Ross River Dena Council Band v. Canada*, [2002] 2 S.C.R. 816. Constitutionally speaking, the exact mechanism for Aboriginal reserve creation in each province often varies depending on the terms of union of the province in question. For reserve creation in the Yukon (as affirmed in *Ross River Dena Council Band*) and the other two federal territories, the royal prerogative – still not displaced – remains well in play.

22 *Royal Proclamation of 1763*, R.S.C. 1985, App. II, No. 1. See also *St. Catherine's Milling and Lumber Co. v. The Queen* (1888), 14 A.C. 46.
23 *Guerin v. The Queen*, [1984] 2 S.C.R. 335. See, more recently, *William v. British Columbia*, 2012 B.C.C.A. 285.
24 See Chapter 5 for a discussion of federal and provincial land ownership, as distinct from federal and provincial legislative powers. I also touch briefly on federal-provincial interjurisdictional immunity in relation to natural resource development and Aboriginal interests; see, for instance, *Keewatin v. Ontario*, 2013 ONCA 158, as well as *William v. British Columbia, supra* note 23.
25 *R. v. Sparrow*, [1990] S.C.J. No. 49.
26 See, for instance, Monahan, *supra* note 5, 461.
27 *Infra* note 35. See, for instance, Tony Fogarassy and KayLynn Litton, "Consultation with Aboriginal Peoples: Impacts on the Petroleum Industry" (2004-5) 41 Alta. L. Rev. 41.
28 *R. v. Adams*, [1996] 3 S.C.R. 101.
29 *R. v. Gladstone*, [1996] 2 S.C.R. 723.
30 *Delgamuukw v. British Columbia*, [1997] 3 S.C.R. 1010.
31 *R. v. Badger*, [1996] 1 S.C.R. 771, and then *R. v. Côté*, [1996] 3 S.C.R. 139, added that treaty rights (not just Aboriginal rights) created bilaterally could also be infringed unilaterally by the Crown, based on the *Sparrow* test. *R. v. Marshall*, [1999] 3 S.C.R. 533, affirmed this logic, noting that there did not need to be any higher standard of justification for infringement of treaties than for infringement of Aboriginal rights. (In some cases, the court suggested, no justification at all was needed for infringement of treaty rights.) See also *Chief Mountain v. Canada*, 2013 B.C.C.A. 49. Peter W. Hogg, *Constitutional Law of Canada*, student ed. (Scarborough: Carswell, 2007), 643n249, protests that, "[w]ith respect, this cannot be right. In the case of a modern land claims agreement, in which the rights and obligations of the Crown and the Indian nation are set out in great detail, and in which there is provision for amendments to be made ..., it seems wrong to me to permit Parliament unilaterally to amend the treaty rights, however strong the justification. At the very least, a higher standard of justification should be demanded for the infringement of treaty rights than for the infringement of aboriginal rights." Hogg's view is persuasively anticipated by Leonard I. Rotman in "Defining Parameters: Aboriginal Rights, Treaty Rights, and the *Sparrow* Justificatory Test" (1997) 36 Alta. L. Rev. 149.
32 Thomas Isaac, *Aboriginal Law: Commentary, Cases and Materials* (Saskatoon: Purich, 2004), 20, suggests that "most of these objectives fall within provincial jurisdiction."

Quaere whether this is altogether true, in strict terms, and whether it is at all true in implied terms. Strictly speaking, environmental protection, infrastructure building, and even foreign population settlement, depending on the specific facts, might well engage federal constitutional responsibility, even frontally; the other objectives might also. More broadly, various criminal law (*Criminal Code*) provisions – all obviously under federal jurisdiction – would typically justify infringement of s. 35 Aboriginal rights (see *R. v. Pamajewon*, [1996] 2 S.C.R. 821), as would war and various species of national emergency. See Brian Slattery, "The Hidden Constitution: Aboriginal Rights in Canada" (1984) 32 Am. J. Comp. L. 361 at 384. One can easily presume, on this logic, that various foreign policy and military or defence objectives would also be satisfactory for such infringement – even if Canadian jurisprudence, for the most part, is predictably silent in this respect. Just as importantly, I argue in this book that national strategy requires that one look at elements of national power (Part I) – and, by implication, the objectives of national power (Part II) – more holistically. This can mean, for instance, that foreign population settlement – a legitimate objective for purposes of infringement – might be in the service of the strategic objective of territorial sovereignty (as, *en passant*, it was at Confederation and in early twentieth century Canada); see Chapter 8 and Case Study C in Part II; also see the 2001 *Mitchell* case in note 34.

33 *R. v. Van der Peet*, [1996] 2 S.C.R. 507.
34 *Mitchell v. Canada*, 2001 S.C.C. 33.
35 *Haida Nation v. British Columbia*, [2004] 3 S.C.R. 511. Building on *Delgamuukw*, *Haida* held that the content of the duty to consult and accommodate varies with the facts of the case at hand, with one end of the "spectrum" of possible circumstances – that of *prima facie* weak title claims, limited Aboriginal rights, and minor infringement – requiring the Crown only to "give notice, disclose information, and discuss any issues raised in response to the notice" (para. 43) and the other end of the spectrum – that of a *prima facie* strong claim, expansive Aboriginal rights, high-impact infringement, and significant risk of "non-compensable damage" – requiring "deep consultation, aimed at finding a satisfactory interim solution" (para. 44). Write Fogarassy and Litton, *supra* note 27, 69: "The law has evolved to such an extent that almost any impact or impairment due to the activities of the Crown or third parties in respect of any possible or probable Aboriginal right, no matter how evidenced, will require consultation with and accommodation of Aboriginal peoples." In this sense, one can also observe that, in recent years, the conception of honour of the Crown has arguably widened at the expense of a strictly enforceable conception of fiduciary duty in the behaviour of the Crown in relation to Aboriginal peoples.
36 *Taku River Tlingit First Nation v. British Columbia*, [2004] 3 S.C.R. 550. See also *Mikisew Cree First Nation v. Canada*, 2005 S.C.C. 69, the third case, along with *Haida* and *Taku River*, in the so-called "consultation trilogy."

37 See the interesting dissent by Kent McNeil from the very idea that provinces can even infringe on Aboriginal rights, let alone be required to consult with Aboriginal groups as a result of infringement, in "Aboriginal Title and the Division of Powers: Rethinking Federal and Provincial Jurisdiction" (1998) 61 Sask. L. Rev. 431. McNeil argues that only Parliament and the federal government may infringe on Aboriginal rights because such rights, including Aboriginal title, inhere in s. 91(24) of the 1867 Act. Writes McNeil at 463: "[G]iven that Aboriginal title is at the heart of federal jurisdiction along with other Aboriginal rights, and so is *inextinguishable* by provincial legislation, it should be *uninfringeable* by provincial legislation as well."

38 See the powerful essay by Douglas Sanderson, "Toward an Aboriginal Grand Strategy" (Spring-Summer 2013) Global Brief 12.

Chapter 2: Diplomacy

1 Hans J. Morgenthau, *Politics among Nations: The Struggle for Power and Peace* (Boston: McGraw-Hill, 1993), 155.

2 L. Wildhaber writes in *Treaty-Making Power and Constitution: An International and Comparative Study* (Basel: Helbing and Lichtenhahn, 1971), at 1: "A cursory examination of the United States Constitution demonstrates that at the end of the 18th century, the conduct of foreign relations included relatively few matters: war, neutrality, and peace; treaties; foreign commerce; transfer of territory; appointment and reception of diplomats; definition and punishment of crimes against international law (piracy). Today, the scope, density and intensity of foreign relations have significantly increased, decision-making techniques have changed, the range of diplomatic instruments has been refined." Indeed, in the United States, since the Second World War, congressional-executive (international) agreements have been used with greater frequency than formal treaties by a significant factor.

3 See, *inter alia*, Torsten H. Strom and Peter Finkle, "Treaty Implementation: The Canadian Game Needs Australian Rules" (1993) 25 Ottawa L. Rev. 39; G.V. La Forest, "The Labour Conventions Case Revisited" (1974) 12 Can. Y.B. Int'l L. 137; R. St. J. Macdonald, "International Treaty Law and the Domestic Law of Canada" (1975) 2 Dalhousie L.J. 307; R.E. Sullivan, "Jurisdiction to Negotiate and Implement Free Trade Agreements in Canada (1987) 24, 2 U.W.O. L. Rev. 63; and the famous piece by F.R. Scott, "Labour Conventions Case: Lord Wright's Undisclosed Dissent?" (1956) 34 Can. Bar Rev. 114. This is but a small sample. In comparison, there are terribly few scholarly pieces on the relationship between the Constitution and foreign affairs or the Constitution and defence, including in the canonical text by Peter W. Hogg, *Constitutional Law of Canada*, student ed. (Scarborough: Carswell, 2007), and none at all, it appears, on the broader, "systemic" relationship between the Constitution and strategy.

4 See *supra*, Introduction, note 5.

5 Note the astrategic, if not *anti*-strategic, implication in the summary of the judgment in *Labour Conventions*, in which the Privy Council states that, though Canada has profited (since 1931) from "her new status as an international person," "[t]reaty legislation, as such, was not dealt with in ss. 91 and 92; the distribution of legislative powers was based on classes of subjects, and as a treaty dealt with a particular class of subjects, so would the legislative power of performing it be ascertained." This seems to affirm, or to be consistent with, the claim made by H. Scott Fairley, *Canada, External Affairs and the Constitution: A Theory of Judicial Review* (S.J.D. diss., Harvard Law School, 1987) [unpublished], that federalism, or notions of "divided autonomy" (between the federal and provincial governments), have been dominant in Canadian constitutional jurisprudence in relation to foreign affairs or strategy.
6 *Commonwealth of Australia Constitution Act, 1900*, 63 & 64 Vict.
7 *Koowarta v. Bjelke-Petersen* (1982), 153 C.L.R. 168.
8 *Commonwealth v. Tasmania* (1983), 158 C.L.R. 1. The US Constitution, for its part, provides for the executive branch of the federal government (the president) to negotiate international treaties and for these treaties to be approved by two-thirds of the members of the Senate (part of the legislative branch). A treaty thus approved by the federal Senate becomes the law of the land, regardless of whether the subject matter of the treaty would traditionally fall under federal or state jurisdiction. Power over funding of treaty obligations lies with the federal legislative branch (all of Congress), not with the executive branch.
9 Comparisons of Canadian and Australian treaty powers with those of the United States are not obviously instructive, though wholly interesting. Article II, s. 2, clause 2 of the US Constitution states that the president "shall have Power, by and with the Advice and Consent of the Senate to make Treaties, provided two thirds of the Senators present concur." As in Australia, concerns in America over federalism, as famously affirmed in *Missouri v. Holland*, 252 U.S. 416 (1920), do not constitute a substantial bar to the subject matter of American treaty making, given that treaties become "the supreme Law of the Land," according to Article VI, clause 2 of the Constitution, and in spite of the aforementioned Tenth Amendment, which reserves to the states (and the American people) constitutional powers not otherwise delegated to the federal government. However, the "advice and consent" requirement often means that the Senate can meaningfully influence or condition executive presidential negotiation of international treaties. The need to satisfy a Senate supermajority for passage of treaties doubtless would be assimilated into executive negotiation. In this sense, the US federal legislative branch could be thought to play a role somewhat akin to that of Canada's provincial governments and legislatures in dulling (though manifestly to a lesser extent) the potency of the federal diplomatic function in regard to treaties.
10 Bill C-60, *An Act to Implement Certain Provisions of the Budget Tabled in Parliament on March 21, 2013 and Other Measures*, 1st Sess., 41st Parl., 2013.

11 *Department of Foreign Affairs and International Trade Act*, R.S.C. 1985, c. E-22. The new *Department of Foreign Affairs and Development Act* (enacted in Bill C-60; see note above) is nineteen sections long – still transactional but longer than the erstwhile, pre-merger version on account of provisions accommodating the merger of CIDA into DFAIT.
12 *Official Development Assistance Accountability Act*, S.C. 2008, c. 17.
13 *Canadian Security Intelligence Service Act*, R.S.C. 1985, c. C-23.
14 Section 12 of the *CSIS Act* restricts CSIS intelligence activities strictly to suspected threats relating to the security of Canada (in other words to *security intelligence*). Yet in the important holding in *Henrie v. Canada*, [1989] 2 F.C. 229, the Federal Court specified that "[t]here are few limits upon the kinds of security information, often obtained on a long-term basis, which may prove useful in identifying a threat." CSIS generally views s. 12 as having no territorial restriction, provided that the intelligence sought is of a "security" nature. (This extraterritorial assumption was questioned in Justice Blanchard's *obiter* in *Re Canadian Security Intelligence Service Act*, [2007] F.C.J. No. 1780.) Section 16 of the *CSIS Act*, for its part, geographically restricts CSIS intelligence activities relating to the defence of Canada and Canadian foreign affairs – the military and diplomatic instruments – to territorial Canada. A proper foreign intelligence agency, on the strength of the royal prerogative, could presumably at least allow for intelligence activities relating to defence and diplomacy *outside* Canada. A decision by the government to launch the agency, whether publicized or not, would not itself be subject to the Charter, for it would be considered an executive decision of high policy. A more controversial question, however, is whether the foreign activities of the agency's employees or operatives would be subject to the Charter. Until the recent *Khadr* holdings, discussed *infra*, Chapter 3, notes 11-13 and 15, one could rely on *Hape*, discussed *infra*, Chapter 3, note 9, and on *Re Canadian Security Intelligence Act*, which affirms *Hape*, to presume that the Charter does not, absent the consent of the host state, apply to Canadian intelligence activities abroad. *Khadr* 2008, *Khadr* 2009, and indeed *Khadr* 2010 seem to have greatly complicated things, apparently implying that involvement by Canadian government agents – even potential foreign intelligence agents – in processes that are illegal at international law could be considered contrary to at least s. 7 of the Charter (the fundamental justice procedural requirement). Of course, perhaps the simplest (and most "elegant"?) solution to creating a human foreign intelligence capacity in Canada would be to simply remove the restriction to territorial Canada (that is, "within Canada") in s. 16 of the *CSIS Act*.
15 In addition to foreign signals intelligence, the CSE is responsible for protection of the Government of Canada's electronic information infrastructure and of information infrastructure of importance to the government. Its legislative basis under the *National Defence Act* (see the next note) was enacted only in 2001 via the *Anti-Terrorism Act*. Prior to that, the agency operated via the royal prerogative. It is also interesting to note that Canada's *geography*, though a factor of power largely too

abstract to capture properly in constitutional terms, is given concrete strategic expression through the signals intelligence function; that is, Canada's vast geography – and indeed its proximity to major strategic players such as Russia, a number of Asian states, as well as the United States – is levered by virtue of the constitutional power of the federal government, previously under the royal prerogative and now under the militia power, to collect signals intelligence in relation to foreign enemies and threats from intercept stations across the territorial sweep of the country. (Of course, CSE assets and capabilities can also be deployed out of Canadian embassies, consulates, and military bases around the world.)

16 *National Defence Act*, R.S.C. 1985, c. N-5.
17 In the United States, the non-justiciability of executive decisions enjoys the moniker political questions – itself doubtless derivative of the British royal prerogative. In the matter of political questions and "strategy" (national security, war and peace, foreign affairs, and so on), there is a live and intense American debate about the nature and scope of the political questions doctrine. The protagonists in this debate have included the likes of John Yoo, *The Powers of War and Peace: The Constitution and Foreign Affairs after 9/11* (Chicago: University of Chicago Press, 2005); Harold Koh, *The National Security Constitution: Sharing Power after the Iran-Contra Affair* (New Haven: Yale University Press, 1990); Michael Glennon, *Constitutional Diplomacy* (Princeton: Princeton University Press, 1990); (the late Canadian) Thomas Franck, *Political Questions/Judicial Answers* (Princeton: Princeton University Press, 1992); Louis Henkin, *Foreign Affairs and the United States Constitution*, 2d ed. (Oxford: Oxford University Press, 1996); Louis Fisher, *Presidential War Power* (Lawrence: University Press of Kansas, 1995); and John Ely Hart, *War and Responsibility: Constitutional Lessons of Vietnam and Its Aftermath* (Princeton: Princeton University Press, 1993).
18 *Council of Civil Service Unions v. Minister for the Civil Service*, [1985] 1 A.C. 374. Lord Radcliffe stated that the exercise of the prerogative is amenable to judicial review if it affects individual rights. This anticipated the subsequent Canadian holding in *Operation Dismantle, infra* note 22.
19 The nuance adduced by Lord Scarman in respect of the peculiar general non-justiciability of national security is notable: "Once the factual basis is established by evidence so that the court is satisfied that the interest of national security is a relevant factor to be considered in the determination of the case, the court will accept the opinion of the Crown or its responsible officer as to what is required to meet it, unless it is possible to show that the opinion was one which no reasonable minister advising the Crown could in the circumstances reasonably have held. There is no abdication of the judicial function, but there is a common sense limitation recognised by the judges as to what is justiciable."
20 Note the irony – strategic irony, as it were – of the British House of Lords exempting British treaties from judicial review – strategically beneficial for the British executive branch – whereas today's Canadian federal executive is strategically handicapped

by the astrategic insistence (astrategic from Canada's standpoint, evidently) of the old Judicial Committee of the Privy Council in *Labour Conventions (A.G. Can. v. A.G. Ont. et al.*, [1937] 1 D.L.R. 673) that treaties signed by the federal government be implementable in law only by that level of Canadian government constitutionally responsible for the particular subject matter of the treaty.

21 *Council of Civil Service Unions v. Minister for the Civil Service*, [1985] 1 A.C. 374, 24.
22 *Operation Dismantle Inc. v. R.*, [1985] 1 S.C.R. 441.
23 See Case Studies A and B in Part II. *Quaere*: can the royal prerogative as it concerns the creation of Aboriginal reserves in certain jurisdictions – say in the three federal territories as part of a federal strategy to assert sovereignty in the Canadian North – be seen, under certain scenarios, as part of such strategic activity or "high policy" so as to make it largely invulnerable to judicial clipping (leaving aside legislative clipping or ouster)? See *supra*, Chapter 1, note 21.
24 *Supra* note 21, 18.
25 *Abassi v. Secretary of State for Foreign and Commonwealth Affairs*, [2002] All E.R. 70. The reasoning of the Supreme Court of Canada, particularly in the concurring opinions of Justices McLachlin and Binnie, in *Mount Sinai Hospital Center v. Quebec*, [2001] S.C.J. No. 43, in respect of administrative review of ministerial discretion, while not dealing with foreign affairs or strategy proper, might also have been instructive in laying some of the jurisprudential foundation leading to *Smith* (see next note).
26 *Smith v. Canada*, [2009] F.C.J. No. 234.
27 Contrast this conscientious balancing of the general non-justiciability of the royal prerogative in relation to foreign affairs with the presumption of justiciability of decisions affecting individuals' rights, obligations, and legitimate expectations with the outright refusal of the Ontario Court of Appeal to consider justiciability, or to countenance balancing of general non-justiciability, of the royal prerogative in relation to the granting of honours in *Black v. Chrétien* (2000), 47 O.R. (3d) 532. See also the interesting critique of this decision by Lorne Sossin in "The Rule of Law and the Justiciability of Prerogative Powers: A Comment on *Black v. Chrétien*" (2002) 47 McGill L.J. 435. Sossin takes an extremely expansive view of the justiciability of prerogative decisions on the basis of two framework questions, posed at 447, both of which he is apparently inclined to answer, in most cases, in the affirmative: "First, can the matter be determined according to objective, judicially cognizable standards and evidence? Second, is the matter appropriate for adjudication given the constitutional, political, and legal systems in Canada? In other words, does the court have the capacity and legitimacy to decide the case?" His view anticipated the 2009 holding in *Smith v. Canada*, *supra* note 26, which has non-negligible precedential import for Canadian strategy.
28 *Supra* note 26 at para. 37.
29 Thomas R. Dye, *Understanding Public Policy*, 3d ed. (Englewood Cliffs, NJ: Prentice-Hall, 1978), 3; Stephen Brooks, *Public Policy in Canada: An Introduction*, 2d ed.

(Toronto: McClelland and Stewart, 2003), 12. On the potentially more inconsistent or *prima facie* incoherent nature of foreign policy, John Kirton, *Canadian Foreign Policy in a Changing World* (Toronto: Nelson, 2007), 3, writes that Canadian foreign policy is "often reactive, internally contradictory, confused and incoherent. But it can also be proactive, centralized, strategic, and unified. In identifying this (foreign) policy, it is important to move beyond the rhetoric that surrounds a government's policy in order to focus on measurable behaviour and uncover the often surprising patterns that lie beneath."

30 *Infra*, Chapter 3, notes 11-13 and 15.
31 See Ed Morgan, "It's a Legal Maze for Canadian Authorities Abroad," *Globe and Mail*, 28 May 2009, A19.
32 *Special Economic Measures Act*, S.C. 1992, c. 17.
33 Canada's sanctions regime, strictly speaking, is a function of a triad of statutes, including the *Special Economic Measures Act*, S.C. 1992, c. 17; the *United Nations Act*, R.S.C. 1985, c. U-2; and the *Export and Import Permits Act*, R.S.C. 1985, c. E-19. The *Special Economic Measures Act* is the dominant statute for purposes of discretionary sanctions. To date, there has been no jurisprudence in relation to it. I discuss the *Export and Import Permits Act* in Chapter 5 in the context of natural resources.

Chapter 3: The Military

1 See, for instance, the unqualified wording of Lord Reid in *Chandler v. Director of Public Prosecutions*, [1964] 1 A.C. 763: "It is in my opinion clear that the disposition and armament of the armed forces are and for centuries have been within the exclusive discretion of the Crown and that no one can seek a legal remedy on the ground that such discretion has been wrongly exercised. I need only refer to the numerous authorities gathered together in *China Navigation Co. Ltd. v. Attorney-General* [(1932) 2 K.B. 197]. Anyone is entitled, in or out of Parliament, to urge that policy in respect of the armed forces should be changed; but until it is changed, on a change of Government or otherwise, no one is entitled to challenge it in court."
2 See Case Study B in Part II on bona fide war. For a "maximalist" view of the justiciability of strategic questions and even high policy, see the *Global Brief* interview with Aharon Barak, former president of the Israeli Supreme Court, in "The Judge as Geokrat and Maximalist" (Spring-Summer 2013) Global Brief 26.
3 *Aleksic v. Canada* (2002), 215 D.L.R. (4th) 720.
4 Even if the issue were justiciable, the Crown would be immune in tort because the bombing decision was one of so-called pure policy as well as because of s. 8 of the *Crown Liability and Proceedings Act*, R.S.C. 1985, c. C-50, which strategically immunizes the Crown from tortious liability "in respect of anything done or omitted in the exercise of any power or authority exercisable for the Crown, whether in time of peace or war, for the purpose of the defence of Canada or of training, or maintaining the efficiency of, the Canadian Forces."

5 See the similar (strategic) logic in the harsh dissent by Justice Scalia of the US Supreme Court in *Rasul v. Bush*, 542 U.S. 466 (2004), in which the majority held that US *habeus corpus* applies to foreign nationals captured abroad in connection with military hostilities and incarcerated at Guantanamo Bay, Cuba. Scalia wrote at para. 498: "The consequence of this holding, as applied to aliens outside the country, is breathtaking. It permits an alien captured in a foreign theater of active combat to bring a [*habeus corpus*] petition against the Secretary of Defense. Over the course of the last century, the United States has held millions of alien prisoners abroad ... A great many of these prisoners would no doubt have complained about the circumstances of their capture and the terms of their confinement. The military is currently detaining over 600 prisoners at Guantanamo Bay alone; each detainee undoubtedly has complaints – real or contrived – about those terms and circumstances. The Court's unheralded expansion of federal-court jurisdiction is not even mitigated by a comforting assurance that the legion of ensuing claims will be easily resolved on the merits ... From this point forward, federal courts will entertain petitions from these prisoners, and others like them around the world, challenging actions and events far away, and forcing the courts to oversee one aspect of the Executive's conduct of a foreign war."
6 *Operation Dismantle Inc. v. R.*, [1985] 1 S.C.R. 441, 443.
7 In the hypothetical event that any military activity of the Canadian government under the prerogative should be found to be in violation of a Charter right, this violation would likely be saved under s. 1 of the Charter, which reads that the rights and freedoms in the Charter are "subject to such reasonable limits prescribed by law as can be demonstrably justified in a free and democratic society." In *obiter*, in *Operation Dismantle*, Justice Wilson mused that, were the government to impose conscription for overseas service in wartime, this would seem to be in violation of s. 7 of the Charter but would meet the reasonable limitation in s. 1. Contrariwise, she supposed, a government decision to seize citizens for military service without enabling legislation would unequivocally violate the Charter, under both ss. 7 and 1.
8 *R. v. Cook*, [1998] 2 S.C.R. 957. The Supreme Court held that a Canadian citizen questioned abroad is still entitled to Charter protection as long as application of the Charter does not interfere with the sovereign authority of the foreign state in question; more precisely, as long as there is no objectionable interference in exercise of the foreign state's jurisdiction.
9 *R. v. Hape* (2007), 280 D.L.R. (4th) 385.
10 Section 32(1) specifies that the Charter applies (a) to the Parliament and Government of Canada in respect of all matters within the authority of Parliament and (b) to the legislature and government of each province in respect of all matters within the authority of the legislature of each province. Section 32(1) does not provide for an explicit territorial limit on application of the Charter.
11 *Canada v. Khadr*, [2008] S.C.J. No. 28. The Supreme Court found, at para. 31, that s. 7 of the Charter, relating to "fundamental justice," was engaged in this case,

thereby imposing "a duty on Canada to provide disclosure of materials in its possession arising from its participation in the foreign process [that is, the questioning of Omar Khadr at Guantanamo Bay] that is contrary to international law and jeopardizes the liberty of a Canadian citizen." This important determination was somewhat anticipated by Justice LeBel for the plurality in *Hape*, *supra* note 9, where he noted at para. 101 that "I would leave open the possibility that, in a future case, participation by Canadian [state actors] in activities in another country that would violate Canada's international human rights obligations might justify a remedy under s. 24(1) of the Charter." Note that the Supreme Court actually relied on two US Supreme Court decisions – *Rasul v. Bush*, *supra* note 5, and *Hamdan v. Rumsfeld*, 126 S. Ct. 2749 (2006) – to determine that the regime under which Khadr was being held at Guantanamo Bay was illegal at American and international law, respectively.
12 *Khadr v. Canada*, 2009 F.C.A. 246.
13 *Khadr v. Canada*, [2009] F.C.J. 462.
14 At para. 63, Justices Evans and Sharlow, writing for the majority and citing Peter W. Hogg, *Constitutional Law of Canada*, 5th ed. (looseleaf) (Toronto: Carswell, 2007), 38-46, note that the Supreme Court has already stated that a breach of s. 7 could only be maintained under s. 1 in exceptional circumstances, such as "natural disasters, the outbreak of war, epidemics and the like."
15 *Canada v. Khadr*, [2010] S.C.J. No. 3.
16 *Amnesty International v. Canada*, 2008 F.C. 336.
17 In *Amnesty International*, *supra* note 16, Justice Mactavish, in *obiter*, suggested that there remains some uncertainty about the possibility that the military, because of its coercive character, might require a *sui generis* test for extraterritorial application of the Charter. In this respect, Mactavish tracked the important British holding in *Al-Skeini et al. v. Secretary of State for Defence*, [2007] U.K.H.L. 26, in which it was determined that the UK *Human Rights Act, 1998*, c. 42, which effectively implemented into British domestic law the *European Convention on Human Rights*, did apply to British public authorities – the British military – to the narrow extent that they exercised effective control on foreign territory through military detention facilities, as with embassies and consulates, operating on the consent of the Iraqi government. Strangely, *Al-Skeini* is not referenced in *Amnesty International* or in the cognate Canadian jurisprudence in *Cook*, *Hape*, or the *Khadr* line of cases.
18 *Amnesty International v. Canada*, [2008] F.C.J. No. 1700.
19 *Amnesty International v. Canada*, [2009] S.C.C.A. No. 63.
20 Craig Forcese, *National Security Law* (Toronto: Irwin Law, 2008), 154. See, however, the dissent in *Aleksic*, *supra* note 3, by Justice Wright, suggesting that the active service provision in the *National Defence Act* should now be seen as having replaced the royal prerogative for military deployments.
21 See the idiosyncratic piece by Ikechi Mgbeoji, who, though searching long and hard through Hansard records for such a constitutional requirement for parlia-

mentary oversight or debate on international troop deployments, concedes that no such requirement exists in Canadian law. (One would be overreaching to ascribe even the status of constitutional convention to the inconsistent votes by recent governments in Ottawa on troop deployments and uses in Afghanistan; see Case Study B in Part II.) Mgbeoji does suggest, however, at 183 that, while "the Crown prerogative on matters of war remains intact, albeit with some modicum of judicial inroads[,]" jurisprudence around this prerogative remains unclear, and some statutes, such as the *National Defence Act*, might have laid the groundwork for future judicial inroads into the prerogative. Ikechi Mgbeoji, "Prophylactic Use of Force in International Law: The Illegitimacy of Canada's Participation in 'Coalitions of the Willing' without United Nations Authorization and Parliamentary Sanction" (2003) 8, 2 Rev. Const. Stud. 170.

22 Forcese, *supra* note 20, at 168-70, observes that two federal orders-in-council were issued in the 1990s, pursuant to the royal prerogative, in relation to domestic deployment of the Canadian Forces, *solely* on the initiative or approval of the federal government: the first, the *Canadian Forces Assistance to Provincial Police Forces Directions* (P.C. 1996-833), addressed federal military assistance to provincial law enforcement agencies; the second, the *Canadian Forces Armed Assistance Directions* (P.C. 1993-624), addressed the deployment of Canadian special forces assets. Both orders-in-council addressed disturbances of the peace, likely or actual, deemed of national interest. Notes Forcese at 170: "Out of an abundance of caution, ... the preferable approach is to treat the order-in-council provisions as procedures governing the application of the [*National Defence Act*] public service powers to the particular circumstances to which they relate."

23 *Emergencies Act*, R.S.C. 1985, c. 22 (4th Supp.).

24 *Human Rights Institute of Canada v. Canada*, [2000] 1 F.C. 475.

25 G.V. La Forest, *Natural Resources and Public Property under the Constitution* (Toronto: University of Toronto Press, 1969), at 155, affirms this on the strength of the 1874 holding in *L'Union St. Jacques de Montréal v. Bélisle* (1874), 6 P.C. 31. The age of the case likely speaks less to the import of the ruling itself than to the aforementioned penury of cases on the strategically important militia and defence power. Note also that there seems to be no constitutional bar to the use of s. 117 of the 1867 Act to convert an Indian reserve in a given province (a reserve otherwise operating on provincial Crown land) into a military base or fortification. The same section, as well as s. 91(7) or the declaratory power – but not s. 91(24), as explained *infra*, Chapter 5, note 23 – could be used by the federal government to infringe on Aboriginal title or treaty lands for the same purpose of erecting a military base or fortification (in the event, say, of expected war or military imperative). In this case, however, one might presume that a certain consultative duty would be triggered, further to *Haida* and the second stage of the justificatory part of the *Sparrow* framework. Granted, this consultative duty would be *de minimis* and perfunctory because of the military implications of the infringement. (See *infra*, Chapter 5, note 18.)

Chapter 4: Government, or Pure Executive Potency

1 See *supra*, Chapter 1, note 2.
2 Craig Forcese, *National Security Law* (Toronto: Irwin Law, 2008), 114.
3 The leading case in this regard is *Reference re Anti-Inflation Act, 1975*, [1976] 2 S.C.R. 373. See Case Study D in Part II.
4 *War Measures Act*, S.C. 1914 (2d sess.), c. 2.
5 *Emergencies Act*, R.S.C. 1985, c. 22 (4th Supp.).
6 Patrick Monahan, *Constitutional Law*, 3d ed. (Toronto: Irwin Law, 2006), 257.
7 *Burmah Oil Co. v. Lord Advocate*, [1965] A.C. 75.
8 *Suresh v. Canada*, [2002] 1 S.C.R. 3. At para. 78, the court stated: "We do not exclude the possibility that in exceptional circumstances, deportation [under the then *Immigration Act*] to face torture might be justified either as a consequence of the balancing process mandated by s. 7 of the Charter or under s. 1." The court went on to say that a violation of s. 7 will be saved by s. 1 "only in cases arising out of exceptional conditions, such as natural disasters, the outbreak of war, epidemics and the like." This last bit seems to speak to the existence in Canadian constitutional law of the doctrine of necessity, discussed in the next note.
9 *Re Manitoba Language Rights*, [1985] 1 S.C.R. 721. Said the court at para. 85 in its unanimous opinion: "Necessity in the context of governmental action provides a justification for otherwise illegal conduct of a government during a public emergency. In order to ensure rule of law, the Courts will recognize as valid the constitutionally invalid Acts of the Legislature." In the *Manitoba Language Rights* case, the constitutionally invalid laws were ones that had not been enacted, printed, and published in French as well as English by the Manitoba legislature, in clear contravention of constitutional requirements.
10 Oren Gross and Fionnuala Ni Aolain, *Law in Times of Crisis: Emergency Powers in Theory and Practice* (Cambridge, UK: Cambridge University Press, 2006), 46-47. The ruling in the *Manitoba Language Rights Reference*, *supra* note 9, affirms the doctrine of necessity not as a proper principle of the Canadian Constitution but as subservient to the constitutional principle of the rule of law.
11 See Case Study D in Part II for an analysis of Canadian emergency powers in the context of counterterrorism.
12 In 1982, this provision replaced virtually identical language, now repealed, in part of s. 91(1) of the *Constitution Act, 1867*. Interestingly, s. 91(1) had been added to the Constitution in 1949, in the midst of the interregnum between the Second World War and the 1950-53 Korean War – a period of time during which the Government of Canada would clearly have had strategy, in one form or other, on its mind.
13 Back in 1985, J.R. Mallory wrote: "The first provision [of the *Constitution Act, 1982*, that might give rise to constitutional challenges on procedural grounds] is subsection 4(2) ... This is clearly a case where a court might have to inquire what Parliament actually was for this purpose." J.R. Mallory, "Beyond 'Manner and

Form': Reading between the Lines in *Operation Dismantle Inc. v. R.*" (1985) 31 McGill L.J. 480, 489. Forcese, *supra* note 2, observes at 122 that it is not clear how and with what degree of activism s. 4(2) would be policed by the courts. Would, for instance, the courts review, or be capable of meaningfully reviewing, the alleged existence of real or apprehended war, invasion, or insurrection? Forcese is also inclined to believe, as noted above, that the courts could well be disposed to save breaches of a number of Charter sections – in particular s. 7 – under s. 1. Drawing on the holding in *Re Gray* (1918), 57 S.C.R. 150, Forcese hints here at an eventual, constitutionally required role for Parliament in checking executive emergency activities, noting at 120 that "a Parliament tempted to delegate indefinitely its full plenary powers, perhaps in response to an emergency, would ... run afoul of a long-established pre-*Charter* constitutional restriction barring complete abdication of Parliament's responsibility in favour of the executive."

14 Of the first fifteen Charter rights, considered the key bulwark of Canada's constitutionalized fundamental rights and freedoms, only ss. 5 (that Parliament will sit at least once every twelve months) and 6 (mobility rights) would effectively be saved under this cocktail. Sections 3 (that every citizen has the right to vote in an election) and 4(1) (that no House of Commons will continue for more than five years) would become moot upon the invocation of s. 4(2).

15 Some scholars, such as Monahan, have pointed to a fourth possible, albeit embryonic, branch of the POGG power relating to interprovincial concerns or matters of interprovincial significance.

16 See *R. v. Crown Zellerbach Canada Ltd.*, [1988] 1. S.C.R. 401. See the critical counterpoint by Henri Brun and Guy Tremblay, *Droit constitutionnel*, 4e éd. (Québec: Éditions Yvon Blais, 2002), at 556-57, in which they note wrily: "Inutile de dire qu'il n'existe pas dans la jurisprudence de préoccupation correspondante de transférer aux provinces les matières, dont les exemples ne manquent pas, qui étaient à l'origine d'intérêt national et qui sont devenues de nature purement locale et privée."

17 *Ontario Hydro v. Ontario*, [1993] 3 S.C.R. 327. Of course, given the security and military considerations associated with nuclear energy, including the need for energy production and secure nuclear energy sites in the event of war or insurrection, and given the magnificent size of Canada's uranium reserves and exports, it stands to reason that this was a strategic coup for the federal government.

18 Peter W. Hogg, *Constitutional Law of Canada*, student ed. (Scarborough: Carswell, 2007), 560. The declaratory power was last used in 1987, and it is seen by some constitutional lawyers today as draconian. (The Charter having been enshrined in 1982, there has been no case to date exploring the relationship between the declaratory power and Charter rights.) Strictly speaking, this characterization speaks to political legitimacy, not constitutional legitimacy. In other words, it speaks to policy-political praxis and not to strategic capacity in constitutional terms. In strictly constitutional terms, the declaratory power is still a perfectly

legitimate tool of strategy. So too is the threat of use of the declaratory power – a type of threat that has doubtless been made (or implied) by the federal government even since 1987 to advance national strategic interests in different matters and at different times.

19 See *Jorgenson v. Canada*, [1971] S.C.R. 725. Contrast this holding with that in the famous 1952 US *Steel Seizure* case, *Youngstown Sheet & Tube Co. v. Sawyer*, 343 U.S. 579, in which the US Supreme Court decided that seizure by the president (the federal executive branch) of a steel mill – strategically important for purposes of military production during the 1950-53 Korean War – was unconstitutional, for it was contrary to the separation of powers doctrine requiring that legislation in respect of such seizure sit with Congress (the legislative branch).

20 *Atomic Energy Control Act*, R.S.C. 1970, c. A-19.

21 *Supra* note 17.

22 Monahan, *supra* note 6, 371. For an expansive and, indeed, critical treatment of the declaratory power, see Andrée Lajoie, *Le pouvoir déclaratoire du Parlement: Augmentation discrétionnaire de la competence fédérale du Canada* (Montréal: Les Presses de l'Université de Montréal, 1969). Exotically, Lajoie suggests at the end of his book that the fact that seven-eighths of historical uses of the declaratory power have related to the rail sector betrays a conspiracy by Macdonald at Confederation not to explicitly regulate *intraprovincial* railways in the formal division of powers of the 1867 Act but through insertion of the *prima facie* innocuous and inconspicuous s. 92(10)(c). Strategy! Writes Lajoie at 112: "Ce n'est pas impossible si l'on considère la structure économique du Canada à la fin du XIXe siècle, de ce pays où des centaines de compagnies ont construit chacune une parcelle de ce qui n'allait devenir un réseau à l'échelle canadienne que beaucoup plus tard."

23 Justice Rand in *Reference re Validity of Section 5(a) of Dairy Industry Act (Canada)*, [1949] S.C.R. 1.

24 See Canada, *Securing an Open Society: Canada's National Security Policy* (Ottawa: Privy Council Office, 2004), 4. I was a member of the Privy Council Office-based team that wrote this policy in 2004.

25 Forcese, *supra* note 2, 8. I should note, however, that the courts have attempted to delimit the terms "danger to the security of Canada" (see *Suresh, supra* note 8, which also treated the definition of "terrorism") and "national security" (see *Canada v. Almalki*, 2010 F.C. 1106). In *Almalki*, Justice Mosley asserted at para. 78: "National security is a broad and inherently vague concept that defies precise definition. I have no doubt, however, that it includes a wider range of interests than territorial integrity or the capacity to respond to the use or threat of force. Among other things, in Canada it has been said to encompass 'the preservation of a way of life acceptable to the Canadian people' and the protection of our values and key institutions." Surely this is too broad or "flexible" a definition, referring as it does to a "way of life." Are economic recessions or depressions, with clear consequences

for a state's "way of life," really national security events? Granted, recessions or depressions can have some discrete national security implications or even causes, but to invoke public psychology as a barometer of national security seems exceedingly overinclusive.
26 *Emergency Management Act*, S.C. 2007, c. 15.
27 The *CSIS Act* is likely based on the federal POGG power or the defence power in s. 91(7), based on the holding in *Attorney-General (Quebec) v. Keable v. Attorney-General (Canada)*, [1979] 1 S.C.R. 218. This holding concerned the activities of the precursor to CSIS, the RCMP's Security Service. (One could reasonably suppose that the POGG head of power is far more plausible than the defence power as a support for the act, given that the act deals only parenthetically with defence interests.) *Quaere*: why do the provinces not erect intelligence services of their own? Why, for instance, does Quebec, while profiting from the Sûreté du Québec (the provincial police force) under s. 92(14) of the 1867 Act, not create its own version of CSIS? Indeed, this was one of the prospective ("strategic") practical-cum-policy challenges or "to do's" envisioned by the sovereigntist camp on the eve of the 1995 referendum on Quebec secession in the event of accession to proper statehood. Constitutionally speaking, the answer is relatively straightforward: provincial spending power aside, the "within the province" limitation of s. 92 (which also exists in ss. 92A, 93, and 95) of the 1867 Act effectively limits the policing-cum-security activities of the provinces to their respective territories.
28 *Royal Canadian Mounted Police Act*, R.S.C. 1985, c. R-10.
29 *Security of Information Act*, R.S.C. 1985, c. O-5.
30 *Canada Evidence Act*, R.S.C. 1985, c. C-5.
31 *Citizenship Act*, R.S.C. 1985, c. C-29.
32 *Immigration and Refugee Protection Act*, S.C. 2001, c. 27. A prominent national security process found in the *Immigration and Refugee Protection Act* is the security certificate, which provides for detention and deportation of foreign nationals and permanent residents deemed to constitute a threat to the security of Canada. These provisions were ruled unconstitutional (variously contrary to ss. 7, 9, and 10(c) of the Charter and not saved by s. 1) in *Charkaoui v. Canada*, [2007] S.C.J. No. 9. The declaration nullifying the certificate regime was suspended for one year. Parliament re-enacted amended provisions in 2007, creating, *inter alia*, an *amicus curiae* regime for those detained under a security certificate.
33 *Aeronautics Act*, R.S.C. 1985, c. A-2.
34 *Canada Transportation Act*, S.C. 1996, c. 10.
35 See the effort by the Supreme Court to delimit "national security" in *Suresh, supra* note 8, in which the court, referring to the then *Immigration Act*, stated with affirmation at para. 5: "We reject the arguments that the terms 'danger to the security of Canada' and 'terrorism' are unconstitutionally vague."
36 *Criminal Code*, R.S.C. 1985, c. C-46.

37 *Anti-Terrorism Act*, S.C. 2001, c. 41.
38 In *R. v. Khawaja*, [2006] O.J. No. 4245, the Ontario Superior Court of Justice found that the motive clause in the definition of terrorism contained in the *Anti-Terrorism Act*, which related to an act or omission "in whole or in part for a political, religious or ideological purpose, objective or cause," was unconstitutional, as contrary to s. 2(b) of the Charter (freedoms of conscience, religion, thought, belief, expression, and association) and not saved by s. 1. (*Prima facie*, this holding did not appear to have any consequence for s. 2(c) of the *CSIS Act*, which defines as threats to the security of Canada "activities within or relating to Canada directed toward or in support of the threat or use of acts of serious violence against persons or property for the purpose of achieving a political, religious or ideological objective within Canada or a foreign state.") The Ontario Court of Appeal subsequently reinstated the motive clause of the terrorism definition in *R. v. Khawaja*, 2010 ONCA 862. Finally, the Supreme Court confirmed the constitutionality of the motive clause in *R. v. Khawaja*, 2012 S.C.C. 69. Note also that, unlike the majority of Canadian laws, as with the terrorism provisions, the *Criminal Code* has a number of provisions with extraterritorial effect (such as hijacking, passport forgery, piracy, and bigamy). The *Security of Information Act*, notably, has extraterritorial effect, in *de facto* "criminal law" terms, in respect of the offence of espionage.
39 Bill S-3, *An Act to Amend the Criminal Code (Investigative Hearings and Recognizance with Conditions)*, 2d Sess., 39th Parl., 2007.
40 Bill C-19, *An Act to Amend the Criminal Code (Investigative Hearings and Recognizance with Conditions)*, 2d Sess., 40th Parl., 2009.
41 Bill C-17, *An Act to Amend the Criminal Code (Investigative Hearings and Recognizance with Conditions)*, 3d Sess., 40th Parl., 2010.
42 Bill S-7, *An Act to Amend the Criminal Code, the Canada Evidence Act and the Security of Information Act*, 1st Sess., 41st Parl., 2013.

Chapter 5: Natural Resources (and Food)

1 Of pure geography, abstraction oblige, and apart from the necessary delineation of physical (provincial, territorial, and national) borders, there is precious little explicit language in the written Constitution. Having conceded this in principle, however, the Constitution is implicitly and doctrinally rich on the subject. (See the discussion in Chapter 1 on Canadian strategy and Aboriginal rights, including Aboriginal title.) One reasonable proxy for geographic power is the concept of territorial integrity or territorial sovereignty. Commenting tangentially, for instance, on the issue of offshore minerals, where the Supreme Court, in the *B.C. Offshore Reference*, [1967] S.C.R. 792, consistent with treatment of this matter in Australia and the United States, confirmed federal legislative jurisdiction and ownership rights over the territorial sea and federal legislative jurisdiction and exploitation rights over the continental shelf, Peter W. Hogg writes: "While the *Constitution Act, 1867* (like the Constitutions of Australia and the United States)

is not explicit on the status of offshore resources, it is noteworthy that all these powers affecting external *sovereignty* [emphasis added] that are mentioned [in the 1867 Act] are, without exception, confided to the federal Parliament. These include trade and commerce (s. 92(2)), military and naval service and defence (s. 91(7)), beacons, buoys, lighthouses and Sable Island (s. 91(9)), navigation and shipping (s. 91(10)), and other major offshore resources, namely, seacoast fisheries (s. 91(12)). In all these matters, the *Constitution Act, 1867* recognizes that 'once the low-water mark is passed, the international domain is reached.' [*United States v. Texas* (1950), 399 U.S. 707, 719.] For domestic constitutional purposes, as well as for international law purposes, the actor in that domain is the federal government, not the provinces." Peter W. Hogg, *Constitutional Law of Canada*, 5th ed. (looseleaf) (Toronto: Carswell, 2007), 30-10. One might add that, where the written Constitution and the courts are otherwise silent on the question of territorial sovereignty, the royal prerogative is in full effect, relating as it does to "the whole catalogue of relations [of the Crown] with foreign nations [including] sovereignty over land, sea, and air." F.A. Mann, *Foreign Affairs in English Courts* (Oxford: Clarendon Press, 1986), 4-5.
2 Prime Minister Harper's speech of 14 July 2007, in the United Kingdom, http://www.ctv.ca/servlet/ArticleNews/story/CTVNews/20060715/g8_harper_060715?s_name=&no_ads=.
3 Hans J. Morgenthau, *Politics among Nations: The Struggle for Power and Peace* (Boston: McGraw-Hill, 1993), 129.
4 More precisely, the section vests public lands with the four founding provinces at Confederation. Equivalent treatment is effectively granted to Manitoba, Saskatchewan, and Alberta in the *Constitution Act, 1930* (U.K.), 20 & 21 Geo. V, c. 26, and to the other provinces via their individual terms of union. The terms of union of every province are part of the Constitution, per s. 52(2)(b) of the 1982 Act.
5 G.V. La Forest, *Natural Resources and Public Property under the Constitution* (Toronto: University of Toronto Press, 1969), 76.
6 Note that rent capture tends to be more pronounced as a government objective in times of high natural resource commodity prices, as in the 1970s and indeed in the global commodity boom that immediately preceded the time of writing. Still, not all governments at all times will see rent capture as their primary policy objective, with some leaving the capture to the private sector and seeing instead, as through much of Canadian history, the principal policy goal as natural resource development as a fillip to economic growth, as per the *staple theory* of economic development. Of course, the tension between rent capture and economic growth speaks to policy choice by governments and not the constitutional *capacity* underpinning either option, which remains, in principle, unchanged.
7 Federal jurisdiction over the territories is constitutionally affirmed in the *Constitution Act, 1871* (U.K.), 34 & 35 Vict., c. 28. The governance structure of each of the three territories – the Yukon, the Northwest Territories, and Nunavut – is

provided (quasi-constitutionally, as it were, on the conception of the Constitution presented here), *inter alia*, by incorporating statutes bearing the name of the territory in question (for example, the *Nunavut Act*, S.C. 1993, c. 28). These acts include the results of some of the devolution, from the 1970s onward, of many "province-like" legislative powers to the territories – a process that, in practical terms, has mitigated, to a certain extent, some of the direct strategic power of the federal government in respect of the natural resources, economic, communications, and population factors of power. (See Case Study C in Part II on Arctic sovereignty.)

8 *R. v. Sparrow*, [1990] S.C.J. No. 49.

9 In addition to s. 92A, I note here, among the relevant s. 92 heads of power, s. 92(13) on property and civil rights, in particular, but also ss. 92(5), 92(10), and 92(16).

10 This fallacy of composition concerning provincial jurisdiction and the national strategic interest is also at play in the recent string of vexed cases of federal-provincial interjurisdictional immunity in respect of Aboriginal title lands. See *Keewatin v. Ontario*, 2013 ONCA 158, and *William v. British Columbia*, 2012 B.C.C.A. 285.

11 La Forest, *supra* note 5, xii-xiii. *En passant*, further to this, an interesting line of enquiry concerns the provincial capacity to erect "sovereign wealth funds" – effectively strategic revenue reserves – from their natural resource revenues. As Alberta has proven with its Heritage Savings Trust Fund, there is evidently no constitutional bar to provinces accumulating natural resource royalties (in addition to other possible provincial revenues) for purposes of strategic expenditures in major projects. The federal government can also evidently create sovereign wealth funds for national strategic purposes, but it clearly does not have available to it the significant royalties from provincial natural resources. It does have, however, on top of many other revenue sources, general access to resource royalties from the territories (except the Yukon) and certain offshore sources (see *supra* note 1). (See also the related discussion on federal and provincial spending powers in Chapter 6.)

12 Strictly speaking, in Canada, at the time of writing, there is no national policy (unlike the old National Energy Policy) for monitoring and ensuring national energy supply or, in ruthlessly strategic terms, adequacy of supply for the strategic instruments of the state. Supply decisions – often market driven, including by dint of the international trading dynamics discussed below – in practice are made *intra*provincially, both by provincial governments and by private suppliers. There is embryonic debate, however, at the time of writing in respect of the construction of a national pipeline to deliver western Canadian oil (principally from the tar sands) to central and eastern Canada. As this by definition would be an interprovincial pipeline, the federal government would have the legislative lead on this initiative. Of course, in practice, this legislative lead on the interprovincial aspect of the pipeline would still have to reckon with provincial jurisdictional lead on

exploration and supply as well as with a number of consultation (honour of the Crown) requirements with Aboriginal groups in respect of Aboriginal title or treaty lands that would be affected by such a pipeline. This means that, while the federal government would have a critical "dog in the fight" in terms of jurisdictional competence for such a pipeline, in practice it would not control all of the constitutional levers necessary for pursuing an articulated national interest. (See the discussion below on the declaratory power and the natural resource factor of power.)

13 There is no case study in Part II on energy supply per se, but I touch on emergency energy supply scenarios in the context of counterterrorism in Case Study D.
14 *Energy Supplies Emergency Act*, R.S.C. 1985, c. E-9.
15 The Article 605 proportionality clause tracks an almost identical proportionality clause in Article 315 in respect of all goods subject to the *NAFTA*.
16 See Stephen McBride, "Quiet Constitutionalism in Canada: The International Political Economy of Domestic Institutional Change" (2003) 36, 2 Cdn J. Pol. Sci. 251, for an interesting discussion of the effectively quasi-constitutional character of *NAFTA* in Canadian governance.
17 See the discussion of this provincial fear in J. Peter Meekison and Roy J. Romanow, "Western Advocacy and Section 92A of the Constitution," in J. Peter Meekison, Roy J. Romanow, and William D. Moull, eds., *Origins and Meaning of Section 92A* (Montreal: Institute for Research on Public Policy, 1985), 18.
18 On this logic, could the declaratory power be used to assume federal legislative control over "works" – consider a strategically important mine – run by First Nations on Aboriginal title or treaty land? Presumably, yes. Still, this would likely only allow the federal government to meet the first stage of the justification part of the *Sparrow* test (requiring a law enacted, on the basis of the declaratory power, for a "compelling and substantial objective"). This means that the second stage – relating to the consultation duty (*Haida*) and the honour of the Crown (increasingly displacing any strict notion of fiduciary duty) – would still apply.
19 *British Columbia v. Lafarge Canada Inc.*, [2007] S.C.J. No. 23; emphasis added.
20 La Forest, *supra* note 5, at 134-35, put it thus: "In a word, the term 'property' in section 91(1A) is used in its broadest sense and includes every kind of asset and partial interest."
21 Recall that the federal spending power, discussed at some length in Chapter 6, is also in part a function of s. 91(1A). The other most relevant head of power for the federal spending power is s. 91(3). Interestingly, Justice Bastarache, again in *Lafarge*, *supra* note 19, waxes "strategical" at para. 123, noting that "a focus on the federal Crown's proprietary interests is consistent with the historical origins and development of federal jurisdiction over public property as a way to ensure that the federal Crown would possess and be the proprietor of sufficient resources to establish and maintain a transcontinental economy in the early years of Confederation."

22 The majority in *Lafarge, supra* note 19, at para. 55, stated: "While federal ownership of land does not create an enclave from which all provincial laws are excluded, provincial law cannot affect the exercise of a 'vital part' of federal property rights."
23 See *Reference re Waters and Water-Powers*, [1929] S.C.R. 200. This case observes that federal expropriation of reserve lands, under s. 91(24), Aboriginal treaty lands, or lands otherwise subject to Aboriginal title, except in the three federal territories, is a more complicated matter than expropriation under most other federal heads of power, as the underlying land, in most cases, belongs to the Crown in right of a given province. The province in question would have to consent to the expropriation, just as it would have to consent to the attempted appropriation of any provincial land for creation by the federal Crown of an Indian reserve. See also *Ontario Mining Company v. Seybold*, [1903] A.C. 73.
24 La Forest, *supra* note 5, at 149-50. Although there is no strict constitutional bar to federal (or indeed provincial) expropriation of private property without compensation, Anglo-Canadian statutory interpretation does require such compensation for the private owner in the absence of explicit statutory language absolving the expropriating government of such an obligation. Hogg, *supra* note 1, at 29-9 and 29-10.
25 See *supra* note 12.
26 See also *Expropriation Act*, R.S.C. 1985, c. E-21.
27 See Case Study D in Part II.
28 *Ontario Hydro v. Ontario*, [1993] 3 S.C.R. 327.
29 *National Energy Board Act*, R.S.C. 1985, c. N-7. Also see *supra* note 12.
30 I do not attempt here to address directly the practical and complex issues relating to the fact that, as in most Western countries, the vast majority of Canadian critical infrastructure – even as it relates to natural resources and food – belongs to the private sector. Strictly speaking, this is a policy matter (policy choice) rather than a constitutional one.
31 *Export and Import Permits Act*, R.S.C. 1985, c. E-19.
32 Sections 16(1), 20, and 21(1) of the *Investment Canada Act*, R.S.C. 1985, c. 28 (1st Supp.), provide for the minister of industry to bar certain purchases of Canadian assets by foreign interests if he or she deems this purchase not to be of "net benefit" to Canada. The criteria informing "net benefit" are broad – even sufficiently broad, one could argue, as to make redundant the "national security" grounds for exclusion of foreign purchasers outlined in ss. 25.1 to 25.6 of the act. The statute could evidently be used to block foreign ownership of certain strategic natural resources – including energy resources – and have the attendant effect of blocking exports of – or, in effect, "domesticating" – that resource, depending on the nature of the ultimate owner of the resource.
33 See Case Study A in Part II for a discussion of Canadian strategic forays into the Americas region, including in just such a scenario.

Notes to pages 68-71   201

Chapter 6: National Economic Might

1 *Defence Production Act*, R.S.C. 1985, c. D-1.
2 *Reference re Alberta Legislation*, [1938] S.C.J. No. 2. The large number of heads of legislative power supporting the *Bank of Canada Act*, R.S.C. 1985, c. B-2, speaks to the breadth and strategic character of the Bank's operations. The preamble to the *Bank of Canada Act* states that the Bank is required to "regulate credit and currency in the best interests of the economic life of the nation, to control and protect the external value of the national monetary unit and to mitigate by its influence fluctuations in the general level of production, trade, prices and employment, so far as may be possible within the scope of monetary action, and generally to promote the economic and financial welfare of Canada." Moreover, in the context of the financial crisis that endures at the time of writing, one could argue that Canadian central banking is also prominently underpinned by the federal purchasing and borrowing power in s. 91(1A) of the 1867 Act, building on the precedents set by the US Federal Reserve in purchasing massive quantities of "bad debt" or "toxic assets" related to sub-prime American mortgage rates. (Given the breadth of these activities, the *Bank of Canada Act* could find a home under the residual or national concern branch of POGG.)
3 See *Global Brief* (Winter 2010), 60, for interesting views on the future roles of central banks in the aftermath of the marked international economic contraction that preceded the time of writing.
4 Other sections likely (arguably) relevant to the constitutional existence of a muscular federal spending power include ss. 102 and 106 of the 1867 Act, both dealing with federal appropriations.
5 One might presume that s. 91(4) of the 1867 Act, referring to the borrowing of money on public credit, would also be a relevant head of power for federal debt. However, the jurisprudence on this section is paltry, and it therefore seems that s. 91(1A) is the dominant supporting head of power.
6 Note the enormous constitutional flexibility of the federal spending power. Peter W. Hogg, *Constitutional Law of Canada*, student ed. (Scarborough: Carswell, 2007), at 174-75, observes that "the better view of the law is that the federal Parliament may spend or lend its funds to any government or institution or individual it chooses; and that it may attach to any grant or loan any conditions it chooses, including conditions it could not directly legislate. There is a distinction, in my view, between compulsory regulation, which can obviously be accomplished only by legislation enacted within the limits of legislative power, and spending or lending or contracting, which either imposes no obligations on the recipient (as in the case of unconditional grants) or obligations that are voluntarily assumed by the recipient (as in the case of a conditional grant, a loan or a commercial contract). There is no compelling reason to confine spending or lending or contracting within the limits of legislative power, because in those functions the government is not

purporting to exercise any peculiar governmental authority over its objects." Even Henri Brun and Guy Tremblay, *Droit constitutionnel*, 4e éd. (Québec: Éditions Yvon Blais, 2002), at 433, concede as much: "Les provinces et le fédéral peuvent donc faire ce qu'ils veulent de leurs avoirs. Ils peuvent les dépenser dans les domaines de l'autre ordre de gouvernement sans régir ceux-ci législativement." However, they add this proviso, at 432, in regard to conditionality attached to the (federal) spending power: "Il n'en reste pas moins que la décision dans *Winterhaven* [*Winterhaven Stables Ltd. v. Attorney General Canada* (1986), A.J. No. 460] laisse croire qu'à partir d'un certain stade, l'imposition de conditions peut changer le caractère véritable d'une législation et la rendre vulnérable. Ainsi, le fédéral était intervenu trop activement dans une matière provinciale lorsqu'il a légiféré sur l'assurance-chômage (avant qu'il ne réussisse à se faire transférer la compétence à cet égard) [*Reference re Employment and Social Insurance Act*, [1937] A.C. 355]. Le fédéral avait plaidé que par son pouvoir de taxer, il pouvait constituer un fonds, et que par son pouvoir relatif à la propriété fédérale, il pouvait ensuite en disposer à sa guise. Mais le Conseil privé jugea la loi invalide parce qu'en réalité elle réglementait ce secteur de la vie sociale. Dans un jugement plus récent, le juge Pigeon, au nom d'une majorité de juges de la Cour suprême, a exprimé l'opinion suivante: '... l'intrusion fédérale dans le commerce local est tout aussi inconstitutionnelle lorsqu'elle se fait par des achats et des ventes que lorsqu'elle se fait d'une autre manière' [*Reference re Agricultural Products Marketing Act*, [1978] 2 S.C.R. 1198]. Cette affirmation laisse voir que le simple droit d'agir (en achetant, en vendant ou en dépensant, par exemple) peut devenir vulnérable s'il fait partie d'une intervention qui se veut régulatrice. Divers *dicta* dans l'affaire Dunbar [*Dunbar v. Attorney-General Saskatchewan* (1984), 11 D.L.R. (4th) 374] accréditent aussi cette approche."

7 Niall Ferguson, *The Cash Nexus: Money and Power in the Modern World, 1700-2000* (New York: Basic Books, 2001), 15.

8 The provincial borrowing power is arguably rooted in s. 92(3) of the 1867 Act, which relates to the borrowing of money on the sole credit of the province.

9 I might also add, in support of the provincial spending power, ss. 109 and 117 of the 1867 Act, both discussed previously.

10 *Reference re Employment and Social Insurance Act*, [1936] S.C.R. 427. The subsequent appeal to the Privy Council, while dismissed on the facts of the case, resulted in *dicta* that famously defended the federal spending power: "That the Dominion may impose taxation for the purpose of creating a fund for special purposes, and may apply that fund for making contributions in the public interest to individuals, corporations or public authorities, could not as a general proposition be denied." *Attorney-General of Canada v. Attorney-General of Ontario*, [1937] A.C. 355. Hogg, *supra* note 6, at 366-67.

11 Hogg, *supra* note 6, at 177. See affirmation of the same in Brun and Tremblay, *supra* note 6.

12 Hogg, *supra* note 6, at 177-78.

13 Michael J. Trebilcock, "The Supreme Court and Strengthening the Conditions for Effective Competition in the Canadian Economy" (2001) 80 Can. Bar Rev. 542 at 550-51.
14 *Ibid.*, 553.
15 *Reference re Securities Act*, 2011 S.C.C. 66. (See also *infra* notes 18 and 22.) The Supreme Court actually determined that the proposed federal *Securities Act* to "create a single scheme governing the trade of securities throughout Canada subject to the oversight of a single national securities regulatory" (para. 2) "overreached" by seeking to use the second or general branch of s. 91(2) of the 1867 Act – the trade and commerce power – to comprehensively regulate the day-to-day activities and transactions relating to contracts, property, and professions in the securities industry – areas that the court saw as readily falling under s. 92(13), the property and civil rights power of the provinces. Said the court at para. 128: "[W]e accept that the economic importance and pervasive character of the securities market may, in principle, support federal intervention that is qualitatively different from what the provinces do. However, as important as the preservation of capital markets and the maintenance of Canada's financial stability are, they do not justify a wholesale takeover of the regulation of the securities industry which is the ultimate consequence of the proposed federal legislation." The court left open the possibility of more modest or limited federal legislation in respect of a national securities commission legitimately falling under the federal trade and commerce power.
16 The nomenclature for the first and second branches of the trade and commerce power comes from the 1881 Privy Council decision in *Citizens' Insurance v. Parsons*, [1881] 7 A.C. 96. See *supra*, Chapter 1, note 18, for discussion of this case and the "grammatical" genesis of the Privy Council's expansive treatment of the provincial property and civil rights power.
17 *General Motors of Canada Ltd. v. City National Leasing*, [1989] 1 S.C.R. 641. The five parts of the test are to be seen as a general guide for constitutionally valid legislation rather than a pedantic checklist of required criteria. These five parts state that constitutional validity exists if the impugned legislation is part of a regulatory scheme; the scheme is administered and overseen by a regulatory agency; the legislation is concerned with trade in the country as a whole rather than trade in a particular industry; the legislation is of such a nature that the provinces jointly or severally would be constitutionally incapable of enacting it; and failure to include one or more provinces in the legislative scheme would jeopardize the successful operation of that scheme.
18 Patrick Monahan, *Constitutional Law*, 3d ed. (Toronto: Irwin Law, 2006), 296. Until the important *Reference re Securities Act*, 2011 S.C.C. 66, what was thought to be the potential (eventual?) expansive force of the federal trade and commerce power had been trickling its way into policy-political praxis. Note the undertaking of the federal Conservative Party in its 2008 general election platform, which drove the eventual proposed national securities legislation and Supreme Court reference:

"A re-elected Conservative government ... will work to eliminate barriers that restrict or impair trade, investment or labour mobility between provinces and territories by 2010. In 2007, the government announced that it was prepared to use the *federal trade and commerce power* to strengthen the Canadian economic union ... We ... are prepared to intervene by exercising federal authority if barriers to trade, investment and mobility remain by 2010." Conservative Party of Canada, *The True North Strong and Free: Stephen Harper's Plan for Canadians* (Ottawa: Conservative Party of Canada, 2008), 16; emphasis added.

19 Monahan, *supra* note 18 at 271-76.
20 The holding in *Gold Seal Ltd. v. Dominican Express Company*, [1922] 62 S.C.R. 424, has proven to have peculiar staying power in this regard.
21 Of course, policy plays hugely here as well, and policy-political context is immensely apposite to the choices made by governments. Notes Thomas Courchene: "[What] is increasingly the essence of nation building are [sic] citizen-based issues as they relate to information empowerment, human capital development, and redressing the actual and potential income-distributional fallout from the new global order. The challenge for some federal systems, and certainly the Canadian federation, is that many of these citizenship issues fall under provincial jurisdiction. In some areas, Ottawa (more generally, central or federal governments) can mount a reasonable case on policy, if not on constitutional grounds, for becoming more involved in some of these areas. For example, with knowledge on the cutting edge of competitiveness, Ottawa will be a meaningful player in human capital development no matter what the [C]onstitution says since the country's competitiveness is at stake. In many other areas, however, federal systems are likely headed for considerable jurisdiction[al] in-fighting as central governments are going to be driven in the direction of catering to the citizen-related issues, traditionally the domain of sub-national governments." Thomas Courchene, "Federalism and the New Economic Order: A Citizen and Process Perspective" (Montreal: Institute for Research on Public Policy, 2002), 12.
22 Monahan, *supra* note 18, at 307-10, writing prior to the 2011 *Reference re Securities Act*, *supra* note 18, is fairly optimistic in his interpretation of the holdings in two cases in particular, *Morguard* and *Hunt*, in respect to the potential efficiency of the economic union, pending further litigation. He asserts at 307 that these holdings suggest that the source of legislation to enhance the proper functioning of the economic union is "the entire framework and structure of the Canadian constitutional order." (This would seem consistent with the thrust of this book – that the framework and structure of the Canadian Constitution are pregnant with immense strategic possibilities, in practice, for the Canadian state.) Monahan suggests that this provides justification for federal legislation to create a national securities commission (something later negatived, as mentioned, by the Supreme Court in the *Securities Reference*), legislation to prevent the establishment or maintenance of restrictions on free interprovincial movement of persons, goods, services,

or investments, as well as legislation to create a common set of rules for mutual recognition of standards and regulations by provinces. For his part, Trebilcock, *supra* note 13, also writing prior to the *Securities Reference*, seems less optimistic about the net verdict emerging from the accumulated jurisprudence to date on negative integration. He notes at 571 that the Supreme Court's "negative integration case-law seems much more equivocal, contradictory, and less well-developed than the counterpart body of U.S. Supreme Court Dormant Commerce Clause jurisprudence ... or for that matter [than] the National Treatment jurisprudence developed under the GATT/WTO."

23 See Trebilcock, *supra* note 13; Robert Howse, "The *Labour Conventions* Doctrine in an Era of Global Interdependence: Rethinking the Constitutional Dimensions of Canada's External Economic Relations" (1990) 16 Can. Bus. L.J. 171; and H. Scott Fairley, *Canada, External Affairs and the Constitution: A Theory of Judicial Review* (S.J.D. diss., Harvard Law School, 1987) [unpublished], as well as in "External Affairs in the Constitution of Canada" (1987) 16 Can. Council Int. L. 220. Note, however, that French Canadian scholarship, including by Brun and Tremblay, *supra* note 6, remains highly laudatory of *Labour Conventions* and would doubtless prove highly critical of any reversal of this holding. Hogg, *supra* note 6, at 505, is agnostic in respect of such an eventuality in his assessment of the evolution of jurisprudence on the second branch of the federal trade and commerce power.

24 Stephen McBride, "Quiet Constitutionalism in Canada: The International Political Economy of Domestic Institutional Change" (2003) 36, 2 Cdn J. Pol. Sci. 251 at 261.

25 See *supra*, Chapter 1, note 19 about anticipatory political considerations in Privy Council and Supreme Court decision making.

26 Note the direct military import accorded to railways in s. 51(xxxvii) of the *Commonwealth of Australia Constitution Act*, which states that the Commonwealth has legislative power over "the control of railways with respect to transport for the naval and military purposes of the Commonwealth." For a persuasive account of the military (defensive) imperative underlying the post-Confederation construction of the Intercolonial Railway, see Jay Underwood, *Built for War: Canada's Intercolonial Railway* (Ottawa: Railfare, 2005). Underwood writes at 2 that "[t]he Intercolonial Railway appears to have been the inevitable compromise, a tacit admission from both sides [Canada and the British Empire] that each bore some measure of responsibility if the Americans [at the time the principal military threat to Canadian sovereignty] were to be held at bay every time they rattled their sabres. But while Britain entered into the project satisfied the empire was financing the construction of a military road, the colonials [Canada] believed they were financing an instrument of commerce." In short, strategic thinking was being outsourced to Westminster, while Canadian thinking or conceptualization of the railway enterprise was purely tactical or inward-looking in nature. See also *supra*, Introduction, note 3.

27 *Johannesson v. West St. Paul*, [1952] 1 S.C.R. 292.
28 Hogg, *supra* note 6, 441.

Chapter 7: Communications

1 For an interesting analysis of the significance of telecommunications to the national economy in the context of the "information revolution," and for a somewhat heretical critique of federal dominance, post-*Alberta Government Telephones* (*infra* note 9), see H.N. Janisch and R.J. Schultz, "Federalism's Turn: Telecommunications and Canadian Global Competitiveness" (1991) 18 Can. Bus. L.J. 161.
2 A perhaps extreme manifestation of communications in the service of the military instrument of the state – but one that makes my point – is called, in military parlance, C4I, or command-control-communications-computers-intelligence, which amalgamates advanced technologies and command-and-control regimes to provide intelligence, or situational awareness, to military actors.
3 Note that statutes such as the *Canadian Railway Act*, R.S.C. 1906, c. 37, once used to cover communications. This is no longer the case, strictly speaking, given technical change. The current federal legislative framework for communications is comprised of the *Telecommunications Act*; the *Broadcasting Act* (*infra* note 22); the *Canadian Radio-television and Telecommunications Commission Act*, R.S.C. 1985, c. C-22; the *Radiocommunication Act*, R.S.C. 1985, c. R-2; the *National Defence Act* (for the CSE); the *Security of Information Act*; the *Privacy Act*, R.S.C. 1985, c. P-21; the *Personal Information Protection and Electronic Documents Act*, S.C. 2000, c. 5; the *Criminal Code*; and, *inter alia*, the *Investment Canada Act*. See the observation by Justice Iacobucci in *Bell ExpressVu Limited Partnership v. Rex et al.* (2002), 212 D.L.R. (4th) 1 at para. 46: "The Broadcasting Act and the Radiocommunication Act must be seen as operating together as part of a single regulatory scheme."
4 Postal service and post offices – doubtless strategic and under federal legislative competence in ss. 91(5) and 108 (Third Schedule, item 8) of the 1867 Act – would also arguably figure on a comprehensive list of communications capabilities.
5 Jacques Baud, *La Guerre asymétrique* (Paris: Éditions du Rocher, 2003), 188-90.
6 Whether total state control of the instruments and content of communication is strategically efficient or inefficient, compared with mixed or more balanced state-non-state control of communications, is greately contested. In the end, however, the "right" balance is a policy-political choice, recognizing that the extreme of total state control of the instruments and content of communication will sooner bump up against serious constitutional constraints than will the reverse extreme of very limited government control of the instruments and contents of communication.
7 Writes Robert Howell in *Canadian Telecommunications Law* (Toronto: Irwin Law, 2011) at 35: "Overall, the pervasiveness of the Internet, touching upon all aspects of society, will attract constitutional comparison with similarly broad areas. These include the environment, health care, and consumer protection. Trends and decisions in areas of broad context provide a clear recognition of the complexity and

pervasiveness that deny any holistic, topical exclusivity to federal and provincial spheres ... Consumer-related measures in other contexts afford a mixed dimension. Features may be brought within federal regulation, as with restrictions and requirements for the advertising of tobacco products, utilizing the federal criminal law power while remaining provincial for other purposes."

8 *Toronto v. Bell Telephone Co.*, [1905] A.C. 52.
9 *Alberta Government Telephones v. CRTC*, [1989] 2 S.C.R. 225. Peter W. Hogg, "Jurisdiction over Telecommunications: *Alberta Government Telephones v. CRTC*" (1990) 35 McGill L.J. 480, stresses the pivotal nature of this case in definitively bringing all of telecommunications "undertakings" (undivided as are undertakings, in the jurisprudence, in terms of the competence of one level of government or the other) under federal jurisdiction.
10 *Téléphone Guèvremont v. Quebec*, [1994] 1 S.C.R. 878. This case ensured that even local telephone companies were interprovincial or international concerns, to be regulated by the federal government under s. 92(10)(a) of the 1867 Act.
11 On the content side, one would evidently exclude from federal regulation, and place under provincial jurisdiction, property and civil rights issues such as commercial advertising.
12 *Radio Reference*, [1932] A.C. 304.
13 *Re CFRB*, [1973] 3 O.R. 819 (C.A.).
14 *Public Service Board v. Dionne*, [1978], 2 S.C.R. 191.
15 *Capital Cities Communications v. CRTC*, [1978] 2 S.C.R. 141. Peter W. Hogg, *Constitutional Law of Canada*, student ed. (Scarborough: Carswell, 2007), notes at 573 that the Supreme Court makes no reference to POGG in its holding in *Capital Cities Communications*. He suggests that this omission is "so striking that it should probably be interpreted as a disapproval of that basis of jurisdiction"; that is, federal jurisdiction is likely rooted only in s. 92(10)(a) of the 1867 Act. Because, as Hogg correctly notes, radio and broadcast television have the same effective constitutional treatment, suggested in *Capital Cities Communications* (with the court relying on the famous *Radio Reference*, *supra* note 12), it naturally follows that both communications modes – whether they are inter- or intraprovincial in character – have the same constitutional underpinnings.
16 As proof of the historical conflation in Canadian constitutional vernacular of the terms "transportation" and "communications," note that telecommunications in Canada was once regulated under the *Canadian Railway Act*, later repealed and replaced by the *Canada Transportation Act*. Section 185(3)(b) of the latter statute reads thus: "[A] reference in those provisions [mentioned in s. 185(2)] to a 'railway, telegraph, telephone and express company,' a 'railway or express company' or a 'carrier by water' shall be interpreted as a reference to a railway company."
17 See s. 7 of the *Telecommunications Act*, which spells out the Canadian Telecommunications Policy. There is not a strategic word in this section, which lists nine policy objectives, ranging from "(a) to facilitate the orderly development

throughout Canada of a telecommunications system that serves to safeguard, enrich and strengthen the social and economic fabric of Canada and its regions," to "(i) ... contribute to the protection of the privacy of the person." Subsection (d) states that one of the objectives of the national telecommunications policy is to promote the ownership and control of Canadian carriers by Canadians. Of course, one might reasonably read this ownership and control as being in aid of the social and economic objectives in (a) rather than in aid of any strategic objectives. Evidently, however, as with the overall Strategic Constitution, there is often strategic effect in astrategic design. As such, as I discuss below, Canadian ownership of and control over certain telecommunications assets do conduce to certain strategic advantages for the Canadian state.

18 *Consolidated Fastfrate Inc. v. Western Canada Council of Teamsters et al.*, 2009 S.C.C. 53.
19 Emphasis added. Of course, influential scholarly articles on the constitutional treatment of communications in Canada – beginning with the W.R. Lederman classic, "Telecommunications and the Federal Constitution of Canada," in H.E. English, ed., *Telecommunications for Canada: An Interface of Business and Government* (Toronto: Methuen, 1973), 339 – are similarly mute on the connection between communications (as a factor of power) and the strategic performance of the Canadian state in international affairs, a connection that is all too plain to the strategic analyst or theorist. The possibly canonical book by Michael Geist, *Internet Law in Canada*, 3d ed. (Toronto: Captus Press, 2002), is similarly silent on this connection.
20 *Telecommunications Act*, S.C. 1993, c. 38.
21 See, for instance, s. 7(1) of the *Radiocommunication Act*: "Her Majesty may assume and, for any length of time, retain possession of any radio station and all things necessary to the sufficient working of it and may, for the same time, require the exclusive service of the operators and other persons employed in working the station."
22 *Broadcasting Act*, S.C. 1991, c. 11.
23 See, for instance, the series of legal and executive decisions concerning the company Globalive, starting with the Canadian Radio-television and Telecommunications Commission (CRTC) – the independent agency of the federal government regulating Canadian telecommunications and broadcasting – negativing, in 2009, Globalive's bid for Canadian spectrum because of excessive foreign leverage in its financial structure (Telecom Decision CRTC 2009-678), followed by a December 2009 order-in-council by the federal cabinet to reverse the CRTC decision, followed yet again by a quashing of this order-in-council by the Federal Court in 2011 (*Public Mobile Inc. v. Canada*, 2011 F.C. 130), and culminating in a reinstatement of cabinet's position through a 2011 Federal Court of Appeal decision (*Globalive Wireless Management Corp. v. Public Mobile Inc.*, 2011 F.C.A. 194).
24 *Investment Canada Act*, R.S.C. 1985, c. 28 (1st Supp.).

25 Section 20 lists the factors to be taken into account for purposes of the net benefit test. They include the macroeconomic and microeconomic impacts of the investment, the intensity of Canadian participation in the business, and, in section 20(e), "the compatibility of the investment with national industrial, economic and cultural policies." There is evidently no mention of foreign policy or Canadian strategy in any of these factors. In other words, the authors of the statute, as it now stands (compare the next note), see no first-order connection between investment in Canada and Canada's capacity (or non-capacity) to perform in international affairs.

26 *Foreign Investment Review Act*, S.C. 1973-74, c. 46. The first use of the *Investment Canada Act* to block a foreign purchase on the basis of a non-cultural sector review occurred in 2008 (the attempted purchase by Alliant Techsystems of the aerospace business of MacDonald Dettwiler and Associates). The second occurred in 2010 (BHP Billiton's attempted purchase of Potash Corporation). In 2012, the federal government approved two cases of acquisition of Canadian energy concerns – both based in Alberta – by foreign state-owned corporations: the $6 billion purchase of Alberta-based Progress Energy by the Malaysian state-owned company Petronas, and the $15.1 billion purchase of Nexen by the China National Offshore Oil Company (CNOOC). In approving these foreign acquisitions, Prime Minister Harper stated on 7 December 2012: "In light of growing trends, and following the decisions made today [in respect of Petronas and CNOOC], the Government of Canada has determined that foreign state control of oil sands development has reached the point at which further such foreign state control would not be of net benefit of Canada. Therefore, going forward, the Minister [of Industry] will find the acquisition of control of a Canadian oil-sands business by a foreign state-owned enterprise to be of net benefit, only in exceptional circumstance[s]." The prime minister also suggested that future amendments to the *Investment Canada Act* would assist in the review of foreign state-owned enterprises seeking to invest in Canada. To this end, he noted three possible future amendments – all apparently sensitive to considerations of strategy: first, provisions authorizing review of "the degree of control or influence a state-owned enterprise would likely exert on the Canadian business that is being acquired"; second, provisions for the review of "the degree of control or influence that a state-owned enterprise would likely exert on the industry in which the Canadian business operates"; and third, provisions for the review of "the extent to which the foreign government in question is likely to exercise control or influence over the state-owned enterprise acquiring the Canadian business." See http://www.pm.gc.ca/eng/media.asp?id=5195.

27 Competition Policy Review Panel, *Compete to Win – Final Report* (Ottawa: Public Works and Government Services Canada, 2008), 29.

28 See *United States Steel Corporation v. Canada*, 2011 F.C.A. 176. The dispute and litigation with US Steel Corporation caused the federal government, in 2012, to include among its amendments to the *Investment Canada Act* an authorization for

the minister of industry, in s. 19(2), to accept security for payment from foreign investors in Canada in the event of possible court-enforced penalties for breaches of undertakings made by those investors before the Government of Canada in regard to the investment.

29 Some commentators, such as Craig Forcese, *National Security Law* (Toronto: Irwin Law, 2008), at 439, argue that, while the Supreme Court has not outright invoked s. 7 of the Charter as protective of privacy rights, there might be a basis for so doing, drawing on the Federal Court of Appeal's rulings in cases such as *Zarzour v. Canada* (2000), 268 N.R. 235.

30 *Hunter v. Southam*, [1984] 2 S.C.R. 145.

31 *R. v. Duarte*, [1990] 1 S.C.R. 30.

32 A perhaps obvious point is worth mentioning here – to wit, that intelligence collection does not, and has not historically had to, meet the standards or thresholds of criminal evidence, as required for prosecution by the state under the *Criminal Code*.

33 Peter W. Hogg, *Constitutional Law of Canada*, 5th ed. (looseleaf) (Toronto: Carswell, 2007), 48-2.

34 *Atwal v. Canada*, [1988] 1 F.C. 107.

35 Forcese, *supra* note 29, 454. Private communication, according to s. 183 of the *Criminal Code*, "means any oral communication, or any telecommunication, that is made by an originator who is in Canada or is intended by the originator to be received by a person who is in Canada and that is made under circumstances in which it is reasonable for the originator to expect that it will not be intercepted by any person other than the person intended by the originator to receive it, and includes any radio-based telephone communication that is treated electronically or otherwise for the purpose of preventing intelligible reception by any person other than the person intended by the originator to receive it."

36 Note that there is an ongoing debate here about the discrepancy – or asymmetry, as it were – between CSIS intercepts or warrants authorized by judges and CSE warrants or intercepts authorized by the executive branch of the federal government – specifically the minister of defence. Note, moreover, that the CSE also has a "meta-data" capability – that is, a capability to monitor foreign communications data, statistics, and trends (including in respect of Internet use), abstracted from individual communications, to divine patterns of strategic interest (such as terrorist networks, espionage relationships, and so on). Insofar as this meta-data mining concerns strictly foreign communications, it appears easily justifiable, in constitutional terms, on the basis of the royal prerogative for foreign affairs as well as the militia and defence power supporting the CSE. Such a program, however, would likely bump up, if ever so slightly, against the nebulous *Khadr* standards in respect of Canadian observation of international law.

37 The minister of defence can intercept such private communications for foreign intelligence purposes if, per s. 273.65(2) of the *National Defence Act*, he or she is satisfied that (a) the interception will be directed at foreign entities located outside

Canada; (b) the information to be obtained could not reasonably be obtained by other means; (c) the expected foreign intelligence value of the information that would be derived from the interception justifies it; and (d) satisfactory measures are in place to protect the privacy of Canadians and to ensure that private communications will only be used or retained if they are essential to international affairs, defence, or security.

38 *Re CSIS Act*, 2009 F.C. 1058. Note that, by implication of this ruling, once again, the greater the geography of a country such as Canada, the larger, *arguendo*, the land surface from which it can intercept communications, and the larger the national economy, the more numerous, *arguendo*, the telecommunications concerns (private or public) that can play a role in routing some of the said communications.

39 *R. v. National Post*, 2010 S.C.C. 16.

40 Recall that s. 2(b) of the Charter guarantees freedom of expression, including freedom of the press and other communications media.

41 Emphasis added. See the Ontario Superior Court of Justice holding in *O'Neill v. Canada* (2006), 82 O.R. (3d) 241, in which certain sections of the *Security of Information Act* barring publication of information deemed "official" or "secret" – including, presumably, national security information – were ruled overly broad and in contravention of s. 7 of the Charter (and not saved by s. 1).

42 Evidently, one variant of state-controlled communications – including in emergency situations – is propaganda or even agitprop.

43 *Infra*, Case Study B, note 26.

44 Granted, apart from the posited general lack of strategic culture in Canadian constitutional jurisprudence and scholarship, one other clearly possible reason for the absence of explicit language on crisis communications might be the disinclination to have a Canadian public broadcaster seem an arm of the state – a "separateness" that is clearly part of the free media bulwark so central to modern democratic systems. One might argue, on this logic, that language that too readily provides for a material federal government "in" or *entrée* into crisis communications in publicly held media would betray an intention to use the media for propaganda. In practice, many of the crisis communications arrangements today in Canada consist of memoranda of understanding (or, at a minimum, in unwritten conventions) between governments and public and private television broadcasters and radio stations, in which these different media concerns – which doubtless have a reciprocal or autonomous professional interest in communicating useful information – agree to communicate, or allow the government to communicate, with the public when an emergency occurs. (If necessary, the government could easily pay private broadcasters for "air time" in the event of emergencies or otherwise compensate a broadcaster for lost advertising dollars.)

45 Evidently, strategically relevant statutes such as the *Criminal Code*, as mentioned, do regulate Internet content and activities.

46 Public Notice CRTC 1999-197.

47 Howell, *supra* note 7, argues at 33: "As a system of telecommunication [the Internet] is utterly global and can present features of traditional broadcasting (point-to-mass) and traditional telecommunications (point-to-point). All of these features are exclusively federal jurisdiction." Contrast this with Craig McTaggart's four-layer decomposition of Internet regulation, variously divided between the federal and provincial governments, depending on whether one is dealing with the physical, operation, application, or content aspects of the Internet. Craig McTaggart, "A Layered Approach to Internet Legal Analysis" (2003) 48 McGill L.J. 571.

48 Section 973.64 of the *National Defence Act*. It stands to reason that any general Canadian federal electronic or cyber-warfare or cyber-espionage capacity – offensive or defensive – would be driven from the CSE, under the federal militia power in s. 91(7).

Chapter 8: Population

1 In practical terms, this spending power has been curtailed by the last several federal governments, by dint of both federal-provincial agreements and unilateral federal restraint (most recently under a doctrine of *soi-disant* "open federalism," even if such restraint has been well short of meeting the standard of constitutional convention).

2 Ukraine, like each of the fifteen post-Soviet states, has a "power-vertical" (*vertikal vlasti*) logic in its unitary constitutional framework that enables the president (through the Presidential Administration, his or her department) to control all important appointments at all levels of government (especially the governors of the provinces, or *oblasts*). Each new president of Ukraine can therefore, in principle, through the national parliament (the Verkhovna Rada), change the national curriculum fairly rapidly (in support of any number of national objectives) and have this change projected across the entire territory and population of the country because of the ready deference of the provincial governors. See Irvin Studin, "Governing in the Ex-Soviet Space" (Fall 2013) Global Brief 12.

3 Consider the question of languages and Canadian strategic leadership in the Americas region – an aspiration articulated by the last Harper government (see Case Study A in Part II). Whence the critical mass of Spanish or Portuguese speakers so clearly necessary – particularly in the diplomatic and military arms of the federal government – for successful advancement of such an aspiration? Absent a major, sustained push by the federal government via its spending power or federal-provincial coordination, the federal government must rely largely on the otherwise independent educational regimes of the various provinces – and the independent policy preferences of their various governments – to generate, over a sustained period, a sufficient number of individuals with the appropriate linguistic training.

4 See, for instance, Irvin Studin, "Canada: Population 100 Million" (Spring-Summer 2010) Global Brief 10. At 100 million, by the end of this century, Canada would likely be bigger in population than every European country with the likely exception

of Russia. It would also be the second most populous country in the Western world, after the United States. Also see Irvin Studin, "When Canada Becomes the West's Second State" (Fall 2013) Global Brief 50.

5 John J. Mearsheimer, *The Tragedy of Great Power Politics* (New York: W.W. Norton, 2003), 60-61.

6 Section 91(25) of the 1867 Act relates to naturalization and aliens. This is a rather idiosyncratic head of power in the sense that few statutes have been enacted on its basis, and, as a consequence, there has been little litigation in regard to it. The *Citizenship Act* arguably falls under this section.

7 Strictly speaking, the federal government has formal agreements with each of the ten provinces on immigration, pursuant to s. 8(1) of the *Immigration and Refugee Protection Act* (and s. 5(1) of the *Department of Citizenship and Immigration Act*, S.C. 94, c. 31). These agreements include provisions for provincial nominees – a class of immigration that is fast growing in importance. However, the Canada-Quebec regime is strategically *sui generis* in respect of the degree to which it transfers upstream policy-making powers (that is, selection and admission) to the province as well as the degree to which it has as one of its express objectives the preservation of the demographic weight of Quebec within Canada.

8 This is perhaps a rebuttable presumption. One might ask why France and the United Kingdom have only, say, two very large cities for population bases of around 60 million each. One could respond to this, *arguendo*, by suggesting that physically vast, populous, and strategically powerful countries such as Russia, the United States, and China, in contrast, have at least half a dozen major urban-cum-industrial centres spread across their respective territories.

9 *Abdelrazik v. Canada*, 2009 F.C. 580, is a fairly recent s. 6 case – and indeed one that deals with the important intersection of royal prerogative and Charter rights – but it treats an altogether incompatible fact pattern and the right to enter into, and remain in, Canada, per s. 6(1), rather than ss. 6(2), 6(3), and 6(4), which are of interest in this chapter.

10 Provinces and territories are one and the same thing for purposes of the application of Charter rights, per s. 30 of the Charter.

11 *Canadian Egg Marketing Agency v. Richardson*, [1998] 3 S.C.R. 157.

12 *R. v. Oakes*, [1986] 1 S.C.R. 103.

13 In "So What Is the Real Legacy of Oakes? Two Decades of Proportionality Analysis under the Canadian *Charter*'s Section 1" (2006) 34 Sup. Ct. L. Rev. 501, Sujit Choudhry interestingly notes the privileging of empirical social science or policy evidence in the context of the *Oakes* test – a hurdle over which strategic considerations would be hard pressed to jump.

14 *Edwards Books & Art Ltd. v. R.*, [1986] 2 S.C.R. 713, para. 126.

15 See Irvin Studin, "Strategy and the Crown Prerogative: Considerations for Justiciability and Judicial Culture" (2013) 7, 1 Journal of Parliamentary and Political Law 63.

Case Study A: Canadian Strategic Leadership in the Americas

1 See Prime Minister Harper's speech of 17 July 2007 in Santiago, Chile, http://www.pm.gc.ca/eng/media.asp?category=2&id=1759. See also Irvin Studin, "Engaging Obama: Canadian Ends, American Means" (2009) 30, 2 Policy Options 18.

2 See, *inter alia*, *Protecting Australia against Terrorism 2006* (Canberra: Department of the Prime Minister and Cabinet, 2006). I was the principal author of this Australian counterterrorism policy, written while on secondment to the Australian Department of the Prime Minister and Cabinet in Canberra from the Canadian Privy Council Office in 2005-6. See also Irvin Studin, "Australian Federalism's Asia Paradox" (2013) 5, 2 Asian Journal of Public Affairs 49; and Irvin Studin, "Australia Shows the West How to Pivot to Asia," *Financial Times*, 7 January 2013, 9.

3 Most of the countries in the Americas follow the civil law tradition. Most of the Caribbean countries, however, follow the common law tradition. English is evidently the official language in most of these common law jurisdictions – the observation plainly being that Canada would, on its current pedagogical structures, have greater ease in "leading" strategically in English-language jurisdictions in the Americas, all the more so because of the common law and comparable Westminster-style political institutions. French-language-cum-civil law jurisdictions such as Haiti would also be reasonably amenable, other things being equal, to Canadian strategic leadership, but there are few such countries in the region (for instance, Guadeloupe and Martinique); that is, the overwhelming majority of countries in the Americas have Spanish (or Portuguese) as the official language and have civilian legal systems.

4 Of course, I oversimplify slightly here, as law faculties themselves are somewhat independent in their curricular decision making within universities (which themselves are quasi-independent, in curricular terms, of the provinces), and players such as provincial bar associations – themselves material to the determination of law school curricula – would have to be thrown into the mix as well.

5 The Faculty of Law at the Université de Moncton in New Brunswick teaches in French but has a common law curriculum.

6 Naturally, the federal government can, and indeed does, actively undertake to provide – via the federal spending power – linguistic and cultural training for federal officials who are to be deployed to foreign postings. But this is easily a suboptimal arrangement, in strategic terms, as such belated language or knowledge acquisition not only fails to guarantee high proficiency or fluency – or an "instinct," as it were, for Hispanic languages or culture, as would be acquired through early life immersion – but also caters to a far smaller, self-selected pool of candidates (generally those who are *already* federal officials) than would be suggested by the far larger pool of pre-employed, Spanish- or Portuguese-speaking candidates who could, in theory, form the recruitment base or aggregate talent pool for the federal diplomatic (and even military) instrument in the event that Spanish and Portuguese were privileged languages in Canada's educational regime.

7   See Irvin Studin, "Process before Product: A New Federal-Provincial Logic for a New Century" (2008) 29, 8 Policy Options 43.
8   See *supra*, Chapter 5, note 21, and Chapter 6, note 4, on the federal spending power.
9   The history of French and English second-language and immersion pedagogy across the provinces is replete with examples of uses of the federal spending power (and federal-provincial cooperation) to advance national linguistic goals. Note also that official bilingualism in federal institutions, such as Parliament, the civil service, the Bank of Canada, and Crown corporations, would also have created over time – though far less potently than the spending power – a need for provincial educational regimes *autonomously* to equip students with second-language capabilities to advance their employment prospects. One could presume, on this logic, that, were an Americas strategy sustained over time, such indirect pressures could also, over time, require certain provinces *autonomously* to make their Spanish- (and Portuguese-) language offerings more robust. In other words, the federal government would create labour market demand for such linguists, thereby forcing the hands of the provinces to modify their curricula accordingly.
10 Kevin Rudd, *Asian Languages and Australia's Economic Future: A Report Prepared for the Council of Australian Governments on a Proposed National Asian Languages/ Studies Strategy for Australian Schools* [the Rudd Report] (Brisbane: Queensland Government Printer, 2004). See also, more recently, Chapter 6 on "Capabilities" – including Asian-language capabilities – in the 2012 Australian Government white paper, *Australia in the Asian Century* (Canberra: Department of the Prime Minister and Cabinet, 2012). Writes Deborah J. Henderson in respect of the Rudd Report in "Meeting the National [Australian] Interest through Asia Literacy: An Overview of the Major Stages and Debates" (2003) 27, 1 Asian Studies Review 23 at 24: "COAG [Council of Australian Governments]'s acceptance of the ... Rudd Report ... was significant. [Rudd's] policy prescription for an 'export culture' that was 'Asia literate' ... was without rival in previous policy struggles about how studies of Asia and its languages might be placed in the education system. The Rudd Report emphasized that a national Asian languages and cultures strategy should be developed in the context of second language provision. Its 15-year plan, aimed at producing an Asia-literate generation to boost Australia's international and regional economic performance, received bipartisan agreement across all levels of state and federal government." See also Irvin Studin, "A Canadian Languages Strategy for the New Century: Foreign Policy, National Unity and the Aboriginal Question" (2011) 32, 5 Policy Options 72.
11 The first and third of these aspects of Canadian strategic engagement are explored in Irvin Studin, "Engaging Obama: Canadian Ends, American Means" (2009) 30, 2 Policy Options 26.
12 *Ibid.*
13 This, *en passant*, is exactly what happened over the past few years. The federal government, at the margin, diverted diplomatic and fiscal resources from regions

such as Africa to the Americas. No legislation was passed in this regard – or needed to be passed – and the provinces played no role whatever in this regard; this was exclusively the province of the royal prerogative. Recall, as mentioned in Part I, that the Canadian International Development Agency (CIDA), in spite of private member legislation to increase oversight of federal development, had no proper enabling legislation until its merger with DFAIT in 2013. Its strategic priorities therefore remained entirely creatures of the royal prerogative.

14 There is no fetter on this flexibility in the highly laconic *Department of Foreign Affairs and International Trade Act*, R.S.C. 1985, c. E-22.

15 Recall that Canadian security intelligence assets could also be deployed to the Americas region, even under the *CSIS Act*, s. 12. Of course, as discussed in Part I, the *Khadr* line of cases appears to impose non-negligible fetters on the "processes" or activities in which Canadian intelligence personnel in CSIS or other agencies or ministries might partake; that is, they may not participate in processes or activities that are illegal at international law. I should also stress that, aside from "human" intelligence assets, Canadian foreign intelligence assets in the form of diplomatic reporting, signals, or communications intelligence (as with the CSE) or, *inter alia*, defence intelligence could also easily be deployed into the region, or otherwise focus on the region (analytically), purely by dint of the royal prerogative. (See the discussion on intelligence in counterterrorism in Case Study D.)

16 Note the mandate of the Australian Secret Intelligence Service (ASIS), which focuses primarily on Australian interests in the Asia-Pacific region, specifically Southeast Asia and the South Pacific. ASIS was created by the Australian government, by royal prerogative, without legislative backing, in 1952. It received enabling legislation only in 2001 via the *Intelligence Services Act, 2001*, in which its mandate is described in s. 6(a) as "to obtain, in accordance with the Government's requirements, intelligence about the capabilities, intentions or activities of people or organisations outside Australia." (Note the absence in the ASIS mandate of any explicit regional affectation for the agency. This absence, by design, leaves to the Australian federal executive the strategic flexibility – royal prerogative oblige – to play with the degree of the agency's immersion in Asia.)

17 Recall that Parliament would have to approve the budget expenditure. Executive dominance of the budget approval process is pronounced in the context of majority government and clearly more mitigated in the context of minority government.

18 In respect of the Americas, diasporic remittances often exceed, by a significant margin, formal development aid money. See, for example, Alan Simmons, Dwaine Plaza, and Victor Piché, "The Remittance Sending Practices of Haitians and Jamaicans in Canada," Report to CIDA, 2005, 5. National regulation of such remittances is typically negligible in Canada; however, were there a policy-political interest in incentivizing increased remittance flows by diasporic Canadians to the Americas, such incentives would flow from the taxation and spending powers of

Parliament as well as from those of the provincial legislatures. This would once again beget the cooperation-cum-coherence challenge of trying to ensure that provincial spending power efforts in international affairs are not at odds with more macro federal efforts.

19 In practice, of course, money or spending aside, the federal government would rely on, or "outsource," many provincial "programmatic" capabilities and assets to deliver its development agenda. These capabilities and assets would include provincial policing or constabulary assets for purposes of training security services in target countries in the Americas as well as provincially regulated lawyers and other legal professionals, both common and civilian.

20 The vast majority of potential immigrants from the Americas are evidently not native French speakers. However, French speakers would be found in significant numbers in Haiti, Guadeloupe, Martinique, and French Guiana. (Note that the very constitutional dynamic that militates against Canadian linguistic-cultural success in the Americas – provincial legislative competence in education – is somewhat replicated in the fettered or conditional capacity of the federal state to select Latin American immigrants to Canada because of the quasi-constitutional need for aggregate immigrant intake not to undermine the general demographic weight of Quebec in the federation.)

21 Canada concluded free-trade agreements with Colombia, Peru, Panama, and Honduras in 2008, 2009, 2010, and 2011 respectively (with a foreign investment protection and promotion agreement, or FIPA, concluded with Peru in 2007), with comparable agreements pending with the Dominican Republic, the Andean Community, the Central America Four (CA-4), and the Caribbean Community (CARICOM).

22 I discussed provincial decision making and the fallacy of composition in Part I. The "Buy American" provisions in the *American Reinvestment and Recovery Act*, part of the American fiscal reaction to the economic crisis that began in 2008, led to the Canadian government and the US government brokering a deal in February 2010 on sub-state or sub-national or sub-federal or sub-central government procurement. The deal specifically addressed s. 1605(a) of the act, which states that "[n]one of the funds appropriated or otherwise made available by this Act may be used for a project for the construction, alteration, maintenance, or repair of a public building or public work unless all of the iron, steel, and manufactured goods used in the project are produced in the United States." The Canada-US agreement called for mutual sub-federal procurement opportunities in iron, steel, and manufactured goods, subject, on the Canadian side, to specific conditions and provisos among different provinces in respect of goods, services, and industries that are affected by these mutual market opportunities. These "tailored" provincial conditions are numerous and indeed cover some 80 percent of the agreement – that is, most of the annexes. This intense tailoring to provincial predilections

and peculiarities again betrays the strategic inefficacy of Canadian bilateral trade and investment negotiations under the *Labour Conventions* framework.

23 Debt relief, programmatically, comes from the World Bank-International Monetary Fund initiative of the mid-1990s, whereby the bilateral and multilateral debt of so-called highly indebted poor countries (HIPCs) is forgiven by wealthy countries to help establish the external sector sustainability of the poor countries in question; that is, to help reduce and stabilize the countries' ratio of external debt to exports and overall GDP.

24 One might wish to call the ratio of the welfare hit on the targeted or sanctioned country to the hit on Canada (the sanctioning country) the *sanctions ratio* or *co-efficient*. To determine the sanctions hit to the target country, consider a so-called sanctions multiplier $1/(E_s+E_d)$, where E_s is the elasticity of national supply and E_d is the elasticity of national demand. In simple terms, the sanctions multiplier multiplied by the initial deprivation equals the hit or welfare loss for the target state. See Gary Clyde Hufbauer et al., *Economic Sanctions Reconsidered: History and Current Policy*, 2d ed. (Washington, DC: Institute of International Economics, 1990).

25 Note the sporadically mooted, exotic, yet strategically non-negligible prospect of Canada annexing the Caribbean island of Turks and Caicos, currently a British overseas territory. While such annexation has historically been mooted by Canadians for apparently "touristic" reasons, one could clearly imagine the use of such a territory for strategic purposes, such as the basing of Canadian military (including naval) and intelligence assets. (The relevance of Canadian geography – land and nautical – as a factor of strategic power again becomes more plain.) On the Canadian side, the simplest and strategically most "elegant" form of the annexation "transaction" would be for Parliament (through the initiative of the federal executive) to pass an act of Parliament to make the Turks and Caicos a federal territory, as with the Yukon, the Northwest Territories, and Nunavut. (See the discussion *supra*, Chapter 5, note 7, as well as in Case Study C below, in respect of the nature of federal governance of the territories.) *Prima facie*, it seems to make little strategic sense to attempt to make Turks and Caicos a bona fide Canadian province, as this form of annexation would require a large degree of deference to the provinces (sub-strategic actors) via the constitutional amending formula required for the granting of such provincial status – seven provinces representing at least fifty percent of the Canadian population – as per ss. 38(1) and 42(1)(f) of the 1982 Act. Moreover, even once past the process of becoming a province, Turks and Caicos as a province would acquire a host of strategic or quasi-strategic constitutional powers, principally in s. 92 of the 1867 Act, but also the "quasi-strategic" education competence, that would, as discussed amply in Part I, dilute the potency of the federal executive – including its capacity to lever the enhanced strategic potential suggested by a Strategic Constitution framework that now incorporated Turks and Caicos.

26 *Smith v. Canada*, [2009] F.C.J. No. 234.

Case Study B: Bona Fide War

1 I do not, strictly speaking, define war, for purposes of this book, as solely a function of a declaration of war by the federal government or Parliament (itself not a constitutional or even yet conventional requirement in Canada). Analytically, in terms of the Strategic Constitution, war can be understood as that strategic end or scenario that maximally, and certainly more than any other scenario, engages the various factors of power of the state.
2 The goals for the Afghan mission arguably morphed over the years since the start of the war in 2001, with the most pronounced inflection point coming when the Canadian military mission moved to the more dangerous theatre of Kandahar province from Kabul in 2005. The priorities cited in this book reflect the most comprehensive statement of the war aims of the Canadian government, as articulated in 2009. See http://www.afghanistan.gc.ca/canada-afghanistan/priorities-priorites/index.aspx?lang=eng.
3 See *infra*, Case Study D, note 11 on the Chief of Defence Intelligence (CDI).
4 See *supra*, Chapter 3, note 25. Also see the discussion of the federal purchase of the Turks and Caicos for military purposes in Case Study A (note 25) as well as the discussion of military bases and expropriation in the Canadian North in Case Study C.
5 *Human Rights Institute of Canada v. Canada*, [2000] 1 F.C. 475.
6 G.V. La Forest, *Natural Resources and Public Property under the Constitution* (Toronto: University of Toronto Press, 1969), 149-50.
7 Again, see note 25 in Case Study A in respect of the possible federal purchase of Turks and Caicos for purposes of a potential military base.
8 Section 36 of the *National Defence Act* states: "The materiel supplied to or used by the Canadian Forces shall be of such type, pattern and design and shall be issued on such scales and in such manner as the Minister, or such authorities of the Canadian Forces as are designated by the Minister for that purpose, may approve." While provinces do not typically engage in pure military procurement, legally and constitutionally, their spending power allows them to purchase a wide variety of assets – "dual-purpose" assets – that would certainly have military utility in both war preparations and military operations (specifically defensive military operations on Canadian soil). First and foremost, they would include local and provincial police and emergency assets. This repeats the issue raised in Part I in respect of strategic coherence (or incoherence) generated by the great and non-mutually exclusive flexibility of the federal and provincial spending powers.
9 John Kenneth Galbraith, *The New Industrial State* (Boston: Houghton Mifflin, 1967), 30. In respect of the "technostructure," Galbraith writes at 71 that, "[w]ith the rise of the modern corporation, the emergence of the organization required by modern technology and planning and the divorce of the owner of the capital from control of the enterprise, the entrepreneur no longer exists as an individual person in the mature industrial enterprise. Everyday discourse, except in the economics textbooks,

recognizes this change. It replaces the entrepreneur, as the directing force of the enterprise, with management. This is a collective and imperfectly defined entity; in the large corporation it embraces chairman, president, those vice presidents with important staff or departmental responsibility, occupants of other major staff positions and, perhaps, division or department heads not included above. It includes, however, only a small proportion of those who, as participants, contribute information to group decisions. This latter group is very large; it extends from the most senior officials of the corporation to where it meets, at the outer perimeter, the white and blue collar workers whose function is to conform more or less mechanistically to instruction or routine. It embraces all who bring specialized knowledge, talent or experience to group decision making. This, not the management, is the guiding intelligence – the brain – of the enterprise. There is no name for all who participate in the group decision making of the organization which they form. I propose to call this organization the Technostructure."

10 See the important but to date publicly overlooked 2013 report by Tom Jenkins et al. on the state-led creation of Canadian military industries for the twenty-first century in *Canada First: Leveraging Defence Procurement through Key Industrial Capabilities* (Ottawa: Department of Public Works and Government Services, 2013).

11 See, for instance, the observation of Chief Justice Lamer in *Ontario Hydro v. Ontario*, [1993] 3 S.C.R. 327, at para. 69: "There is no authority supporting the view that the declaratory power should be narrowly construed. Quite the contrary. It might, I suppose, have been possible to interpret s. 92(10)(c) so as to confine it to works related to communications and transportation such as those specifically listed in s. 92(10)(a) and (b) but the courts, including this Court, have never shown any disposition to so limit its operation, and a wide variety of works – railways, bridges, telephone facilities, grain elevators, feed mills, atomic energy and munition factories – have been held to have been validly declared to be for the general advantage of Canada."

12 Recall, from Part I, that the *Emergencies Act* coexists with the predecessor *Energy Supplies Emergency Act*, also rooted in the federal emergency power, which states at s. 15(1), specifically in relation to petroleum resources, that when "the Governor in Council is of the opinion that a national emergency exists by reason of actual or anticipated shortages of petroleum or disturbances in the petroleum markets that affect or will affect the national security and welfare and the economic stability of Canada, and that it is necessary in the national interest to conserve the supplies of petroleum products within Canada, the Governor in Council may, by order, so declare and by that order authorize the establishment of a program for the mandatory allocation of petroleum products within Canada in accordance with this Act." Note also that the *Emergencies Act* states, laconically, in s. 40(1), that only in the event of a declared war emergency "the Governor in Council may make such orders or regulations as the Governor in Council believes, on reasonable grounds, are necessary or advisable for dealing with the emergency." This is the

total extent of what is written in the "orders and regulations" part for this type of emergency, compared with more extensive descriptions of "orders and regulations" for the other three types of emergency – public welfare, public order, and international. This suggests that the act intends for there to be expansive *marge de manoeuvre* for the executive to do whatever is "necessary or advisable" to address the war emergency. To be sure, such *de maximis marge de manoeuvre* does not eclipse or oust or exhaust the overarching emergency or national security prerogative availed to the executive beyond the act. Moreover, to the extent that the government wishes to resort to or cite the specific "orders and regulations" made explicit under the other three types of emergency, there is nothing in the act to stop it from declaring more than one type of emergency. Indeed, it seems natural that a war emergency should also beget an international emergency, which would then entail, according to s. 30 of the act, orders and regulations relating to, *inter alia*, control or regulation or "any specified industry or service, including the use of equipment, facilities and inventory," and "the appropriation, control, forfeiture, use and disposition of property or services." See *infra*, Case Study D, note 30 for commentary on the old *War Measures Act*.

13 Note, however, that the Canadian government could not rely on the *Emergencies Act* for purposes of conscription. Section 40(2) of the *Emergencies Act* states: "The power ... to make order and regulations [under the war emergency] may not be exercised for the purpose of requiring persons to serve in the Canadian Forces." This means that Parliament would have to pass an explicit law on conscription.

14 The federal government also did not seek Parliamentary approval for the post-2011 non-combat training and technical support role for Canadian Forces (and the diplomatic instrument, to be sure) in Afghanistan.

15 Laskin J.A. writes in *Black v. Chrétien* (2000), 47 O.R. (3d) 532, at paras. 52 and 53: "I will briefly discuss prerogative powers that lie at the opposite ends of the spectrum of judicial reviewability. At one end of the spectrum lie executive decisions to sign a treaty or to declare war. These are matters of 'high policy.' *R. v. Secretary of State for Foreign and Commonwealth Affairs, ex parte Everett*, [1989] 1 All E.R. 655 at 660, *per* Taylor L.J. Where matters of high policy are concerned, public policy and public interest considerations far outweigh the rights of individuals or their legitimate expectations [Laskin is referring here to the standard from *Council of Civil Service Unions v. Minister for the Civil Service*, [1985] 1 A.C. 374]. At the other end of the spectrum lie decisions like the refusal of a passport or the exercise or mercy." Indeed, in *Council of Civil Service Unions v. Minister for the Civil Service*, Lord Roskill, at 148, famously invokes the broad category of "the defence of the realm" as one of the select few prerogative powers that are not "susceptible to judicial review because their nature and subject matter are such as not to be amenable to the judicial process" – noting that the courts are not (institutionally) best placed to determine whether the "armed forces [should be] disposed in a particular manner." One might presume, in the Canadian context, that this is so to the extent

that "the defence of the realm" does not engage Charter rights; if it did, upon judicial review, the Charter claim would have little chance of success.

16 The second extension vote in Parliament came with several conditions, one of which was that other NATO allies must send at least 1,000 troops to southern Afghanistan. However, as this vote did not override the royal prerogative, this condition cannot have been regarded as constitutionally – or legally or indeed, for my purposes, strategically – binding.

17 Canada, *Independent Panel on Canada's Future Role in Afghanistan* (Ottawa: Public Works and Government Services, 2008), 34. Compare this *ad hoc* war cabinet with the standing National Security Committee of cabinet employed in the Australian government, which makes decisions on everything ranging from declaration of war (and conclusions of peace) to military procurement.

18 Alexander Hamilton, James Madison, and John Jay, *The Federalist Papers* (New York: Bantam, 2003), 109. In Canada, certain provinces – and often Quebec – have strong views in respect of the strategic or policy-political wisdom of the federal state engaging in hostilities with foreign states. These provincial views can carry moral or political weight, but their significance, in strict constitutional terms, is nugatory. (See the discussion on Quebec's influence in Canadian federalism as well as *supra*, Chapter 1, note 19.)

19 *Amnesty International v. Canada*, 2008 F.C. 336.

20 The concept and vernacular are those of Hedley Bull, *The Anarchical Society: A Study of Order in World Politics* (New York: Columbia University Press, 1977).

21 Consider, for instance, as mentioned in Chapter 3, a federal decision to initiate or participate in a war that is illegal at international law. This could arguably have been the case in Kosovo in 1999 or Iraq in 2003 (had Canada decided to participate) or in the prospective event of, say, a federal intervention in a foreign country, *sans* Security Council mandate, to stanch, say, a genocide or humanitarian disaster.

22 *Smith v. Canada*, [2009] F.C.J. No. 234 at para. 29.

23 The provinces, given the "dual-purpose" assets at their disposal and their massive legislative jurisdiction in a number of annex areas (such as microeconomics), would have to be coordinated for them to play an important supporting role in domestic military defence. Recall that the *Emergencies Act* states that federal orders and regulations made under its auspices cannot "unduly impair the ability of any province to take measures ... for dealing with an emergency in the province" or, in regard to command and control, that nothing in the act should be construed or applied "so as to derogate from ... the control or direction of the government of a province or municipality over any police force over which it normally has control or direction."

24 Emphasis added. A majority government evidently makes successful invocation of s. 4(2) of the Charter easier.

25 *Canada Elections Act*, S.C. 2000, c. 9.

26 Note the *dicta* from Chief Justice Laskin – for all intents and purposes about the principle of constitutional necessity in times of war – in *Reference re Anti-Inflation Act, 1975*, [1976] 2 S.C.R. 373, referring to the *Fort Frances* case (*Fort Frances Pulp and Paper Co. v. Manitoba Free Press Co.*, [1923] A.C. 695), perhaps the first Canadian case to make use of the word *emergency*: "The *Fort Frances* case is curious in an important respect because the reasons appear to suggest that in time of war there is a power implicit in the Constitution which, irrespective of what is in ss. 91 and 92, endows the Parliament of Canada with extraordinary authority to protect the general interest."

Case Study C: Arctic Sovereignty

1 The Canadian Arctic as a region is a territorial subset of the Canadian North, which includes the Yukon, the Northwest Territories, and Nunavut. The Arctic can be said to refer to the Arctic archipelago as well as to the islands and waters lying north of Canada's mainland (together known as Inuit Nunaat).
2 The United States, for instance, has not signed the UN Convention on the Law of the Sea, though it arguably regards UNCLOS as customary international law.
3 Compare this strategic approach with the question of Arctic sovereignty with a strictly legal one, as taken by Michael Byers in *Who Owns the Arctic? Understanding Sovereignty Disputes in the North* (Vancouver: Douglas and McIntyre, 2009). He takes a similar approach in "Pax Arctica" (Winter 2010) Global Brief 50. At 7 in *Who Owns the Arctic?* Byers writes: "No country will ever 'own' the North Pole, which is located roughly 750 km to the north of any land, including Ellesmere Island, Greenland and the Russian archipelago of Franz Josef Land. This is because coastal states cannot possess full sovereignty more than 12 nautical miles (22 km) from shore. Instead, they have certain 'sovereign rights' out to 200 nautical miles (370 km) and sometimes farther, depending on the shape and sediments of the seabed. If Canada, Denmark or Russia can scientifically demonstrate [in the context of the UN Commission on the Limits of the Continental Shelf, discussed just below] that the North Pole is a 'natural prolongation' of its continental shelf, the country in question will have the exclusive right to exploit the resources of the seabed there – and nothing more. The water and sea-ice will remain part of the 'high seas,' meaning that ships and planes will be able to travel freely, and tourists and adventurers from anywhere in the world will be able to visit without producing passports or paying fees." However, Byers concedes at 92 that the UN Commission on the Limits of the Continental Shelf, assessing different countries' claims to the continental shelf based on scientific evidence, does not issue binding decisions, only recommendations given "considerable weight" in interstate negotiations on sovereign waters or, more precisely, sovereign rights to waters. Moreover, he concedes at 92 that there are possible overlaps among countries' claims to water rights under the commission process and at 93 that "[t]he UN commission will not make

recommendations with regard to any overlaps between claims. It is up to the countries involved to negotiate a solution, refer the matter to an international court or arbitral tribunal, or simply agree to disagree and not issue exploration licenses for the contested area." Strange that Byers does not allow for the possibility of direct military or diplomatic competition or conflict in the event of such disagreements (or differing judgments or interpretations?) – particularly where there might be significant economic (especially resource) rents at stake and where there might be glaring asymmetries in raw strategic power among the different states involved. This, of course, is where strategy and power are at play. See Charles Emmerson, *The Future History of the Arctic* (London: Random House, 2010), and his online article for *Global Brief* on March 11, 2010, entitled "Pax Arctica? Not Quite," http://globalbrief.ca/blog/2010/03/11/pax-arctica-not-quite/.

4   Ken Coates et al., *Arctic Front: Defending Canada in the Far North* (Toronto: Thomas Allen, 2008), 44.
5   In principle, more geography also evidently creates increased capacity for more Canadians – that is, for a greater aggregate population. And while such increased capacity would be non-theoretical, given Canada's extremely small population to geography ratio, the practical degree of stimulus that such additional geography, on its own, would provide to the population factor of power is likely negligible.
6   Byers, *supra* note 3, 6.
7   The Arctic might contain some 25 percent of the world's remaining undiscovered oil and gas deposits, based on a July 2008 US Geological Survey. Arctic waters also contain gas hydrates, a potentially very important future source of energy. Onshore, the Arctic has iron ore, base metals, and, *inter alia*, diamonds. Note that both P. Whitney Lackenbauer and Franklyn Griffiths downplay the existence of an actual or prospective "threat" to Canadian Arctic sovereignty from foreign states; see, respectively, P. Whitney Lackenbauer, "From Polar Race to Polar Sage: An Integrated Strategy for Canada and the Circumpolar World" (Toronto: Canadian International Council Working Paper, 2009), and Franklyn Griffiths, "Towards a Canadian Arctic Strategy" (Toronto: Canadian International Council Working Paper, 2009).
8   See the next note. As mentioned, in my analysis of "constitutional statics," I treat international law as a given or exogenous factor; that is, it has no explanatory role for Canada's overall capacity to achieve its ends in regard to Arctic sovereignty but is one of a number of external structural parameters (which can include, for instance, the behaviour or strategic power of other Arctic countries) that form the general context in which Canada pursues its sovereignty imperative. At the time of writing, I am finalizing a paper entitled "Constitutional Statics, International Law, and Canada's Arctic Game" and exploring the "statics" between the Strategic Constitution and international law in relation to Canadian strategic behaviour in the Arctic.
9   Rob Huebert, "Canadian Arctic Sovereignty and Security in a Transforming Circumpolar World" (Canadian International Council Working Paper, 2009), 3.

Huebert reminds us that, in international law, sovereignty consists of three principal elements: a defined territory, an existing system of governance, and a people within the defined territory. He posits the absence of a defined territory – the absence of defined borders or indeed the presence of contested borders – as the key *enjeu*, as it were, in Canada's sovereignty game. He writes at 6: "Ultimately whether it is dividing the Arctic Ocean seabed, determining the boundaries of Canadian sections of the Beaufort and Lincoln Sea or shipping in the Northwest Passage, the issue is control. What are the Arctic maritime boundaries that Canada can control and what can it do within these boundaries?"

10 Lackenbauer, *supra* note 7, 41-42. Indeed, the "Canadianness" of the geography in question suggests the strategic issue at hand. The United States, for instance, does not dispute Canadian "sovereign rights" to the NWP – Canada's right to resource exploration within the waters of the NWP – but rather Canadian "ownership" of the NWP and therefore Ottawa's capacity to enforce Canadian law in the NWP. Sensitive to setting a precedent in respect of other archipelagic regions of the world, the United States currently views the NWP as an "international strait," meaning that US and indeed other foreign commercial and naval vessels ought to have free right of transit passage.

11 In November 2012, Canada reached a tentative agreement with Denmark on the maritime boundary for the Lincoln Sea; see http://www.international.gc.ca/media/aff/news-communiques/2012/11/28a.aspx.

12 The Lomonosov Ridge is an underwater mountain ridge bisecting the Arctic Ocean north of Ellesmere Island and Greenland.

13 See *supra*, Chapter 5, note 7.

14 *B.C. Offshore Reference*, [1967] S.C.R. 792.

15 Peter W. Hogg, *Constitutional Law of Canada*, 5th ed. (looseleaf) (Toronto: Carswell, 2007), 30-10.

16 F.A. Mann, *Foreign Affairs in English Courts* (Oxford: Clarendon Press, 1986), 4-5.

17 See, for instance, *Canada's Northern Strategy* (Ottawa: Department of Public Works and Government Services, 2009), at 12: "Canada's North is a vast region still yet to be fully mapped and studied. As a result of the ratification of the United Nations Convention on the Law of the Sea (UNCLOS), Canada is in the process of conducting scientific studies to determine the full extent of our continental shelf as defined under UNCLOS."

18 Strictly speaking, Canada, like all states, has an Exclusive Economic Zone (EEZ) from 12 to 200 nautical miles offshore: that is, exclusive rights over the resources in the water, ocean floor, and seabed. All states have a twelve nautical mile territorial sea, per UNCLOS.

19 The diplomatic instrument under the royal prerogative would be in effect, naturally, with all the accompanying provisos – that the potency of this instrument is a function of the strength of the economy and population factors, first and

foremost, with due consideration given to the less treated question of how diplomats are educated or "trained."
20 Article 76 of UNCLOS specifies that coastal states can claim rights over an "extended continental shelf," beyond the EEZ, if the depth and shape of the seabed and the thickness of underlying sediments indicate a "natural prolongation" of the shelf closer inshore.
21 I am speaking most evidently here of Indian and Northern Affairs Canada (INAC), Natural Resources Canada, and Transport Canada (specifically the Coast Guard).
22 See Irvin Studin, "Changing Luck and North American Wars" (Spring-Summer 2011) Global Brief 20, and Irvin Studin, "The Melting of the Polar Ice Signals the End of the 'Pax Arctica,'" *Financial Times*, 29 August 2012, 9.
23 Strictly counterfactually, there is no constitutional bar to the federal government creating, on the strength of the royal prerogative, new Indian reserves in any or all of the three federal territories, or even new territories in the North, with the possible motive of increasing Canada's northern demographic footprint.
24 The three territories could also, independently of the federal spending power, arguably use their own spending powers to incentivize increased birth rates in the North.
25 I have written widely on the policy and strategic case for 100 million Canadians by the year 2100. On current projections, such a national population would make Canada more populous than any European country, save Russia, and, by implication, the second most populous country in the West, after the United States. Clearly, if Canada is to meet its Arctic sovereignty imperative this century, some of this increased population will have to live in the North. See Studin, "Canada: Population 100 Million" (Spring-Summer 2010) Global Brief 10. Also see Studin, "When Canada Becomes the West's Second State" (Fall 2013) Global Brief 50.
26 See s. 30 of the Charter.
27 *Canadian Egg Marketing Agency v. Richardson*, [1998] 3 S.C.R. 157.
28 *R. v. Oakes*, [1986] 1 S.C.R. 103.
29 See *supra*, Chapter 8, note 14.
30 See *supra*, Chapter 5, note 7.
31 Shelagh Grant, *Polar Imperative: A History of Arctic Sovereignty in North America* (Vancouver: Douglas and McIntyre, 2010), 24.
32 U.S. Geological Survey Arctic Oil and Gas Report (July 2008), http://geology.com/usgs/arctic-oil-and-gas-report.shtml.
33 http://www.aadnc-aandc.gc.ca/eng/1100100036087/1100100036091.
34 Use of force in international conflict aside, for purposes of domestic constitutional organization, the federal government would already have regulatory power over assets such as interprovincial oil and gas pipelines or pipelines that cross between territories and provinces. See *supra*, Chapter 5, note 12 for discussion of the ancillary role of provinces and First Nations in respect of such pipelines.

35 Note that a small-scale aggressive move by Canada to seize or threaten to seize assets or territories or seas controlled by countries (or agents of countries) that are far larger and strategically more powerful than Canada, such as the United States or Russia, would not necessarily be met with outright and immediate retaliation by these countries. This is a calculation to be made by Canada, of course (according to a certain game-theoretic framework), but Canada could well make the aggressive move with the anticipation or expectation that the other country would not want to retaliate for fear of escalation, disproportionate response, or simply because the Canadian move did not meet a certain minimal threshold for aggressive response. Strategic self-deterrence, as it were, might therefore be decisive in regard to this country's response. It is conceivable that Canada could align itself with one great power – the United States or, arguably, even Russia – on Arctic matters, thereby possibly deterring other great powers from responding to its aggressive acts, particularly if they do not cross any particular "red line." See Irvin Studin, "Canada's Four-Point Game" (Spring-Summer 2012) Global Brief 20, as well as Studin, "Melting," *supra* note 22.

36 Bill C-15, *An Act to Replace the Northwest Territories Act to Implement Certain Provisions of the Northwest Territories Lands and Resources Devolution Agreement and to Repeal or Make Amendments to the Territorial Lands Act, the Northwest Territories Waters Act, the Mackenzie Valley Resource Management Act, Other Acts and Certain Orders and Regulations*, 2d Sess., 41st Parl., 2013.

Case Study D: National Security/Counterterrorism since 9/11

1 As mentioned in Part I, see the exceptional effort by the Supreme Court to delimit "national security" as a concept in *Suresh v. Canada*, [2002] 1 S.C.R. 3, in which the court, referring to the then *Immigration Act*, stated with affirmation: "We reject the arguments that the terms 'danger to the security of Canada' and 'terrorism' are unconstitutionally vague." Note the definitional issue posited in *Freedom and Security under the Law*, Second Report, Vol. 1, of the (McDonald) Commission of Inquiry Concerning Certain Activities of the Royal Canadian Mounted Police (Ottawa: Department of Supply and Services, 1981) at 39: "The terms of reference do not explain what is meant by the phrase 'the security of Canada,' and yet some explanation is surely required ... [T]here has been a tendency in some quarters to reject the concept of 'national security' entirely and to rely instead on concepts that are more readily understood, such as 'national defence' and 'law enforcement.' But we question whether these alternative phrases adequately cover the security activities that, in our view, need to be carried out in all states, including Canada." At 40, the report builds on its conceptualization of national security from the first report of the commission, identifying two basic security imperatives for Canada: "first, the need to protect Canadians and their governments against attempts by foreign powers to use coercive or clandestine means to advance their own interests

in Canada, and second, the need to protect the essential elements of Canadian democracy against attempts to destroy or subvert them." For a good review of the evolution of Canada's security environment and responses (and its implicit conceptualization of "national security"), see Commission of Inquiry into the Actions of Canadian Officials in Relation to Maher Arar, *A New Review Mechanism for the RCMP's National Security Activities* (Ottawa: Department of Public Works and Government Services, 2006).

2 Canada, *Securing an Open Society: Canada's National Security Policy* (Ottawa: Privy Council Office, 2004).

3 In the technical or professional parlance, these two phases subdivide into four overlapping phases: prevention, preparedness, response, and recovery (PPRR). The first two of these four phases could be identified with the pre-attack phase that I have posited and the latter two, for all practical intents and purposes, with the post-attack phase.

4 One might expand this category to include the entire so-called CBRN, or chemical-biological-radiological-nuclear, spectrum of terrorist attacks.

5 See *infra* note 15 on Crown and third-party (for instance, police) disclosure obligation in criminal cases.

6 The classical statutory articulation of security intelligence as a concept is found in s. 12 of the *CSIS Act* (see *supra*, Chapter 2, note 14): "The Service [CSIS] shall collect, by investigation or otherwise, to the extent that it is strictly necessary, and analyse and retain information and intelligence respecting activities that may on reasonable grounds be suspected of constituting threats to the security of Canada and, in relation thereto, shall report to and advise the Government of Canada."

7 *Supra*, Chapter 4, note 27.

8 *Re CSIS Act*, [2007] F.C.J. No. 1780.

9 *R. v. Hape* (2007), 280 D.L.R. (4th) 385.

10 See the holding in *Re CSIS Act*, 2009 F.C. 1058, in which the Federal Court held that the CSE could assist CSIS in intercepting foreign telecommunications within territorial Canada.

11 CDI is nowhere mentioned in the *National Defence Act*. However, within the Canadian Department of National Defence, as Stéphane Lefebvre explains, "CDI has functional authority for common policy, oversight, doctrine, and procedures for the entire defence intelligence function ... The CDI is focused on the collection of information on the military capabilities and intentions of foreign states and entities. Its ability to collect information domestically is limited, and conducted either in support of domestic Canadian Forces operations or in support of other departments and agencies under their legal authorities." Stéphane Lefebvre, "Canada's Legal Framework for Intelligence" (2010) 23, 2 Journal of Intelligence and Counterintelligence 247 at 263.

12 Until its recent merger into DFAIT, the Canadian International Development Agency (CIDA) would also have played an informational intelligence role for the

federal government. It now surely continues to play this role, albeit with less autonomy, within the DFAIT fold.

13 "Terrorist activity" is defined in s. 83.01(1) of the *Criminal Code*. See *supra*, Chapter 4, note 38 for discussion of the *Khawaja* line of cases and the constitutionality of this definition.

14 A total of twenty-eight security certificates have been issued in Canada since 1991. At the time of writing, three people in Canada have been named in security certificates.

15 Bill C-3, *An Act to Amend the Immigration and Refugee Protection Act and to Make a Consequential Amendment to Another Act*, 2d Sess., 39th Parl., 2007. I should note also that general Crown ("first party") constitutional disclosure obligations in criminal cases were classically established in *R. v. Stinchcombe*, [1991] 3 S.C.R. 326. More recently, in *R. v. McNeil*, [2009] 1 S.C.R. 66, the Supreme Court confirmed and clarified the common law regime established in *R. v. O'Connor*, [1995] 4 S.C.R. 411, for disclosure of information to a criminally accused by so-called third parties of the state, including the police. (See also the 2007 Federal Court holding in *Canada v. Khawaja*, below, for analysis of Crown disclosure obligations under s. 38 of the *Canada Evidence Act*.) While the security certificate regime does not fall under criminal law – meaning that neither *Stinchcombe* nor *O'Connor* strictly applies to it in respect of the disclosure burdens on the Crown or state-related third parties – the 2007 and 2008 *Charkaoui* decisions affirmed that the disclosure burden on the Crown and state-related third parties is not insignificant even in an administrative law context, given the need to satisfy s. 7 of the Charter. In non-security certificate cases, the *O'Connor* third-party burden could apply to Canadian security agencies such as CSIS or the CSE in respect of appeals from those criminally accused. This could condition some of the behaviour of these agencies, which are neither designed for, nor culturally accustomed to, collecting security information in a way, or at a standard, that lends itself easily to criminal prosecutions by the Crown; that is, these strategic agencies have not historically been mandated as "evidence-gathering" organizations, in the criminal law sense. One basic manifestation of such "conditioned" behaviour could be a heightened preference of CSIS or the CSE to avoid retention of information that might be susceptible to such a disclosure burden. The Supreme Court holding in *Charkaoui No. 2*, 2008 S.C.C. 38, which requires CSIS to preserve all operational notes (*contra* its previous practice of destroying them), supporting security certificate applications doubtless amplified this dynamic, providing CSIS with a not inconsiderable incentive to avoid seeking or continuing with certain security certificates where the Service might fear that the potential disclosure risk in respect of confidential information by the court is material. Such increased risk aversion or conservatism could mean, in practice, that a number of security certificate candidates posing a threat to Canadian interests in Canada might not be detained and/or deported.

As for Crown disclosure obligations under s. 38 of the *Canada Evidence Act* (concerning international relations, national defence, and national security), in *Canada v. Khawaja*, [2007] F.C.J. No. 622, Justice Mosley confirmed the three-step process, outlined in *Canada v. Ribic*, [2005] 1 F.C.R. 33, for disclosure of such evidence to the accused in criminal trials (including counterterrorism trials, as with *Khawaja*): first, *Stinchcombe* had to be applied to identify any information for the accused that could be thought reasonably useful to his or her defence (third-party standards applying, evidently, as in *McNeil*, above); second, there had to be a determination as to whether such information might be injurious to Canadian national security, international relations, or national defence; and third, there had to be a balancing between the general public interest in disclosure and the public (security) interest in non-disclosure, with Justice Mosley determining that such balancing – the key step in the s. 38 proceeding – should take place on a case-by-case basis. This decision was upheld by the Federal Court of Appeal in *Canada v. Khawaja*, 2007 F.C.A. 342, on the matter of the necessary balancing of public interest in disclosure and non-disclosure and on the specific decision of the judge to disclose to the defence a descriptive summary of relevant information. (The court held that the specific information in the summary revealed material injurious to Canada's national security, international relations, and defence.) The Federal Court holding was also upheld in *Canada v. Khawaja*, 2007 F.C.A. 388, which found that the *ex parte* representation availed to the attorney general and to Khawaja during the trial, under s. 38.11(2) of the *Canada Evidence Act*, was not contrary to s. 7 of the Charter. See also *Harkat v. Canada*, 2012 F.C.A. 122.

16 *Charkaoui v. Canada*, [2007] S.C.J. No. 9. No doubt, as with police forces and all other "repressive" arms of the state, there are numerous permutations of Charter limitations on what Canadian intelligence or intelligence-related services can do domestically. I cannot treat even most of them – nor is such treatment necessary – since I am interested primarily in *nexa* between such constitutional limitations and what the Canadian state might wish to accomplish internationally or strategically.

17 Compare this regime with that in Australia, where citizens and non-citizens alike are subject to preventative detentions of up to forty-eight hours by the Commonwealth (federal) government in terrorist situations, with complementary state and territory legislation allowing for such detention for up to fourteen days. To perform a preventative arrest, the Australian Federal Police (AFP) must have reasonable grounds to suspect that the subject will engage in a terrorist act; possesses a thing that is connected with the preparation for, or engagement of an individual, in a terrorist act; or has done something in preparation or planning for a terrorist act. The AFP must also be satisfied that the preventative detention will substantially assist in preventing a terrorist attack, and that detaining the individual is reasonably necessary for such prevention, or that the detention will preserve evidence relating to a terrorist act, and that detaining the individual is reasonably necessary

for such prevention. *Protecting Australia against Terrorism 2006* (Canberra: Department of the Prime Minister and Cabinet, 2006), 35. In Canada, as discussed in Part I, provisions related to two of the pivotal criminal law processes enacted in the *Anti-Terrorism Act* – so-called investigative hearings and recognizance with conditions, including preventative arrests in the context of potential terrorist acts – sunsetted in 2006. The federal government attempted to reinstate these provisions, without substantial amendment, in 2007 via Bill S-3. This bill was passed by the Senate but was at second reading in the House of Commons when it recessed in June 2008. An election was called in September 2008, and the bill was subsequently reintroduced by the government in the House of Commons – this time as Bill C-19. The House of Commons was subsequently prorogued. The bill was again tabled in March 2010 as Bill C-17. A federal general election was called for May 2011. The provisions were finally successfully reinstated in April 2013 in Bill S-7, which also included *Criminal Code* amendments creating offences in regard to, *inter alia*, people who leave or attempt to leave Canada for purposes of committing a terrorist act outside Canada as well as those who harbour or conceal a person involved in terrorist activity to facilitate such activity.

18 Modern counterterrorism in particular, and intelligence in general, rely heavily on the technical and technological, but they are still led, with little doubt, by the human brain (or "controlling mind"). And while it is uncontroversial that the federal government has direct constitutional and practical capabilities in creating the technical-technological apparatus necessary for much counterterrorism intelligence – partnering, evidently, with the provinces, the private sector, and international players – the more interesting observation here is arguably about the capabilities of the federal government in "forming" the human brains that create these technologies, use them, and, most importantly, provide them with relevant inputs (that is, intelligence data).

19 See Canada, *Canada's Cyber Security Strategy* (Ottawa: Department of Public Works and Government Services, 2010).

20 To be fair, many governments today employ an "all-hazards" approach to counterterrorism, particularly in relation to critical infrastructure (including transportation infrastructure), such that, in certain cases, they are not practically interested in differentiating (or, indeed, in some cases, even able to differentiate) between human-made (say terrorist) harm and harm deriving from natural causes (such as natural disasters) or indeed between intentional and inadvertent human-caused harm.

21 In contrast to the federal trade and commerce power in s. 91(2) of the 1867 Act, federal legislative jurisdiction over transportation is not "segmented"; that is, as Patrick Monahan states, "the Privy Council's determination that jurisdiction over transportation undertakings was to be undivided has led to quite different results in the transportation field [compared with internal trade]. Once an undertaking is classified as interprovincial, federal jurisdiction immediately extends to all aspects

of the enterprise, including any features that are strictly local. This has meant that federal authority to regulate transportation undertakings has been much more extensive and therefore more effective than in many other areas of federal jurisdiction. In particular, the Privy Council's undivided approach to transportation undertakings has meant that this is one of the few areas in which the federal government is capable of effective action without the necessity of involving provincial governments." Patrick Monahan, "Constitutional Jurisdiction over Transportation: Recent Developments and Proposals for Change," in Canada, *Royal Commission on National Passenger Transportation*, vol. 3 (Ottawa: Royal Commission on National Passenger Transportation, 1992), 791, 796. Writes Peter W. Hogg, *Constitutional Law of Canada*, 5th ed. (looseleaf) (Toronto: Carswell, 2007), at 22-36: "[I]n each case the courts have held that a significant amount of 'continuous and regular' interprovincial business turns the entire enterprise into an interprovincial undertaking."

22 *Johannesson v. West St. Paul*, [1952] 1 S.C.R. 292.

23 Until recently, the federal government had tried on several occasions to purchase the Windsor-Detroit Ambassador Bridge from private American interests to advance Canadian objectives in expanding traffic and trade capacity along the Windsor-Detroit border. These attempts failed, and in 2012 the federal government signed an agreement with the state of Michigan to construct a new bridge (the Detroit River International Crossing) across the border. In fact, the Government of Canada agreed to pay the entire cost of construction. (The bigger the economic factor of power of a country, the more international bridges it can finance on its own.)

24 *Reference re Anti-Inflation Act, 1975*, [1976] 2 S.C.R. 373.

25 *Co-Operative Committee on Japanese-Canadians v. Canada*, [1947] A.C. 87.

26 In the event of a terrorist attack on national strategic energy assets – for instance one or more nuclear power plants, critical pipelines, or critical provincial electrical grids – the *Emergencies Act* coexists with the predecessor *Energy Supplies Emergency Act*, also rooted in the federal emergency power, which states at s. 15(1), specifically in relation to petroleum resources, that when "the Governor in Council is of the opinion that a national emergency exists by reason of actual or anticipated shortages of petroleum or disturbances in the petroleum markets that affect or will affect the national security and welfare and the economic stability of Canada, and that it is necessary in the national interest to conserve the supplies of petroleum products within Canada, the Governor in Council may, by order, so declare and by that order authorize the establishment of a program for the mandatory allocation of petroleum products within Canada in accordance with this Act."

27 Note that the *Emergencies Act* specifies at s. 4 that the executive cannot use the *Emergencies Act* in and of itself to amend or alter that act. This is a strange provision: how can the executive alter legislation without Parliament?

28 *Reference re Anti-Inflation Act, 1975*, [1976] 2 S.C.R. 373 at 378.

29 *Ibid.* at 412.
30 Recall that the *Emergencies Act* defines "national emergency" in s. 3 as "an urgent and critical situation of a temporary nature that (a) seriously endangers the lives, health or safety of Canadians and is of such proportions as to exceed the capacity or authority of a province to deal with it, or (b) seriously threatens the ability of the Government of Canada to preserve the sovereignty, security and territorial integrity of Canada." This definition makes clear that certain *temporary* – though *prima facie* sweeping – executive emergency measures are essential, in certain situations, to restore the capacity of the government to pursue strategic interests – described as sovereignty, security, and territorial integrity. These measures ("orders and regulations"), depending on the nature of the declared emergency, include everything from prohibitions on travel to requisition or seizure of property, control of specified industries, and removal from Canada of non-citizens.

Let me briefly compare the current *Emergencies Act* with the old (largely pre-Charter) *War Measures Act, 1914* that it replaced in 1988. That act was quite laconic in general and specifically less comprehensive in defining different types of emergency, privileging as it did, in s. 2, "war, invasion, or insurrection, real or apprehended." Critical differences exist: for instance, in s. 2 of that act, the government could invoke emergency powers simply by issuing a proclamation which in itself "shall be conclusive evidence that [said] war, invasion, or insurrection, real or apprehended, exists and has existed for any period of time therein stated, and of its continuance, until such issue of a further proclamation it is declared that the war, invasion or insurrection no longer exists." Unlike the *Emergencies Act*, there was no scope for parliamentary review or checks of this declaration or of the executive powers flowing therefrom. (For the *War Measures Act*, as with the extant *Emergencies Act*, all these powers would be subject to *ex post* judicial review but doubtless at a highly deferential standard of review.) Non-exhaustive executive powers (orders and regulations, in the vernacular of the modern *Emergencies Act*) under s. 3 included censorship of writing and communications; arrest, detention, and deportation; control of the harbours, ports, and territorial waters of Canada as well as the movements of vessels; controls over land, air, and water transportation; controls over imports and exports as well as production and manufacturing; and appropriation, control, forfeiture, and disposition of property and the use thereof. These orders and regulations are naturally most similar to those found under the "war emergency" in the *Emergencies Act*.
31 Recall that the 2006 Ontario Superior Court of Justice holding in *R. v. Khawaja*, [2006] O.J. No. 4245, does not *prima facie* threaten the constitutionality of s. 2(c) of the *CSIS Act*.
32 Of the first fifteen Charter rights, considered the key bulwark of Canada's constitutionalized fundamental rights and freedoms, only ss. 5 (that Parliament will sit at least once every twelve months) and 6 (mobility rights) would effectively be

saved under this cocktail. Sections 3 (that every citizen has the right to vote in an election) and 4(1) (that no House of Commons will continue for more than five years) would become moot upon the invocation of s. 4(2).
33 One can note the common use of "colour coding" or national alerts – often via broadcasting or radio concerns – by different countries around the world (*inter alia*, the United States and Australia) to communicate different states of national threat and readiness in respect of terrorism.
34 See *supra* note 19.

Conclusion
1 *Turp v. Canada*, 2012 FC 893. The court found that the *Kyoto Protocol Implementation Act*, S.C. 2007, c. 30, not supported by the federal government, was deemed not to eclipse, exhaust, or otherwise displace the prerogative of the executive to withdraw from the *Kyoto Protocol*. The act was repealed in 2012.

Bibliography

Books, Articles, and Reports

Asch, Michael, and Catherine Bell. "Definition and Interpretation of Fact in Canadian Aboriginal Title Litigation: An Analysis of *Delgamuukw*" (1993-94) 19 Queen's L.J. 503.

Asch, Michael, and Patrick Macklem. "Aboriginal Rights and Canadian Sovereignty: An Essay on *R. v. Sparrow*" (1991) 12, 2 Alta. L. Rev. 498.

Australian Government. *Australia in the Asian Century*. Canberra: Department of the Prime Minister and Cabinet, 2012.

–. *Protecting Australia against Terrorism 2006*. Canberra: Department of the Prime Minister and Cabinet, 2006.

Bankes, Nigel. "*Delgamuukw*, Division of Powers and Provincial Land and Resource Laws: Some Implications for Provincial Resource Rights" (1998) 32, 2 UBC L. Rev. 317.

Barak, Aharon. "The Judge as Geokrat and Maximalist" (2013) Global Brief 26.

Baud, Jacques. *La Guerre asymétrique*. Paris: Éditions du Rocher, 2003.

Beaudoin, Gérald-A. *La Constitution du Canada: Institutions, partage des pouvoirs, Charte canadienne des droits et libertés*. Montréal: Wilson and Lafleur, 2004.

Binnie, W.I.C. "The *Sparrow* Doctrine: Beginning of the End or End of the Beginning?" (1990) 14 Queen's L.J. 217.

Blackshield, Tony, and George Williams. *Australian Constitutional Law: Law and Theory*. Sydney: Federation Press, 2002.

Blackstone, Sir William. *Commentaries on the Laws of England*. Oxford: Clarendon Press, 1765-69. http://www.lonang.com/exlibris/blackstone/bla-107.htm.

Bobbitt, Philip. *The Shield of Achilles: War, Peace and the Course of History*. New York: Anchor Books, 2002.
Borrows, John. "Constitutional Law from a First Nations Perspective: Self-Government" (1994) 29 UBC L. Rev. 1.
–. "A Genealogy of Law: Inherent Sovereignty and First Nations Self-Government" (1992) 20 Osgoode Hall L.J. 291.
–. "Sovereignty's Alchemy: An Analysis of *Delgamuukw v. British Columbia*" (1999) 37, 3 Osgoode Hall L.J. 537.
Bowker, Andrea. "*Sparrow's* Promise: Aboriginal Rights in the BC Court of Appeal" (1995) 53, 1 U.T. Fac. L. Rev. 1.
Brooks, Stephen. *Public Policy in Canada: An Introduction*. 2d ed. Toronto: McClelland and Stewart, 2003.
Brun, Henri, et Guy Tremblay. *Droit constitutionnel*. 4e éd. Québec: Éditions Yvon Blais, 2002.
Bull, Hedley. *The Anarchical Society: A Study of Order in World Politics*. New York: Columbia University Press, 1977.
Byers, Michael. "Pax Arctica" (Winter 2010) Global Brief 50.
–. *Who Owns the Arctic? Understanding Sovereignty Disputes in the North*. Vancouver: Douglas and McIntyre, 2009.
Canada. *Canada's Cyber Security Strategy*. Ottawa: Department of Public Works and Government Services, 2010.
–. *Canada's Northern Strategy*. Ottawa: Department of Public Works and Government Services, 2009.
–. *Independent Panel on Canada's Future Role in Afghanistan*. Ottawa: Department of Public Works and Government Services, 2008.
–. *Securing an Open Society: Canada's National Security Policy*. Ottawa: Privy Council Office, 2004.
–. Statement of Policy Priorities in Afghanistan, 2009. http://www.afghanistan.gc.ca/canada-afghanistan/priorities-priorites/index.aspx?lang=eng.
–. "2010 Budget, Leading the Way on Jobs and Growth." Ottawa: Department of Public Works and Government Services, 2010.
Choudhry, Sujit. "So What Is the Real Legacy of Oakes? Two Decades of Proportionality Analysis under the Canadian *Charter*'s Section 1" (2006) 34 Sup. Ct. L. Rev. 501.
Clausewitz, Carl von. *Vom Kriege*. Berlin: Die Deutsche Bibliothek, 2010.
Coates, Ken, et al. *Arctic Front: Defending Canada in the Far North*. Toronto: Thomas Allen, 2008.
Commission of Inquiry Concerning Certain Activities of the Royal Canadian Mounted Police. *Freedom and Security under the Law*. Second Report, vol. 1. Ottawa: Department of Supply and Services, 1981.
Commission of Inquiry into the Actions of Canadian Officials in Relation to Maher Arar. *A New Review Mechanism for the RCMP's National Security Activities*. Ottawa: Department of Public Works and Government Services, 2006.

Competition Policy Review Panel. *Compete to Win – Final Report*. Ottawa: Public Works and Government Services Canada, 2008.

Conservative Party of Canada. *The True North Strong and Free: Stephen Harper's Plan for Canadians*. Ottawa: Conservative Party of Canada, 2008.

Courchene, Thomas. "Federalism and the New Economic Order: A Citizen and Process Perspective." Montreal: Institute for Research on Public Policy, 2002.

Coutau-Bégarie, Hervé. *Traité de stratégie*. Paris: Economica, 2002.

Department of Justice Canada. *The Constitution Acts, 1867 to 1982*. Ottawa: Department of Public Works and Services, 2001.

Dye, Thomas R. *Understanding Public Policy*. 3d ed. Englewood Cliffs, NJ: Prentice-Hall, 1978.

Emmerson, Charles. *The Future History of the Arctic*. London: Random House, 2010.

–. "Pax Arctica. Not Quite" (March 11, 2010) Global Brief. http://globalbrief.ca/blog/2010/03/11/pax-arctica-not-quite/.

Émond, André. "Partenaire des peuples autochtones du Canada: Les différents visages de la Couronne" (1997-98) 29 Ottawa L. Rev. 63.

Fairley, H. Scott. *Canada, External Affairs and the Constitution: A Theory of Judicial Review*. SJD diss., Harvard Law School, 1987 [unpublished].

–. "External Affairs in the Constitution of Canada" (1987) 16 Can. Council Int. L. 220.

Favoreau, Louis, et al. *Droit constitutionnel (de la France)*. Paris: Dalloz, 2008.

Ferguson, Niall. *The Cash Nexus: Money and Power in the Modern World, 1700-2000*. New York: Basic Books, 2001.

Fisher, Louis. *Presidential War Power*. Lawrence: University Press of Kansas, 1995.

Fogarassy, Tony, and KayLynn Litton. "Consultation with Aboriginal Peoples: Impacts on the Petroleum Industry" (2004-5) 41 Alta. L. Rev. 41.

Forcese, Craig. *National Security Law*. Toronto: Irwin Law, 2008.

Franck, Thomas. *Political Questions/Judicial Answers*. Princeton: Princeton University Press, 1992.

Galbraith, John Kenneth. *The New Industrial State*. Boston: Houghton Mifflin, 1967.

Galloway, Donald. *Immigration Law*. Toronto: Irwin Law, 1997.

Geist, Michael. *Internet Law in Canada*. 3d ed. Toronto: Captus Press, 2002.

Glennon, Michael. *Constitutional Diplomacy*. Princeton: Princeton University Press, 1990.

Grammond, Sébastian. "La protection constitutionelle des droits ancestraux des peuples autochtones et l'arrêt *Sparrow*" (1990-91) 36 McGill L.J. 1382.

Granatstein, Jack. *Canada's Army: Waging War and Keeping the Peace*. Toronto: University of Toronto Press, 2002.

Grant, Shelagh. *Polar Imperative: A History of Arctic Sovereignty in North America*. Vancouver: Douglas and McIntyre, 2010.

Gray, Colin S. *Modern Strategy*. New York: Oxford University Press, 1999.
Griffiths, Franklyn. "Towards a Canadian Arctic Strategy." Toronto: Canadian International Council Working Paper, 2009.
Gross, Oren, and Fionnuala Ni Aolain. *Law in Times of Crisis: Emergency Powers in Theory and Practice*. Cambridge, UK: Cambridge University Press, 2006.
Gwyn, Richard. *John A., the Man Who Made Us – Volume 1*. Toronto: Random House, 2007.
Hamilton, Alexander. "Federalist No. 70." In *The Federalist Papers*, 426. New York: Bantam Dell, 1982.
Hamon, Francis, and Michel Troper. *Droit constitutionnel (de la France)*. Paris: LGDJ, 2007.
Hart, John Ely. *War and Responsibility: Constitutional Lessons of Vietnam and Its Aftermath*. Princeton: Princeton University Press, 1993.
Henderson, Deborah J. "Meeting the National [Australian] Interest through Asia Literacy: An Overview of the Major Stages and Debates" (2003) 27, 1 Asian Studies Review 23.
Henkin, Louis. *Foreign Affairs and the United States Constitution*. 2d ed. Oxford: Oxford University Press, 1996.
Hogg, Peter W. *Constitutional Law of Canada*. 4th ed. (looseleaf). Toronto: Carswell, 1997.
–. *Constitutional Law of Canada*. 5th ed. (looseleaf). Toronto: Carswell, 2007.
–. *Constitutional Law of Canada*. Student ed. Scarborough: Carswell, 2007.
–. "Jurisdiction over Telecommunications: *Alberta Government Telephones v. CRTC*" (1990) 35 McGill L.J. 480.
–, and Patrick Monahan. *Liability of the Crown*. 4th ed. Toronto: Carswell, 2011.
Howell, Robert. *Canadian Telecommunications Law*. Toronto: Irwin Law, 2011.
Howse, Robert. "The *Labour Conventions* Doctrine in an Era of Global Interdependence: Rethinking the Constitutional Dimensions of Canada's External Economic Relations" (1990) 16 Can. Bus. L.J. 171.
Huebert, Rob. "Canadian Arctic Sovereignty and Security in a Transforming Circumpolar World." Toronto: Canadian International Council Working Paper, 2009.
Hufbauer, Gary Clyde, et al. *Economic Sanctions Reconsidered: History and Current Policy*. 2d ed. Washington, DC: Institute of International Economics, 1990.
Hurley, James Ross. *La modification de la Constitution du Canada*. Ottawa: Privy Council Office, 1996.
Huyer, Timothy. "Honour of the Crown: The New Approach to Crown-Aboriginal Reconciliation" (2006) 21 Windsor Rev. Legal Soc. Issues 33.
Isaac, Thomas. *Aboriginal Law: Commentary, Cases and Materials*. Saskatoon: Purich, 2004.
Janisch, H.N., and R.J. Schultz. "Federalism's Turn: Telecommunications and Canadian Global Competitiveness" (1991) 18 Can. Bus. L.J. 161.

Jenkins, David. "The Lockean Constitution: Separation of Powers and the Limits of the Prerogative" (2011) 56 McGill L.J. 543.

Jenkins, Tom, et al. *Canada First: Leveraging Defence Procurement through Key Industrial Capabilities*. Ottawa: Department of Public Works and Government Services, 2013.

Joint Chiefs of Staff. *D.O.D. Dictionary of Military and Associated Terms*. JCS Joint Pub 1-02. Washington, DC: GPO, 23 March 1994.

Kirton, John. *Canadian Foreign Policy in a Changing World*. Toronto: Nelson, 2007.

–. "The 10 Most Important Books on Canadian Foreign Policy" (2009) 64, 2 International Journal 553.

Kissinger, Henry. *Does America Need a Foreign Policy? Toward a Diplomacy for the 21st Century*. New York: Simon and Schuster, 2001.

Koh, Harold. *The National Security Constitution: Sharing Power after the Iran-Contra Affair*. New Haven: Yale University Press, 1990.

La Forest, G.V. "The *Labour Conventions* Case Revisited" (1974) 12 Can. Y.B. Int'l L. 137.

–. *Natural Resources and Public Property under the Constitution*. Toronto: University of Toronto Press, 1969.

Lackenbauer, P. Whitney. "From Polar Race to Polar Sage: An Integrated Strategy for Canada and the Circumpolar World." Toronto: Canadian International Council Working Paper, 2009.

Lafontaine, Alain. "La coexistence de l'obligation de fiduciaire de la Couronne et du droit à l'autonomie gouvernementale des peuples autochtones" (1995) 36, 1 Les cahiers de droit 669.

Lagassé, Philippe. "Parliamentary and Judicial Ambivalence toward Executive Prerogative Powers in Canada" (2012) 55, 2 Canadian Public Administration 157.

Lajoie, Andrée. *Le pouvoir déclaratoire du Parlement: Augmentation discrétionnaire de la competence fédérale du Canada*. Montréal: Les Presses de l'Université de Montréal, 1969.

Laskin, Bora. *Canadian Constitutional Law*. 4th ed. Toronto: Carswell, 1975.

Lederman, W.R. "Telecommunications and the Federal Constitution of Canada." In H.E. English, ed., *Telecommunications for Canada: An Interface of Business and Government*, 339. Toronto: Methuen, 1973.

Lefebvre, Stéphane. "Canada's Legal Framework for Intelligence" (2010) 23, 2 Journal of Intelligence and Counterintelligence 247.

Macdonald, R. St. J. "International Treaty Law and the Domestic Law of Canada" (1975) 2 Dalhousie L.J. 307.

MacKay, R.A., and E.B. Rogers. *Canada Looks Abroad*. Toronto: Oxford University Press, 1938.

Macklem, Patrick. "Aboriginal Rights and State Obligations" (1997-98) 36, 1 Alta. L. Rev. 97.

Mallory, J.R. "Beyond 'Manner and Form': Reading between the Lines in *Operation Dismantle Inc. v. R.*" (1985) 31 McGill L.J. 480.
Mann, F.A. *Foreign Affairs in English Courts.* Oxford: Clarendon Press, 1986.
McBride, Stephen. "Quiet Constitutionalism in Canada: The International Political Economy of Domestic Institutional Change" (2003) 36, 2 Cdn J. Pol. Sci. 251.
McNeil, Kent. "Aboriginal Title and the Division of Powers: Rethinking Federal and Provincial Jurisdiction" (1998) 61 Sask. L. Rev. 431.
–. "Envisaging Constitutional Space for Aboriginal Governments" (1993-94) 19 Queen's L.J. 95.
McTaggart, Craig. "A Layered Approach to Internet Legal Analysis" (2003) 48 McGill L.J. 571.
Mearsheimer, John J. *The Tragedy of Great Power Politics.* New York: W.W. Norton, 2003.
Meekison, J. Peter, and Roy J. Romanow. "Western Advocacy and Section 92A of the Constitution." In J. Peter Meekison, Roy J. Romanow, and William D. Moull, eds., *Origins and Meaning of Section 92A*, 18. Montreal: Institute for Research on Public Policy, 1985.
Mgbeoji, Ikechi. "Prophylactic Use of Force in International Law: The Illegitimacy of Canada's Participation in 'Coalitions of the Willing' without United Nations Authorization and Parliamentary Sanction" (2003) 8, 2 Rev. Const. Stud. 170.
Monahan, Patrick. "Constitutional Jurisdiction over Transportation: Recent Developments and Proposals for Change." In Canada, *Royal Commission on National Passenger Transportation*, vol. 3, 791. Ottawa: Royal Commission on National Passenger Transportation, 1992.
–. *Constitutional Law.* 3d ed. Toronto: Irwin Law, 2006.
Morabito, Marcel. *Histoire constitutionnelle de la France (1789-1958).* Paris: Montchrestien, 2008.
Morgan, Ed. "It's a Legal Maze for Canadian Authorities Abroad." *Globe and Mail*, 28 May 2009, A19.
Morgan, Michael Cotey. "Between War and Peace" (May 2009) Global Brief 42.
Morgenthau, Hans J. *Politics among Nations: The Struggle for Power and Peace.* Boston: McGraw-Hill, 1993.
Nye, Joseph Jr. *The Paradox of American Power: Why the World's Only Superpower Can't Go It Alone.* Oxford: Oxford University Press, 2002.
–. *Soft Power: The Means to Success in World Politics.* New York: Perseus, 2004.
Pollard, David, et al. *(British) Constitutional and Administrative Law.* London: Oxford University Press, 2007.
Rémillard, Gil. *Le Fédéralisme canadien – Tome I: La Loi constitutionnelle de 1867.* Montréal: Québec/Amérique, 1983.
Rotman, Leonard I. "Defining Parameters: Aboriginal Rights, Treaty Rights, and the *Sparrow* Justificatory Test" (1997) 36 Alta. L. Rev. 149.

–. "Taking Aim at the Canons of Treaty Interpretation in Canadian Aboriginal Rights Jurisprudence" (1997) 46 U.N.B. L.J. 11.

Rudd, Kevin. *Asian Languages and Australia's Economic Future: A Report Prepared for the Council of Australian Governments on a Proposed National Asian Languages/ Studies Strategy for Australian Schools* [the Rudd Report]. Brisbane: Queensland Government Printer, 2004.

Russian Academy of Sciences – Economic Institute. *Strategicheskiy otvet Rossiyi na vysovy novovo veka* (Russia's Strategic Response to the Challenges of the New Century). Moscow: Examen, 2004.

Sanderson, Douglas. "Toward an Aboriginal Grand Strategy" (Spring-Summer 2013) Global Brief 12.

Scott, F.R. "Expanding Concepts of Human Rights." In *Essays on the Constitution*, 358. Toronto: University of Toronto Press, 1977.

–. "Labour Conventions Case: Lord Wright's Undisclosed Dissent?" (1956) 34 Can. Bar Rev. 114.

Simmons, Alan, Dwaine Plaza, and Victor Piché. "The Remittance Sending Practices of Haitians and Jamaicans in Canada." Report to CIDA, 2005.

Slattery, Brian. "The Hidden Constitution: Aboriginal Rights in Canada" (1984) 32 Am. J. Comp. L. 361.

–. "Some Thoughts on Aboriginal Title" (1999) 48 U.N.B. L.J. 19.

Sossin, Lorne. "The Duty to Consult and Accommodate: Procedural Justice as Aboriginal Rights" (2010) 23 Can. J. Admin. L. & Prac. 93.

–. "The Rule of Law and the Justiciability of Prerogative Powers: A Comment on *Black v. Chrétien*" (2002) 47 McGill L.J. 435.

Speech by the Prime Minister in the United Kingdom, 14 July 2007. http://www.ctv.ca/servlet/ArticleNews/story/CTVNews/20060715/g8_harper_060715?s_name=&no_ads=.

Speech by the Prime Minister of Canada in Santiago, Chile, 17 July 2007. http://www.pm.gc.ca/eng/media.asp?category=2&id=1759.

Statement by the Prime Minister of Canada on Foreign Investment, 7 December 2012. http://www.pm.gc.ca/eng/media.asp?id=5195.

Stein, Janice Gross, and Eugene Lang. *The Unexpected War: Canada in Afghanistan*. Toronto: Viking, 2007.

Strom, Torsten H., and Peter Finkle. "Treaty Implementation: The Canadian Game Needs Australian Rules" (1993) 25 Ottawa L. Rev. 39.

Studin, Irvin. "Australia Shows the West How to Pivot to Asia." *Financial Times*, 7 January 2013, 9.

–. "Australian Federalism's Asia Paradox" (2013) 5, 2 Asian Journal of Public Affairs 49.

–. "Canada: Population 100 Million" (Spring-Summer 2010) Global Brief 10.

–. "Canada's Four-Point Game" (Spring-Summer 2012) Global Brief 20.

—. "A Canadian Languages Strategy for the New Century: Foreign Policy, National Unity and the Aboriginal Question" (2011) 32, 5 Policy Options 72.
—. "Canadian Leadership in the Americas – in Constitutional Terms" (2012) 30, 1 N.J.C.L. 1.
—. "Changing Luck and North American Wars" (Spring-Summer 2011) Global Brief 20.
—. "Constitution and Strategy: Understanding Canadian Power in the World" (2010) 28, 1 N.J.C.L. 1.
—. "Constitutional Statics, International Law, and Canada's Arctic Game" (forthcoming 2014).
—. "Engaging Obama: Canadian Ends, American Means" (2009) 30, 2 Policy Options 26.
—. "Governing in the Ex-Soviet Space" (Fall 2013) Global Brief 12.
—. "The Melting of the Polar Ice Signals the End of the 'Pax Arctica.'" *Financial Times*, 29 August 2012, 9.
—. "Process before Product: A New Federal-Provincial Logic for a New Century" (2008) 29, 8 Policy Options 43.
—. "Revisiting the Democratic Deficit: The Case for Political Party Think Tanks" (2008) 29, 2 Policy Options 62.
—. "The Strategic Constitution in Action: Canada's Afghan War as a Case Study" (2012) 13 German L.J. 419.
—. "Strategy and the Crown Prerogative: Considerations for Justiciability and Judicial Culture" (2013) 7, 1 Journal of Parliamentary and Political Law 63.
—. "When Canada Becomes the West's Second State" (Fall 2013) Global Brief 50.
Sullivan, Kathleen M., and Gerald Gunther. *[American] Constitutional Law*. New York: Foundation Press, 2007.
Sullivan, R.E. "Jurisdiction to Negotiate and Implement Free Trade Agreements in Canada" (1987) 24, 2 U.W.O. L. Rev. 63.
Trebilcock, Michael J. "The Supreme Court and Strengthening the Conditions for Effective Competition in the Canadian Economy" (2001) 80 Can. Bar Rev. 542.
Trudeau, Pierre Elliott. *Federalism and the French Canadians*. Toronto: Macmillan, 1968.
Underwood, Jay. *Built for War: Canada's Intercolonial Railway*. Ottawa: Railfare, 2005.
U.S. Geological Survey Arctic Oil and Gas Report (July 2008). http://geology.com/usgs/arctic-oil-and-gas-report.shtml.
Wildhaber, L. *Treaty-Making Power and Constitution: An International and Comparative Study*. Basel: Helbing and Lichtenhahn, 1971.
Yoo, John. *The Powers of War and Peace: The Constitution and Foreign Affairs after 9/11*. Chicago: University of Chicago Press, 2005.

Legal Cases

Abassi v. Secretary of State for Foreign and Commonwealth Affairs, [2002] All E.R. 70.
Abdelrazik v. Canada, 2009 F.C. 580.
A.G. Can. v. A.G. Ont. et al., [1937] 1 D.L.R. 673.
Alberta Government Telephones v. CRTC, [1989] 2 S.C.R. 225.
Aleksic v. Canada (2002), 215 D.L.R. (4th) 720.
Al-Skeini et al. v. Secretary of State for Defence, [2007] UKHL 26.
Amnesty International v. Canada, 2008 F.C. 336.
Amnesty International v. Canada, [2008] F.C.J. No. 1700.
Amnesty International v. Canada, [2009] S.C.C.A. No. 63.
Atwal v. Canada, [1988] 1 F.C. 107.
Bell ExpressVu Limited Partnership v. Rex et al. (2002), 212 D.L.R. (4th) 1.
B.C. Offshore Reference, [1967] S.C.R. 792.
Black v. Chrétien (2000), 47 O.R. (3d) 532.
British Columbia v. Lafarge Canada Inc., [2007] S.C.J. No. 23.
Burmah Oil Co. v. Lord Advocate, [1965] A.C. 75.
Calder v. British Columbia, [1973] S.C.R. 313.
Canada v. Almalki, 2010 F.C. 1106.
Canada v. Khadr, [2008] S.C.J. No. 28.
Canada v. Khadr, [2010] S.C.J. No. 3.
Canada v. Khawaja, [2007] F.C.J. No. 622.
Canada v. Khawaja, 2007 F.C.A. 342.
Canada v. Khawaja, 2007 F.C.A. 388.
Canada v. Ribic, [2005] 1 F.C.R. 33.
Canadian Egg Marketing Agency v. Richardson, [1998] 3 S.C.R. 157.
Capital Cities Communications v. CRTC, [1978] 2 S.C.R. 141.
Chandler v. Director of Public Prosecutions, [1964] 1 A.C. 763.
Charkaoui v. Canada, [2007] S.C.J. No. 9.
Charkaoui v. Canada, 2008 S.C.C. 38.
Chief Mountain v. Canada, 2013 B.C.C.A. 49.
China Navigation Co. Ltd. v. Attorney-General (1932), 2 K.B. 197.
Citizens' Insurance v. Parsons, [1881] 7 A.C. 96.
Commonwealth v. Tasmania (1983), 158 C.L.R. 1.
Consolidated Fastfrate Inc. v. Western Canada Council of Teamsters et al., 2009 S.C.C. 53.
Co-Operative Committee on Japanese-Canadians v. Canada, [1947] A.C. 87.
Council of Civil Service Unions v. Minister for Civil Service, [1985] 1 A.C. 374.
Croft v. Dunphy, [1933] A.C. 156.
Dehghani v. Canada, [1993] 1 S.C.R. 1053.
Delgamuukw v. British Columbia, [1997] 3 S.C.R. 1010.

Dunbar v. Attorney-General Saskatchewan (1984), 11 D.L.R. (4th) 374.
Edwards Books & Art Ltd. v. R., [1986] 2 S.C.R. 713.
Exemption Order for New Media Broadcasting Undertakings, Public Notice CRTC 1999-197.
Fort Frances Pulp and Paper Co. v. Manitoba Free Press Co., [1923] A.C. 695.
General Motors of Canada Ltd. v. City National Leasing, [1989] 1 S.C.R. 641.
Globalive Wireless Management Corp. v. Public Mobile Inc., 2011 F.C.A. 194.
Haida Nation v. British Columbia, [2004] 3 S.C.R. 511.
Hamdan v. Rumsfeld, 126 S. Ct. 2749 (2006).
Harkat v. Canada, 2012 F.C.A. 122.
Henrie v. Canada, [1989] 2 F.C. 229.
Human Rights Institute of Canada v. Canada, [2000] 1 F.C. 475.
Hunter v. Southam, [1984] 2 S.C.R. 145.
Johannesson v. West St. Paul, [1952] 1 S.C.R. 292.
Jorgenson v. Canada, [1971] S.C.R. 725.
Keewatin v. Ontario, 2013 ONCA 158.
Khadr v. Canada, 2009 F.C.A. 246.
Khadr v. Canada, [2009] F.C.J. 462.
Khadr v. Canada, 2010 F.C. 715.
Koowarta v. Bjelke-Petersen (1982), 153 C.L.R. 168.
Liquidators of the Maritime Bank v. Receiver General of New Brunswick, [1892] A.C. 437.
L'Union St. Jacques de Montréal v. Bélisle (1874), 6 P.C. 31.
Mikisew Cree First Nation v. Canada, 2005 S.C.C. 69.
Missouri v. Holland, 252 U.S. 416 (1920).
Mitchell v. Canada, 2001 S.C.C. 33.
Mount Sinaï Hospital Center v. Quebec, [2001] S.C.J. No. 43.
Mowat v. Casgrain (1897), 6 Que. Q.B. 12.
New Brunswick Broadcasting Co. v. Nova Scotia (Speaker of the House of Assembly), [1993] 1 S.C.R. 319.
Nunavut Tunngavik Inc. v. Canada, 2009 NUCA.
O'Neill v. Canada (2006), 82 O.R. (3d) 241.
Ontario Hydro v. Ontario, [1993] 3 S.C.R. 327.
Ontario Mining Company v. Seybold, [1903] A.C. 73.
Operation Dismantle Inc. v. R., [1985] 1 S.C.R. 441.
Public Mobile Inc. v. Canada, 2011 F.C. 130.
Public Service Board v. Dionne, [1978], 2 S.C.R. 191.
Quebec v. Canada, [1979] 1 S.C.R. 218.
Radio Reference, [1932] A.C. 304.
Rasul v. Bush, 542 U.S. 466 (2004).
Re CFRB, [1973] 3 O.R. 819 (C.A.).
Re CSIS Act, [2007] F.C.J. No. 1780.

Re CSIS Act, 2009 F.C. 1058.
Re Gray (1918), 57 S.C.R. 150.
Re Manitoba Language Rights, [1985] 1 S.C.R. 721.
Re Resolution to Amend the Constitution, [1981] 1 S.C.R. 753.
Reference re Agricultural Products Marketing Act, [1978] 2 S.C.R. 1198.
Reference re Alberta Legislation, [1938] S.C.J. No. 2.
Reference re Anti-Inflation Act, 1975, [1976] 2 S.C.R. 373.
Reference re Employment and Social Insurance Act, [1936] S.C.R. 427.
Reference re Employment and Social Insurance Act, [1937] A.C. 355.
Reference re Securities Act, 2011 S.C.C. 66.
Reference re Validity of Section 5(a) of Dairy Industry Act (Canada), [1949] S.C.R. 1.
Reference re Waters and Water-Powers, [1929] S.C.R. 200.
R. v. Adams, [1996] 3 S.C.R. 101.
R. v. Badger, [1996] 1 S.C.R. 771.
R. v. Cook, [1998] 2 S.C.R. 957.
R. v. Côté, [1996] 3 S.C.R. 139.
R. v. Crown Zellerbach Canada Ltd., [1988] 1. S.C.R. 401.
R. v. Duarte, [1990] 1 S.C.R. 30.
R. v. Gladstone, [1996] 2 S.C.R. 723.
R. v. Hape (2007), 280 D.L.R. (4th) 385.
R. v. Khawaja, [2006] O.J. No. 4245.
R. v. Khawaja, 2010 ONCA 862.
R. v. Khawaja, 2012 S.C.C. 69.
R. v. McNeil, [2009] 1 S.C.R. 66.
R. v. National Post, 2010 S.C.C. 16.
R. v. Oakes, [1986] 1 S.C.R. 103.
R. v. O'Connor, [1995] 4 S.C.R. 411.
R. v. Pamajewon, [1996] 2 S.C.R. 821.
R. v. Secretary of State for Foreign and Commonwealth Affairs, ex parte Everett, [1989] 1 All E.R. 655.
R. v. Sparrow, [1990] S.C.J. No. 49.
R. v. Stinchcombe, [1991] 3 S.C.R. 326.
R. v. Van der Peet, [1996] 2 S.C.R. 507.
Review of Globalive Wireless Management Corp. under the Canadian Ownership and Control Regime, CRTC Telecom Decision 2009-678.
Smith v. Canada, [2009] F.C.J. No. 234.
St. Catherine's Milling and Lumber Co. v. The Queen (1888), 14 A.C. 46.
Suresh v. Canada, [2002] 1 S.C.R. 3.
Taku River Tlingit First Nation v. British Columbia, [2004] 3 S.C.R. 550.
Téléphone Guèvremont v. Quebec, [1994] 1 S.C.R. 878.
Toronto v. Bell Telephone Co., [1905] A.C. 52.
Turp v. Canada, 2012 F.C. 893.

United States v. Texas (1950), 399 U.S. 707.
United States Steel Corporation v. Canada, 2011 F.C.A. 176.
USA Foundation v. United States, 242 F.3d 1300 (11th Cir. 2001).
William v. British Columbia, 2012 B.C.C.A. 285.
Winterhaven Stables Ltd. v. Attorney General Canada (1986), A.J. No. 460.
Youngstown Sheet & Tube Co. v. Sawyer, 343 U.S. 579.
Zarzour v. Canada (2000), 268 N.R. 235.

Government Statutes
Aeronautics Act, R.S.C. 1985, c. A-2.
Anti-Terrorism Act, S.C. 2001, c. 41.
Atomic Energy Control Act, R.S.C. 1970, c. A-19.
Bank of Canada Act, R.S.C. 1985, c. B-2.
Bill C-3, *An Act to Amend the Immigration and Refugee Protection Act and to Make a Consequential Amendment to Another Act*, 2d Sess., 39th Parl., 2007.
Bill C-15, *An Act to Replace the Northwest Territories Act to Implement Certain Provisions of the Northwest Territories Lands and Resources Devolution Agreement and to Repeal or Make Amendments to the Territorial Lands Act, the Northwest Territories Waters Act, the Mackenzie Valley Resource Management Act, Other Acts and Certain Orders and Regulations*, 2d Sess., 41st Parl., 2013.
Bill C-17, *An Act to Amend the Criminal Code (Investigative Hearings and Recognizance with Conditions)*, 3d Sess., 40th Parl., 2010.
Bill C-19, *An Act to Amend the Criminal Code (Investigative Hearings and Recognizance with Conditions)*, 2d Sess., 40th Parl., 2009.
Bill C-60, *An Act to Implement Certain Provisions of the Budget Tabled in Parliament on March 21, 2013 and Other Measures*, 1st Sess., 41st Parl., 2013.
Bill S-3, *An Act to Amend the Criminal Code (Investigative Hearings and Recognizance with Conditions)*, 2d Sess., 39th Parl., 2007.
Bill S-7, *An Act to Amend the Criminal Code, the Canada Evidence Act and the Security of Information Act*, 1st Sess., 41st Parl., 2013.
Broadcasting Act, S.C. 1991, c. 11.
Canada Elections Act, S.C. 2000, c. 9.
Canada Evidence Act, R.S.C. 1985, c. C-5.
Canada-Newfoundland Atlantic Accord Implementation Act, S.C. 1987, c. 3.
Canada Transportation Act, S.C. 1996, c. 10.
Canadian Radio-television and Telecommunications Commission Act, R.S.C. 1985, c. C-22.
Canadian Railway Act, R.S.C. 1906, c. 37.
Canadian Security Intelligence Service Act, R.S.C. 1985, c. C-23.
Citizenship Act, R.S.C. 1985, c. C-29.
Commonwealth of Australia Constitution Act, 1900, 63 & 64 Vict.
Constitution Act, 1867 (U.K.), 30 & 31 Vict., c. 3.

Bibliography 247

Constitution Act, 1871 (U.K.), 34 & 35 Vict., c. 28.
Constitution Act, 1930 (U.K.), 20 & 21 Geo. V, c. 26.
Constitution Act, 1982, enacted as Schedule B to the *Canada Act, 1982* (U.K.), 1982, c. 11.
Contempt of Court Act, 1981 (U.K.), c. 49.
Criminal Code, R.S.C. 1985, c. C-46.
Crown Liability and Proceedings Act, R.S.C. 1985, c. C-50.
Defence Production Act, R.S.C. 1985, c. D-1.
Department of Foreign Affairs and International Trade Act, R.S.C. 1985, c. E-22.
Department of Citizenship and Immigration Act, S.C. 94, c. 31.
Emergencies Act, R.S.C. 1985, c. 22 (4th Supp.).
Emergency Management Act, S.C. 2007, c. 15.
Energy Supplies Emergency Act, R.S.C. 1985, c. E-9.
Export and Import Permits Act, R.S.C. 1985, c. E-19.
Expropriation Act, R.S.C. 1985, c. E-21.
Foreign Investment Review Act, S.C. 1973-74, c. 46.
Human Rights Act, 1998 (U.K.), c. 42.
Hupacasath v. Canada, 2013 FC 900.
Immigration and Refugee Protection Act, S.C. 2001, c. 27.
Indian Act, R.S.C. 1985, c. I-5.
Intelligence Services Act 2001 (Cth).
Investment Canada Act, R.S.C. 1985, c. 28 (1st Supp.).
Kyoto Protocol Implementation Act, S.C. 2007, c. 30. [Repealed, 2012, c. 19, s. 699].
Letters Patent Constituting the Office of the Governor-General of Canada, 1947, R.S.C. 1985, Appendix II, No. 31, Art. II.
National Defence Act, R.S.C. 1985, c. N-5.
National Energy Board Act, R.S.C. 1985, c. N-7.
Nunavut Act, S.C. 1993, c. 28.
Official Development Assistance Accountability Act, S.C. 2008, c. 17.
Personal Information Protection and Electronic Documents Act, S.C. 2000, c. 5.
Privacy Act, R.S.C. 1985, c. P-21.
Quebec Act, 1774 (U.K.), R.S.C. 1985, Appendix II, No. 2.
Radiocommunication Act, R.S.C. 1985, c. R-2.
Royal Canadian Mounted Police Act, R.S.C. 1985, c. R-10.
The Royal Proclamation, 1763 (U.K.), R.S.C. 1985, Appendix II, No. 1.
Security of Information Act, R.S.C. 1985, c. O-5.
Special Economic Measures Act, S.C. 1992, c. 17.
Statute of Westminster, 22 & 23 Geo. V, c. 4.
Telecommunications Act, S.C. 1993, c. 38.
Territorial Lands Act, R.S.C. 1985, c. T-7.
United Nations Act, R.S.C. 1985, c. U-2.
War Measures Act, S.C. 1914 (2d sess.), c. 2.

Indexes

.... Subject Index ....

Aboriginal peoples: duty to consult with (consultation duty), 27, 182n35, 199n18; fiduciary duty of Crown regarding, 25-28, 174, 182n35, 199n18; honour of the Crown to consult with, 27, 174, 182n35, 198-99n12, 199n18; infringement of rights of, 25-28, 57, 127, 174, 181n31, 182n32, 182n35, 183n37, 191n25; and natural resources (*see* Natural resources); reserves, 180n21, 187n23, 226n23; rights of, 8, 19n(a), 24-28, 104, 174, 181-82nn31-32, 182n35, 183n37, 196n1; treaties, 15, 19n(a), 25, 57, 122, 160, 191n25, 199n12, 199n18, 200n23

Administrative law, 25, 130, 155, 172, 187n25, 229n15

Aeronautics, 53, 79, 117, 146, 159, 195n33

Aid of the civil power/military call-out, 43-44, 48, 131, 140, 166. *See also* Emergencies; Militia (and defence) power

Afghanistan (war in), 8, 42, 105, 120, 124, 127-28, 191, 219n2, 221n14, 222nn16-17. *See also* War

Agriculture. *See* Food

Alberta, 83, 84, 146-47, 197n4, 198n11, 201n2, 206n1, 207n9, 209n26, 238, 243, 245

Amendment (of the Constitution), 15, 18, 21, 179-80n18

Americas/Americas strategy, 8, 105, 109-19, 170, 179n11, 200n33, 212n3, 214n3, 215n9, 215-16n13, 216n15, 216n18, 217nn19-20

Arctic/Arctic sovereignty, 8, 101, 105, 114, 135-49, 174, 178n7, 197-98n7, 223n1, 223n3, 223-24nn3-4, 224nn7-8, 224-25n9, 225n12, 226n22, 226n25, 226nn31-32, 227n35; domain awareness and, 139-40; natural resources of, 136-39, 147-50 (*see also*

Natural resources); population of, 98, 101, 141, 143, 145, 224n5, 225n19, 226n25 (*see also* Population); territorial integrity, 135-50 (*see also* Geography/territory)
Argentina, 118. *See also* Americas/Americas strategy
Australia, 6, 30, 31, 52, 75, 109, 111, 138, 177n11, 183n3, 184n6, 184n9, 196n1, 205n26, 214n2, 215n10, 216n16, 222n17, 230-31n17, 234n33
Bank of Canada, 71, 201n2, 215n9. *See also* Monetary policy
Banks, 71-72, 201n3; central banking (*see* Bank of Canada; Monetary policy)
Barak, Aharon, 188n2
Barnes J., 34
Bastarache J., 63, 199n21
Beaudoin, Gérald-A., 180n19
Beaufort Sea, 138. *See also* Arctic/Arctic sovereignty
Beetz J., 162, 179n11
Binnie J., 27, 84, 90, 187n25
Blackstone, Sir William, 17, 178n10
Blanchard J., 153-54, 185n14
Bobbitt, Philip, 5, 176n6
Borders, 42, 135, 137, 153, 178n6, 196n1, 224-25n9. *See also* Arctic/Arctic sovereignty; Geography/territory
Borrowing (public). *See* Credit
Brazil, 115, 117-18. *See also* Americas/Americas strategy
Bridges, 65, 158-59, 220n11, 232n23
British Columbia, 45, 63, 85, 147, 178n4, 180n20, 181nn23-24, 181n30, 182nn35-36
Broadcasting, 82-83, 85, 91-93, 167, 178n4, 206n3, 208nn22-23, 212n47, 234n33, 243, 244, 246. *See also* Communications

Brun, Henri (and Guy Tremblay), 180n19, 193n16, 201-2n6
Byers, Michael, 136, 223-24n3
Cabinet, 35, 36, 112, 113, 128, 133, 208n23, 214n2, 215n10, 222n17, 230-31n17
Canada-European Union free trade agreement. *See Comprehensive Economic and Trade Agreement (CETA)*
Canada-Quebec Accord (immigration), 97-98, 114, 173, 179n16, 213n7. *See also* Immigration
Canada-United States Trade Agreement (CUSTA), 61. *See also North American Free Trade Agreement (NAFTA)*
Canadian Forces. *See* Militia (and defence) power
Canadian International Development Agency (CIDA), 31-32, 185n11, 216n13, 216n18, 228n12
Canadian Radio-television and Telecommunications Commission (CRTC), 83, 92, 172, 207n9, 207n15, 208n23, 211n46
Caribbean Community (CARICOM), 217n21. *See also* Americas/Americas strategy
Cartier, G.E., 179n17
Chakaoui, Adil, 155-56, 195n32, 229n15, 230n16
Charter of Rights and Freedoms: and Crown prerogative, 33, 36, 39-42, 50, 104, 165, 172, 213n9; s. 1, 18-19, 50, 93, 101, 127, 132, 144, 155, 165, 174, 189n7, 192n1, 193n13, 196n38, 211n41, 213n13; s. 4(2), 19, 50-51, 131-33, 166, 193n14, 222n24, 234n32; s. 6, 19, 50, 74, 98m 100-1, 114, 141, 143-44, 164, 166, 174, 193n14, 213n9, 233n32; s. 7, 19, 33, 39-42, 50, 127, 129, 131, 155-56, 165-66, 185n14,

189n7, 189n11, 192n8, 193n13, 195n32, 210n29, 211n41, 229n15, 230n15; s. 8, 19, 50, 87, 89, 131, 166; s. 9, 19, 50, 131, 155, 166, 195n32; s. 10, 19, 50, 131, 155, 166, 195n32; s. 11, 19, 50, 131, 166; s. 12, 19, 50, 131, 166; s. 13, 19, 50, 131, 166; s. 14, 19, 50, 131, 166; s. 33 (notwithstanding clause), 18-19, 50, 98, 131-32, 166
Civil code/civil law, 23, 100, 179-80n18, 214n3
Clausewitz, Carl von, 175n1, 177n13
Colombia, 217n21. *See also* Americas/Americas strategy
Command(er) in chief, 5
Communications, 8, 16, 19, 32-33, 52-53, 70, 74, 78, 80-93, 103, 114, 117, 122, 124-25, 140, 158, 166-69, 172, 198n7, 206-12nn1-48
Comprehensive Economic and Trade Agreement (CETA), 115
Conservative Party of Canada, 32, 203-4n18
Constitution (definition of), 14-15
Constitution Act, 1867: peace, order and good government (POGG)/general power, 19, 47-48, 51, 53, 60, 65-66, 75, 77, 79, 83, 92, 99, 124, 131, 146, 153, 159-63, 167, 190n15, 195n27, 201n2, 207n15; preamble, ix, x, 3, 6, 17, 19; s. 9, 19; s. 15, 5, 19, 38; s. 91(1A), 19, 63, 65, 71, 85, 95, 111, 124, 211nn20-21, 201n2, 201n5; s. 91(2), 19, 24, 53, 65-66, 71, 74-75, 77, 79, 83-84, 124, 138, 197n1, 203nn15-16, 203n18, 204n18, 205n23, 231n21; s. 91(3), 19, 71, 96, 111, 199n21, 202n6, 216n18; s. 91(7) (*see* Militia (and defence) power); s. 91(11), 19, 47; s. 91(24), 19, 24, 183n37, 191n25, 200n23; s. 91(25), 19, 213n6; s. 91(27), 19; s. 91(29), 19; s. 92A, 19, 21, 23, 58-59, 62, 64-66, 195n27, 198n9, 199n17; s. 92(10)(c) (*see* Declaratory power); s. 92(13) (*see* Property and civil rights); s. 92(16), 19, 193n16, 198n9; s. 93 (*see* Education); s. 94, 179-80n18; s. 95, 19, 21, 96; s. 108, 16, 19, 38, 57, 206n4; s. 109, 19, 45, 57, 202n9; s. 117, 16, 19, 38, 44-45, 54, 57, 79, 122, 125, 159, 191n25, 202n9; s. 121, 19, 74, 76; s. 122, 19; s. 132 (*see* Treaties, International treaties)
Constitution Act, 1982: Charter of Rights and Freedoms (*see* Charter of Rights and Freedoms); s. 35, 19, 24-27, 116, 182n32; s. 52, 15, 176n10, 178n4, 197n4
Counterterrorism. *See* National security
Credit, 71-72, 124, 201n2, 201n5, 202n8
Criminal law, 19, 21, 52-54, 155, 180n18, 182n33, 196n38, 207n7, 229n15, 231n17
Critical infrastructure, 65-66, 70, 93, 125, 140, 151-52, 158-60, 168, 185n15, 200n30, 231n20
Crown liability, 188n4
Crown prerogative. *See* Royal prerogative
Culture, 6, 16, 22, 26, 63, 86, 110, 121, 211n44, 213n15, 214n6, 215n10
Currency, 71, 74, 201n2
Davis Strait, 137. *See also* Arctic/Arctic sovereignty
Declaratory power, 19, 45, 51-52, 62, 64-66, 79, 85, 124-25, 134, 146-47, 159-60, 167, 191n25, 193-94n18, 194n22, 199n12, 199n18, 220n11
Defence power. *See* Militia (and defence) power

Democratic rights (according to the *Charter of Rights and Freedoms*), 50, 131, 166. *See also* Charter of Rights and Freedoms
Demographics. *See* Population
Denmark, 136-38, 148, 223n3, 225n11
Department of Defence, 140, 220n10. *See also* Militia (and defence) power; War
Development (aid/assistance), 30-33, 112-13, 185nn11-12, 216n13, 216n18, 217n18, 228n12
Dickson J., 75, 101, 144
Diplomacy, 5-6, 8, 14-21, 23, 28-37, 41, 45-46, 55-59, 66-67, 70, 73-74, 77-82, 94-95, 103, 110, 112-14, 117-18, 129-30, 134, 139, 145, 148, 157, 169-71, 175n1, 176n7, 176n10, 177n13, 179n11, 183-88nn1-33, 212n3, 214n6, 215n13, 216n15, 221n14, 224n3, 225-26n19
Disallowance, federal power of, 21
Domain awareness. *See* Arctic/Arctic sovereignty
Dominican Republic, 217n21. *See also* Americas/Americas strategy
Duff J., 72
Economy/economics, 4, 8, 16, 19, 21, 26, 28-30, 37, 45, 53, 56-57, 59-60, 64, 66-81, 84, 86, 95-96, 98, 100-1, 103, 109, 113-18, 124-26, 134-36, 142-44, 147, 153, 157-58, 169, 171-72, 175n1, 188nn32-33, 194n22, 194-95n25, 197n6, 198n7, 199n21, 201-6nn1-28
Education, 21, 94-96, 110-12, 115, 120-21, 132, 157, 170-71, 212n3, 214n6, 215nn9-10, 217n20, 218n25. *See also* Languages
Ellesmere Island, 223n3, 225n12. *See also* Arctic/Arctic sovereignty
Emergencies, 6, 21, 44, 46-51, 53, 59-61, 65-66, 68-69, 85, 90-93, 104, 118, 124-26, 131, 134, 140, 149, 151-52, 156-57, 160-68, 172-73, 182n33, 191n23, 192n5, 192nn9-11, 193n13, 195n26, 199nn13-14, 211n42, 211n44, 219n8, 220-21n12, 221n13, 222n23, 223n26, 232nn26-27, 233n30. *See also* Emergency management; Public health emergencies; War
Emergency management, 53, 151-52, 160-68, 195n26. *See also* Emergencies; National security; Public health emergencies
Energy, 21, 28, 51-52, 56, 58-63, 66-67, 78, 122, 147, 149-50, 158, 162, 172, 193n17, 194n19, 198n12, 199n13, 199n14, 200n29, 200n32, 209n26, 220nn11-12, 224n7, 232n26. *See also* Critical infrastructure; Natural resources
Evans J., 190n14
Exclusive Economic Zone (EEZ), 135, 139, 225n18, 226n20
Exports, 56-59, 61, 66-67, 70, 149, 188n33, 193n17, 200nn31-32, 215n10, 218n23, 233n30. *See Constitution Act, 1867*, s. 91(2); Imports
Expropriation, 26, 44, 54, 64-66, 79, 85, 92, 122-25, 134, 146, 159-60, 167, 219n4, 200nn23-24, 200n26
Federalism, school of Canadian constitutional scholarship, 4. *See also Constitution Act, 1867*
Ferguson, Niall, 72, 202n7
Fiduciary duty. *See* Aboriginal peoples
Fiscal policy. *See Constitution Act, 1867*, ss. 91(1A) and 91(3); Economy/economics; Monetary policy
Food, 8, 19, 21, 62, 65-66, 69-70, 78, 103, 116, 125-26, 200n30

Forcese, Craig, 46-47, 190n20, 191n22, 192n2, 193n13, 194n25, 210n29, 210n35
Forts/fortification, 16, 44, 122-23, 191n25
French Guiana, 217n20. *See also* Americas/Americas strategy
Galbraith, John K., 122, 219n9
General advantage of Canada. *See* Declaratory power
General power. *See Constitution Act, 1867*, peace, order and good government (POGG)/general power
Geography/territory, 16, 27, 39-40, 55, 95, 98, 110, 122, 135-36, 139, 145, 153, 173-74, 183n2, 185n15, 190n17, 196n1, 211n38, 212n2, 218n25, 224n5, 225nn9-10
Government Communications Headquarters (UK) (GCHQ), 33
Governor general, 15, 176n10
Grandpré J., 162
Guadeloupe, 214n3, 217n20. *See also* Americas/Americas strategy
Haiti, 120, 214n3, 217n20. *See also* Americas/Americas strategy
Hans Island, 136-38, 140. *See also* Arctic/Arctic sovereignty
Harper, Stephen, 73, 109, 111, 197n2, 204n18, 209n26, 212n3, 214n1
Heeney J., 39
Henkin, Louis, 186n17
Hogg, Peter W., ix, 72, 138, 181n31, 183n3, 190n14, 193n14, 196-97n1, 200n24, 201n6, 202nn10-12, 205n23, 206n28, 207n9, 207n15, 210n33, 225n15, 232n21
Honduras, 217n21. *See also* Americas/Americas strategy
Iacobucci J., 206n3
Immigration, 21, 53, 95-99, 114-15, 141-43, 154-56, 173-74, 179n16, 192n8, 195n32, 195n35, 213n7, 217n20, 227n1, 229n15
Imports, 59, 61, 66-67, 69, 118, 126, 233n30. *See Constitution Act, 1867*, s. 91(2); Exports
Industrial capacity. *See* Economy/economics
Intelligence: Canadian Security Intelligence Service (CSIS), 32, 53, 88-89, 113, 153-54, 157, 163, 185n14, 195n27, 196n38, 210n36, 211n38; Chief of Defence Intelligence (CDI), 32, 154, 219n3, 228n11; Canadian Security Establishment (CSE), 32, 33, 53-54, 83, 88-89, 93, 140, 154, 163, 185-86n15, 206n3, 210n36, 212n48, 216n15, 228n10, 229n15; foreign intelligence, 32, 89, 113, 153-54, 157, 185n14, 210n37, 211n37, 216n15; security certificate, 155-56, 195n32, 229n14, 229-30n15. *See also* National security
International law, 40-41, 116, 118, 136-38, 146, 154, 171, 183n2, 185n14, 190n11, 191n21, 197n1, 210n36, 216n15, 222n21, 223n2, 224n8, 224-25n9
International Monetary Fund (IMF), 218n23
Internet, 80-82, 92-93, 125, 158, 168, 172, 206n7, 208n19, 210n36, 211n45, 212n47, 231n19
Inuit, 25, 223n1. *See also* Arctic/Arctic sovereignty
Investment, 30, 36, 70, 74, 76-78, 85-87, 115-16, 123-24, 133, 150, 171, 200n32, 204n18, 204-5n22, 206n3, 208n24, 209nn25-26, 209-10n28, 217-18n22. *See also* Economy/economics
Iraq, ix, 23, 41, 120, 190n17, 222n21
Justice, 5, 28, 33, 52, 87, 153, 156, 185n14, 189n11

Khadr, Omar, 36, 40-42, 88, 104, 113, 118-19, 129, 134, 154, 171-72, 185n14, 189-90n11, 190nn12-13, 190n15, 190n17, 210n36, 216n15. *See also* Intelligence; National security
Khawaja, Momin, 196n38, 229n13, 229-30n15, 233n31
King. *See also* Crown prerogative; Queen
Kissinger, Henry, 5, 176n7
Koh, Harold, 186n17
Kosovo, 39, 41, 120, 222n21
La Forest, G.V., 57-59, 64-66, 122, 183n3, 191n5, 197n5, 198n11, 199n20, 200n24, 219n6
Lamer J., 26, 220n11
Languages, 49, 110-11, 162, 192nn9-10, 212n3, 214n3, 214n6, 215nn9-10. *See also* Education
Laskin, Bora, 6, 18, 38, 163, 177n12, 179n13, 223n26
LeBel J., 190n11
Lieutenant governor, 21, 48
Lincoln Sea, 138, 225n9, 225n11. *See also* Arctic/Arctic sovereignty
Lomonosov Ridge, 138, 225n12. *See also* Arctic/Arctic sovereignty
Macdonald, Sir John A., 178n6, 179n17, 194n22
Macroeconomics. *See* Economy/economics
Mactavish J., 190n17
Majority government, 19n(b), 46, 216n17, 222n24
Manitoba, 49, 91, 146-47, 162, 192nn9-10, 197n4
Manley report (2008), 128. *See also* Afghanistan
Mann, F.A., 139, 197n1, 225n16
Martin, Paul, 151
Martinique, 214n3, 217n20. *See also* Americas/Americas strategy

Martland J., 161
McLachlin J., 155-56, 187n25
Mexico, 61, 67, 115
Microeconomics. *See* Economy/economics
Militia (and defence) power, 6, 16, 18-19, 38, 42, 45, 64, 68, 83, 88, 121-26, 133, 138, 146, 186, 191n25, 195n27, 197n1, 210n36, 212n48
Mining/minerals/mines, 21, 57-58, 62, 117, 160, 200n23
Minority government, 14, 19n(b), 46, 216n17
Mobility rights. *See Charter of Rights and Freedoms*, s. 6
Monahan, Patrick, x, 15, 75, 178n5, 181n26, 192n6, 193n15, 194n22, 203n18, 204n19, 204n22, 231-32n21
Monetary policy, 71-72, 201n2. *See also* Bank of Canada; Economy/economics; Fiscal policy
Montana, 34, 130
Morale (national), 16
Mosley J., 89, 194n25, 230n15
Munitions, 16, 68, 123-24. *See also* War
National concern. *See Constitution Act, 1867*, peace, order and good government (POGG)/general power
National securities commission, 74, 77, 180n18, 203n15, 203n18, 204n22. *See also* Economy/economics
National security, xi, 33-34, 48, 50, 53-55, 60-61, 85-90, 96, 99-101, 105, 126, 131, 134, 140, 144, 186n17, 186n19, 190n20, 192n2, 194n24, 194-95n25, 195n32, 195n35, 200n32, 203n15, 210n29, 211n41, 220-21n12, 222n17, 227-28nn1-2, 230n15, 232n26. *See also* Intelligence
Nationalization, 21, 117
Natural resources: forestry, 21, 26, 28, 56, 58; minerals (*see* Mines/mining);

nuclear (see Nuclear energy; oil and gas (see Oil and gas)
Necessity, 49-50, 61, 131, 162, 165, 192nn8-10, 223n26
New Brunswick, 177n2, 178n4, 180n18, 214n5
New Zealand, 94
North American Free Trade Agreement (NAFTA), 61, 67, 115, 124, 149-50, 199n14, 199n16
Northwest Passage, 137-38, 146, 149, 225nn9-10. See also Arctic/Arctic sovereignty
Northwest Territories, 146, 148-49, 197-98n7, 218n25, 223n1, 227n36
Notwithstanding clause. See Charter of Rights and Freedoms, s. 33
Nova Scotia, 178n4, 180n18
Nuclear energy, 51-52, 56, 61-62, 65, 125, 160, 193n17, 232n26.
Nunavut, 146, 148-49, 197-98n7, 218n25, 223n1, 227n36
Nye, Joseph, 13, 177n1
Oakes test. See Charter of Rights and Freedoms, s. 1
Oil and gas, 49, 52, 56, 59-62, 67, 71, 116, 124, 148-49, 172, 181n27, 192n7, 198n12, 209n26, 220n12, 224n7, 226n32, 226n34, 232n26. See also Energy
Ontario, 180nn18-19
Pakistan, 120
Panama, 217n21. See also Americas/Americas strategy
Paramountcy (federal), 21, 58, 64, 66, 73, 172
Peace, order and good government (POGG). See Constitution Act, 1867, peace, order and good government (POGG)/general power
Peru, 217n21. See also Americas (or Americas Strategy)

Pigeon J., 161
Pipelines, 58, 65-66, 198-99n12, 226n34, 232n26
Political questions (doctrine), 33, 39, 186n17
Population, 8, 16, 18-19, 21, 26, 45, 55-56, 74, 76, 94-103, 113-15, 118, 121, 126, 134, 141, 143, 145, 157, 166, 169, 173-74, 182n32, 198n7, 212n2, 212n4, 213n8, 218n25, 224n5, 225n19, 226n25
Power (strategic power) (definition), 8, 13-14
Prerogative powers. See Royal prerogative
Prestige, 14
Prime minister, 30, 36, 73, 109, 111, 151, 197n2, 209n26, 214nn1-2, 215n10, 231n17. See also Cabinet; Harper, Stephen; Macdonald, Sir John A.; Martin, Paul; Trudeau, Pierre Elliott
Privy Council, Judicial Committee of, 21-22, 24, 30, 75, 91, 161-62, 170, 179n13, 179n18, 180n19, 184n5, 186-87n20, 202n10, 203n16, 205n25, 231n21
Privy Council Office (PCO), xi, 32, 128, 154, 194n24, 214n2
Procurement, 69, 115-16, 112, 126, 201n2, 217n22, 219n8, 220n10, 222n17
Property and civil rights, 19, 23, 53, 72, 75, 94, 123, 142, 170, 179n17, 179-80n18, 180n19, 198n9, 203nn15-16, 207n11
Provinces (as foreign affairs actors), 22-23, 43-45, 48, 72-73, 111, 114, 116, 128, 140, 153, 195n27, 217n19, 219n8, 222n18
Public health emergencies, 151-52, 160-68. See also Emergencies;

Emergency management; National Security
Public policy (definition), 35-36
Quebec, 8, 22-24, 77, 96-98, 110, 114, 173, 178n6, 179-80nn15-18, 180n19, 198n27, 213n7, 217n20, 222n18
Queen, 5, 17;
Radio, 80-83, 85, 91-92, 167, 206n3, 207n12, 207n15, 208n21, 208n23, 210n35, 211n44, 234n33. *See also* Communications
Rand J., 194n23
Rémillard, Gil, 178n5
Ritchie J., 161
Royal Canadian Mounted Police (RCMP), 53, 154, 163, 195nn27-28, 227n1, 228n1
Royal prerogative, 17, 19, 30-44, 49-50, 61, 63, 66, 85, 103-4, 112-13, 115, 117, 118-19, 121, 126, 128-34, 139-40, 146, 153, 156, 162, 165-66, 171-72, 176n10, 178n9, 180-81n21, 185-86nn14-15, 186nn17-18, 187n23, 187n27, 189n7, 190n20, 191nn21-22, 197n1, 210n36, 213n9, 213n15, 216n13, 216nn15-16, 221n12, 221-22nn15-16, 225n19, 226n23
Residual powers. *See Constitution Act, 1867*, peace, order and good government (POGG)/general power
Rights, school of Canadian constitutional scholarship. *See also Charter of Rights and Freedoms*
Rudd, Kevin, 215n10. *See also* Australia
Rule of law, 49, 162, 187n27, 192nn9-10
Russia, 135, 137-38, 148, 186, 212-13n4, 213n8, 223n3, 226n25, 227n35
Sanctions, 30, 36-37, 56, 79, 112, 117-18, 188n33, 218n24
Saskatchewan, 146-47, 197n4
Scalia, Antonin, 189n5
Scott, F.R., x, 6, 176n9, 183n3

Second World War, 5, 51, 62, 125, 133, 183n2, 192n12
Sharlow J., 190n14
Shipping. *See* Transportation
Singapore, 94, 135
Smith, Ronald, 34-36, 104, 119, 130-31, 134, 172, 187n25, 187n27, 218n26, 222n22
Sovereignty. *See also* Geography/territory; Arctic/Arctic sovereignty
Spending power. *See Constitution Act, 1867*, ss. 91(1A) and 91(3); Fiscal policy
Stinchcombe, 229-30n15
Strategic Constitution (definition of), 3-20. *See also* Constitution (definition of)
Strategy (definition of), x, 3-20, 175n1
Taché, E.P., 179n17
Taxation/taxes, 57-58, 71-72, 74, 95-96, 114, 116, 124, 202n6, 202n10
Technology, 16, 89, 123, 137, 206n2, 219n9, 231n18
Telephone/telecommunications, 81-83, 85, 87, 206n1, 207nn8-10, 207n16, 210n35, 220n11. *See also* Communications
Territory. *See* Geography/territory
Terrorism. *See* National Security
Title, Aboriginal. *See* Aboriginal peoples
Trade and commerce power. *See Constitution Act, 1867*, s. 91(2); United States Constitution
Transportation: air/aviation, 66, 68, 78-79, 125, 145-47, 158-60, 223n3, 233n30; rail/railways, 52, 65-66, 74, 78-79, 83, 85, 138-39, 145-47, 194n22, 205n26, 206n3, 207n16, 220n11; shipping (including ports), 158
Treaties: Aboriginal (*see* Aboriginal peoples); international, 3-4, 17, 25,

30-31, 36-37, 61, 77, 121, 132-33, 171, 183nn2-3, 184n5, 184nn8-9, 187n20, 221n15
Treaty rights (Aboriginal). *See* Aboriginal peoples
Tremblay, Guy. *See* Brun, Henri (and Guy Tremblay)
Trudeau, Pierre Elliott, 24, 180n19
Turks and Caicos, 218n25, 219n4, 219n7
Ukraine, 94, 212n2
United Kingdom (Great Britain), 10, 17, 95, 104, 137, 197n2, 205n26, 213n8
United Nations, 139, 148, 188n33, 191n21, 225n17
United Nations Convention on the Law of the Sea (UNCLOS), 135, 139, 223n2, 225nn17-18, 226n20
United States: Constitution, 75, 180n18, 184nn7-9, 186n17, 190n11;

The Federalism Papers, 128, 177n3, 222n18
Uranium. *See* Nuclear energy
War, ix, 4-5, 8, 16-18, 23, 29, 5, 47-48, 50-51, 56, 62, 64, 68-69, 71-72, 91, 104-5, 118-34, 140, 162-66, 171, 174, 175n1, 175n3, 177n13, 182n32, 183n2, 186n17, 188-91n2-25, 192n4, 192n8, 192nn12-13, 193n17, 194n19, 205n26, 219-23nn1-26, 226n22, 233n30. *See also Constitution Act, 1867*, s. 91(7); National Security
Wilson J., 39, 127, 165, 186n17, 189n7
World Bank, 218n23
Wright J., 190n20
Yoo, John, 186n17
Yukon, 148-49, 180-81n21, 191n7, 198n11, 218n25, 223n1

.... Index of Cases ....

Abassi v. Secretary of State for Foreign and Commonwealth Affairs, [2002] All E.R. 70: 187n25
Abdelrazik v. Canada, 2009 F.C. 580: 213n9
A.G. Can v. A.G. Ont. et al., [1937] 1 D.L.R. 673: 178n8, 186-87n20
Alberta Government Telephones v. CRTC, [1989] 2 S.C.R. 225: 83, 206n1, 207n9
Aleksic v. Canada (2002), 215 D.L.R. (4th) 720: 38, 40-41, 188n3, 190n20
Al-Skeini et al. v. Secretary of State for Defence, [2007] UKHL 26: 190n17
Amnesty International v. Canada, 2008 F.C. 336: 190n16, 222n19
Amnesty International v. Canada, [2008] F.C.J. No. 1700: 190n18
Amnesty International v. Canada, [2009] S.C.C.A. No. 63: 190n19

Atwal v. Canada, [1988] 1 F.C. 107: 210n34
Bell ExpressVu Limited Partnership v. Rex et al. (2002), 212 D.L.R. (4th) 1: 206n3
B.C. Offshore Reference, [1967] S.C.R. 792: 196n1, 225n14
Black v. Chrétien (2000), 47 O.R. (3d) 532: 187n27, 221n15
British Columbia v. Lafarge Canada Inc., [2007] S.C.J. No. 23: 63, 199n19
Burmah Oil Co. v. Lord Advocate, [1965] A.C. 75: 49, 192n7
Calder v. British Columbia, [1973] S.C.R. 313: 180n20
Canada v. Almalki, 2010 F.C. 1106: 194n25
Canada v. Khadr, [2008] S.C.J. No. 28: 189n11

Canada v. Khadr, [2010] S.C.J. No. 3: 190n15
Canada v. Khawaja, [2007] F.C.J. No. 622: 229-30n15
Canada v. Khawaja, 2007 F.C.A. 342: 229-30n15
Canada v. Khawaja, 2007 F.C.A. 388: 229-30n15
Canada v. Ribic, [2005] 1 F.C.R. 33: 229-30n15
Canadian Egg Marketing Agency v. Richardson, [1998] 3 S.C.R. 157: 100, 143, 213n11, 26n27
Capital Cities Communications v. CRTC, [1978] 2 S.C.R. 141: 83, 207n15
Chandler v. Director of Public Prosecutions, [1964] 1 A.C. 763: 188n1
Charkaoui v. Canada, [2007] S.C.J. No. 9: 155-56, 195n32, 229-30n15, 230n16
Charkaoui v. Canada, 2008 S.C.C. 38: 229-30n15
Chief Mountain v. Canada, 2013 B.C.C.A. 49: 181n31
China Navigation Co. Ltd. v. Attorney-General (1932), 2 K.B. 197: 188n1
Citizens' Insurance v. Parsons, [1881] 7 A.C. 96: 179n18, 203n16
Commonwealth v. Tasmania (1983), 158 C.L.R. 1: 184n8
Consolidated Fastfrate Inc. v. Western Canada Council of Teamsters et al., 2009 S.C.C. 53: 83, 208n18
Co-operative Committee on Japanese-Canadians v. Canada, [1947] A.C. 87: 232n25
Council of Civil Service Unions v. Minister for Civil Service, [1985] 1 A.C. 374: 33-34, 104, 186n18, 187n21, 221n15
Croft v. Dunphy, [1933] A.C. 156: 176n8

Dehghani v. Canada, [1993] 1 S.C.R. 1053: 156
Delgamuukw v. British Columbia, [1997] 3 S.C.R. 1010: 26, 181n30, 182n35
Dunbar v. Attorney-General Saskatchewan (1984), 11 D.L.R. (4th) 374: 201-2n6
Edwards Books & Art Ltd. v. R., [1986] 2 S.C.R. 713: 213n14
Fort Frances Pulp and Power Co. v. Manitoba Free Press Co., [1923] A.C. 695: 91, 223n26
General Motors of Canada Ltd. v. City National Leasing, [1989] 1 S.C.R. 641: 75, 203n17
Globalive Wireless Management Corp. v. Public Mobile Inc., 2011 F.C.A. 194: 208n23
Haida Nation v. British Columbia, [2004] 3 S.C.R. 511: 182n35
Hamdan v. Rumsfeld, 126 S. Ct. 2749 (2006): 189-90n11
Harkat v. Canada, 2012 F.C.A. 122: 229-30n15
Henrie v. Canada, [1989] 2 F.C. 229: 185n14
Human Rights Institute of Canada v. Canada, [2000] 1 F.C. 475: 191n24, 219n5
Hunter v. Southam, [1984] 2 S.C.R. 145: 210n30
Johannesson v. West St. Paul, [1952] 1 S.C.R. 292: 79, 159, 206n27, 232n22
Jorgenson v. Canada, [1971] S.C.R. 725: 194n19
Keewatin v. Ontario, 2013 ONCA 158: 181n24, 198n10
Khadr v. Canada, 2009 F.C.A. 246: 190n12
Khadr v. Canada, [2009] F.C.J. 462: 190n13

Koowarta v. Bjelke-Petersen (1982), 153 C.L.R. 168: 31, 184n7
Liquidators of the Maritime Bank v. Receiver General of New Brunswick, [1892] A.C. 437: 177n2
L'Union St. Jacques de Montréal v. Bélisle (1874), 6 P.C. 31: 191n25
Mikisew Cree First Nation v. Canada, 2005 S.C.C. 69: 182n36
Missouri v. Holland, 252 U.S. 416 (1920): 184n9
Mitchell v. Canada, 2001 S.C.C. 33: 27, 181-82n32, 182n34
Mount Sinai Hospital Center v. Quebec, [2001] S.C.J. No. 43: 187n25
Mowat v. Casgrain (1897), 6 Que. Q.B. 12: 177n2
New Brunswick Broadcasting Co. v. Nova Scotia (Speaker of the House of Assembly), [1993] 1 S.C.R. 319: 178n4
O'Neill v. Canada (2006), 82 O.R. (3d) 241: 211n41
Ontario Hydro v. Ontario, [1993] 3 S.C.R. 327: 193n17, 200n28, 220n11
Ontario Mining Company v. Seybold, [1903] A.C. 73: 200n23
Operation Dismantle Inc. v. R., [1985] 1 S.C.R. 441: 33, 39, 104, 127, 165, 186n18, 187n22, 189nn6-7, 192-93n13
Public Mobile Inc. v. Canada, 2011 F.C. 130: 208n23
Public Service Board v. Dionne, [1978], 2 S.C.R. 191: 83, 207n14
Quebec v. Canada, [1979] 1 S.C.R. 218: 195n27
Radio Reference, [1932] A.C. 304: 83, 207n12, 207n15
Rasul v. Bush, 542 U.S. 466 (2004): 189n5, 189-90n11
Re CFRB, [1973] 3 O.R. 819 (C.A.): 207n13

Re CSIS Act, [2007] F.C.J. No. 1780: 228n8
Re CSIS Act, 2009 F.C. 1058: 211n38, 228n10
Re Gray (1918), 57 S.C.R. 150: 192-93n13
Re Manitoba Language Rights, [1985] 1 S.C.R. 721: 49, 162, 192n9
Re Resolution to Amend the Constitution, [1981] 1 S.C.R. 753: 178n9
Reference re Agricultural Products Marketing Act, [1978] 2 S.C.R. 1198: 201-2n6
Reference re Alberta Legislation, [1938] S.C.J. No. 2: 201n2
Reference re Anti-Inflation Act, 1975, [1976] 2 S.C.R. 373: 223n26, 232nn24-25
Reference re Employment and Social Insurance Act, [1936] S.C.R. 427: 202n10
Reference re Employment and Social Insurance Act, [1937] A.C. 355: 201-2n6
Reference re Securities Act, 2011 S.C.C. 66: 74, 77, 203n15, 203n18, 204n22
Reference re Validity of Section 5(a) of Dairy Industry Act (Canada), [1949] S.C.R. 1: 194n23
Reference re Waters and Water-Powers, [1929] S.C.R. 200: 200n23
R. v. Adams, [1996] 3 S.C.R. 101: 181n28
R. v. Badger, [1996] 1 S.C.R. 771: 181n31
R. v. Cook, [1998] 2 S.C.R. 957: 189n8
R. v. Côté, [1996] 3 S.C.R. 139: 181n31
R. v. Crown Zellerbach Canada Ltd., [1988] 1. S.C.R. 401: 193n16
R. v. Duarte, [1990] 1 S.C.R. 30: 210n31
R. v. Gladstone, [1996] 2 S.C.R. 723: 26, 181n29

R. v. Hape (2007), 280 D.L.R. (4th) 385: 185n14, 189n9, 189-90n11, 190n17, 228n9

R. v. Khawaja, [2006] O.J. No. 4245: 196n38, 233n31

R. v. Khawaja, 2010 ONCA 862: 196n38

R. v. Khawaja, 2012 S.C.C. 69: 196n38

R. v. McNeil, [2009] 1 S.C.R. 66: 229-320n15

R. v. National Post, 2010 S.C.C. 16: 89, 211n39

R. v. Oakes, [1986] 1 S.C.R. 103: 93, 101, 127, 144-45, 213nn12-13, 226n28

R. v. O'Connor, [1995] 4 S.C.R. 411: 229n15

R. v. Pamajewon, [1996] 2 S.C.R. 821: 181-82n32

R. v. Secretary of State for Foreign and Commonwealth Affairs, ex parte Everett, [1989] 1 All E.R. 655: 221n15

R. v. Sparrow, [1990] S.C.J. No. 49: 19n(a), 25-26, 57, 174, 181n25, 198n8

R. v. Stinchcombe, [1991] 3 S.C.R. 326: 229-30n15

R. v. Van der Peet, [1996] 2 S.C.R. 507: 26, 182n33

Smith v. Canada, [2009] F.C.J. No. 234: 34-36, 104, 119, 130-31, 134, 172, 187nn25-26, 187n27, 218n26, 222n22

St. Catherine's Milling and Lumber Co. v. The Queen (1888), 14 A.C. 46: 181n22

Suresh v. Canada, [2002] 1 S.C.R. 3: 49, 156, 192n8, 194n25, 195n35, 227n1

Taku River Tlingit First Nation v. British Columbia, [2004] 3 S.C.R. 550: 182n36

Téléphone Guèvremont v. Quebec, [1994] 1 S.C.R. 878: 83, 207n10

Toronto v. Bell Telephone Co., [1905] A.C. 52: 83, 207n8

Turp v. Canada, 2012 F.C. 893: 171, 234n1

United States v. Texas (1950), 399 U.S. 707: 138, 197

United States Steel Corporation v. Canada, 2011 F.C.A. 176: 209n28

William v. British Columbia, 2012 B.C.C.A. 285: 181nn23-24, 198n10

Winterhaven Stables Ltd. v. Attorney General Canada (1986), A.J. No. 460: 201-2n6

Youngstown Sheet & Tube Co. v. Sawyer, 343 U.S. 579: 192n19

Zarzour v. Canada (2000), 268 N.R. 235: 210n29

............................Index of Statutes............................

Aeronautics Act, R.S.C. 1985, c. A-2: 53, 79, 146, 159, 195n33

Anti-Terrorism Act, S.C. 2001, c. 41: 54, 185n15, 196nn37-38, 230-231n17

Atomic Energy Control Act, R.S.C. 1970, c. A-19: 52, 194n20

Bank of Canada Act, R.S.C. 1985, c. B-2: 201n2

Bill C-3, An Act to Amend the Immigration and Refugee Protection Act and to Make a Consequential Amendment to Another Act, 2d Sess., 39th Parl., 2007: 156, 201n2

Bill C-15, An Act to Replace the Northwest Territories Act to Implement Certain Provisions of the Northwest

Territories Lands and Resources Devolution Agreement and to Repeal or Make Amendments to the Territorial Lands Act, the Northwest Territories Waters Act, the Mackenzie Valley Resource Management Act, Other Acts and Certain Orders and Regulations, 2d Sess., 41st Parl., 2013: 227n36

Bill C-17, *An Act to Amend the Criminal Code (Investigative Hearings and Recognizance with Conditions)*, 3d Sess., 40th Parl., 2010: 231, 196n41

Bill C-19, *An Act to Amend the Criminal Code (Investigative Hearings and Recognizance with Conditions)*, 2d Sess., 40th Parl., 2009: 54, 196n40

Bill C-60, *An Act to Implement Certain Provisions of the Budget Tabled in Parliament on March 21, 2013 and Other Measures*, 1st Sess., 41st Parl., 2013: 184n10, 185n11

Bill S-3, *An Act to Amend the Criminal Code (Investigative Hearings and Recognizance with Conditions)*, 2d Sess., 39th Parl., 2007: 54, 196n39, 231n17

Bill S-7, *An Act to Amend the Criminal Code, the Canada Evidence Act and the Security of Information Act*, 1st Sess., 41st Parl., 2013: 54, 196n42, 231n17

Broadcasting Act, S.C. 1991, c. 11: 85, 91, 167, 206n3, 208n22

Canada Elections Act, S.C. 2000, c. 9: 133, 222n25

Canada Evidence Act, R.S.C. 1985, c. C-5: 53, 195n30, 196n42, 229n15, 230n15

Canada Transportation Act, S.C. 1996, c. 10: 53, 79, 146, 159, 195n34, 207n16

Canadian Radio-television and Telecommunications Commission Act, R.S.C. 1985, c. C-22: 206n3

Canadian Railway Act, R.S.C. 1906, c. 37: 206n3, 207n16

Canadian Security Intelligence Service Act, R.S.C. 1985, c. C-23: 32, 53, 88-89, 113, 153, 163, 185nn13-14, 195n27, 196n38, 211n38, 216n15, 228n6, 228n10, 233n31

Citizenship Act, R.S.C. 1985, c. C-29: 53, 195n31, 213n6

Commonwealth of Australia Constitution Act, 1900, 63 & 64 Vict.: 31, 75, 177n11, 184n6

Constitution Act, 1867 (U.K.), 30 & 31 Vict., c. 3: ix, 3-6, 14-19, 21, 23-24, 30-31, 38, 42, 44-45, 47, 51-52, 54, 57-58, 60, 62-64, 68, 71-72, 74-77, 79, 83-85, 92, 94, 96, 99, 110-11, 121-25, 133, 137-38, 142, 146, 158-59, 175n2, 178nn5-6, 178n9, 179n13, 179-80n18, 180n19, 183n37, 191n25, 192n12, 194n22, 195n27, 196-97n1, 201n2, 201nn4-5, 202nn8-9, 203n15, 206n4, 207n10, 207n15, 213n6, 218n25, 231n21

Constitution Act, 1871 (U.K.), 34 & 35 Vict., c. 28: 138, 197-98n7

Constitution Act, 1930 (U.K.), 20 & 21 Geo. V, c. 26: 197n4

Constitution Act, 1982, enacted as Schedule B to the *Canada Act, 1982* (U.K.), 1982, c. 11: 4, 6, 14-15, 17-18, 21-25, 58, 62, 65, 116, 175n4, 176n10, 178nn4-5, 192nn12-13, 193n18, 197n4, 218n25

Criminal Code, R.S.C. 1985, c. C-46: 54, 82, 87-88, 157, 182, 195n36, 196nn38-42, 206n3, 210n32, 210n35, 211n45, 229n13, 231n17

Crown Liability and Proceedings Act, R.S.C. 1985, c. C-50: 188n4
Defence Production Act, R.S.C. 1985, c. D-1: 68-69, 123, 125, 201n1
Department of Foreign Affairs and International Trade Act, R.S.C. 1985, c. E-22: 31, 185n11, 216n14
Department of Citizenship and Immigration Act, S.C. 94, c. 31: 213n7
Emergencies Act, R.S.C. 1985, c. 22 (4th Supp.): 53, 60-61, 69, 85, 91, 125-26, 131, 134, 140, 156-57, 160, 162, 191n23, 192n5, 220n12, 221n13, 222n23, 232nn26-27, 233n30
Emergency Management Act, S.C. 2007, c. 15: 53, 195n26
Energy Supplies Emergency Act, R.S.C. 1985, c. E-9: 60-61, 199n14, 220n12, 232n26
Export and Import Permits Act, R.S.C. 1985, c. E-19: 66, 188n33, 200n31
Expropriation Act, R.S.C. 1985, c. E-21: 200n26
Foreign Investment Review Act, S.C. 1973-74, c. 46: 86, 209n26
Human Rights Act, 1998 (U.K.), c. 42: 190n17
Immigration and Refugee Protection Act, S.C. 2001, c. 27: 53, 96-97, 155, 195n32, 213n7, 229n15
Indian Act, R.S.C. 1985, c. I-5: 24, 180-81n21
Intelligence Services Act 2001 (Cth): 216n16
Investment Canada Act, R.S.C. 1985, c. 28 (1st Supp.): 50, 86-87, 200n32, 206n3, 208n24, 209n26, 209-10n28
Kyoto Protocol Implementation Act, S.C. 2007, c. 30. [Repealed, 2012, c. 19, s. 699]: 234n1
Letters Patent Constituting the Office of the Governor-General of Canada, *1947,* R.S.C. 1985, Appendix II, No. 31, Art. II: 15, 176n10
National Defence Act, R.S.C. 1985, c. N-5: 32, 42-44, 53-54, 83, 88, 121-22, 131, 133, 166, 185n15, 186n16, 190n20, 191nn21-22, 206n3, 210n37, 212n48, 219n8, 228n11
National Energy Board Act, R.S.C. 1985, c. N-7: 66, 200n29
Nunavut Act, S.C. 1993, c. 28: 198n7
Official Development Assistance Accountability Act, S.C. 2008, c. 17: 31-32, 185n12
Personal Information Protection and Electronic Documents Act, S.C. 2000, c. 5: 206n3
Privacy Act, R.S.C. 1985, c. P-21: 206n3
Quebec Act, 1774 (U.K.), R.S.C. 1985, Appendix II, No. 2: 23, 179n15, 179n17
Radiocommunication Act, R.S.C. 1985, c. R-2: 206n3, 208n21
Royal Canadian Mounted Police Act, R.S.C. 1985, c. R-10: 53, 195n28
The Royal Proclamation, 1763 (U.K.), R.S.C. 1985, Appendix II, No. 1: 15, 24, 181n22
Security of Information Act, R.S.C. 1985, c. O-5: 53, 195n29, 196n38, 196n42, 206n3, 211n41
Special Economic Measures Act, S.C. 1992, c. 17: 37, 66, 188nn32-33
Statute of Westminster, 22 & 23 Geo. V, c. 4: 5, 15, 176n8, 176n10
Telecommunications Act, S.C. 1993, c. 38: 84-86, 206n3, 207n17, 208n20
Territorial Lands Act, R.S.C. 1985, c. T-7: 227n36
United Nations Act, R.S.C. 1985, c U-2: 188n33
War Measures Act, S.C. 1914 (2d sess.), c. 2: 47, 91, 192n4, 221n12, 233n30

Dale Brawn
Paths to the Bench: The Judicial Appointment Process in Manitoba, 1870-1950 (2014)

Dominique Clément
Equality Deferred: Sex Discrimination and British Columbia's Human Rights State, 1953-84 (2014)

Irvin Studin
The Strategic Constitution: Understanding Canadian Power in the World (2014)

Elizabeth A. Sheehy
Defending Battered Women on Trial: Lessons from the Transcripts (2014)

Carmela Murdocca
To Right Historical Wrongs: Race, Gender, and Sentencing in Canada (2013)

Donn Short
"Don't Be So Gay!" Queers, Bullying, and Making Schools Safe (2013)

Melissa Munn and Chris Bruckert
On the Outside: From Lengthy Imprisonment to Lasting Freedom (2013)

Emmett Macfarlane
Governing from the Bench: The Supreme Court of Canada and the Judicial Role (2013)

Ron Ellis
Unjust by Design: The Administrative Justice System in Canada (2013)

David R. Boyd
The Right to a Healthy Environment: Revitalizing Canada's Constitution (2012)

David Milward
Aboriginal Justice and the Charter: Realizing a Culturally Sensitive Interpretation of Legal Rights (2012)

Shelley A.M. Gavigan
Hunger, Horses, and Government Men: Criminal Law on the Aboriginal Plains, 1870-1905 (2012)

Steven Bittle
Still Dying for a Living: Corporate Criminal Liability after the Westray Mine Disaster (2012)

Jacqueline D. Krikorian
International Trade Law and Domestic Policy: Canada, the United States, and the WTO (2012)

Michael Boudreau
City of Order: Crime and Society in Halifax, 1918-35 (2012)

David R. Boyd
The Environmental Rights Revolution: A Global Study of Constitutions, Human Rights, and the Environment (2012)

Lesley Erickson
Westward Bound: Sex, Violence, the Law, and the Making of a Settler Society (2011)

Elaine Craig
Troubling Sex: Towards a Legal Theory of Sexual Integrity (2011)

Laura DeVries
Conflict in Caledonia: Aboriginal Land Rights and the Rule of Law (2011)

Jocelyn Downie and Jennifer J. Llewellyn (eds.)
Being Relational: Reflections on Relational Theory and Health Law (2011)

Grace Li Xiu Woo
Ghost Dancing with Colonialism: Decolonization and Indigenous Rights at the Supreme Court of Canada (2011)

Fiona Kelly
Transforming Law's Family: The Legal Recognition of Planned Lesbian Motherhood (2011)

Colleen Bell
The Freedom of Security: Governing Canada in the Age of Counter-Terrorism (2011)

Andrew S. Thompson
In Defence of Principles: NGOs and Human Rights in Canada (2010)

Aaron Doyle and Dawn Moore (eds.)
Critical Criminology in Canada: New Voices, New Directions (2010)

Joanna R. Quinn
The Politics of Acknowledgement: Truth Commissions in Uganda and Haiti (2010)

Patrick James
Constitutional Politics in Canada after the Charter: Liberalism, Communitarianism, and Systemism (2010)

Louis A. Knafla and Haijo Westra (eds.)
Aboriginal Title and Indigenous Peoples: Canada, Australia, and New Zealand (2010)

Janet Mosher and Joan Brockman (eds.)
Constructing Crime: Contemporary Processes of Criminalization (2010)

Stephen Clarkson and Stepan Wood
A Perilous Imbalance: The Globalization of Canadian Law and Governance (2009)

Amanda Glasbeek
Feminized Justice: The Toronto Women's Court, 1913-34 (2009)

Kim Brooks (ed.)
Justice Bertha Wilson: One Woman's Difference (2009)

Wayne V. McIntosh and Cynthia L. Cates
Multi-Party Litigation: The Strategic Context (2009)

Renisa Mawani
Colonial Proximities: Crossracial Encounters and Juridical Truths in British Columbia, 1871-1921 (2009)

James B. Kelly and Christopher P. Manfredi (eds.)
Contested Constitutionalism: Reflections on the Canadian Charter of Rights and Freedoms (2009)

Catherine Bell and Robert K. Paterson (eds.)
Protection of First Nations Cultural Heritage: Laws, Policy, and Reform (2008)

Hamar Foster, Benjamin L. Berger, and A.R. Buck (eds.)
The Grand Experiment: Law and Legal Culture in British Settler Societies (2008)

Richard J. Moon (ed.)
Law and Religious Pluralism in Canada (2008)

Catherine Bell and Val Napoleon (eds.)
First Nations Cultural Heritage and Law: Case Studies, Voices, and Perspectives (2008)

Douglas C. Harris
Landing Native Fisheries: Indian Reserves and Fishing Rights in British Columbia, 1849-1925 (2008)

Peggy J. Blair
Lament for a First Nation: The Williams Treaties of Southern Ontario (2008)

Lori G. Beaman
Defining Harm: Religious Freedom and the Limits of the Law (2007)

Stephen Tierney (ed.)
Multiculturalism and the Canadian Constitution (2007)

Julie Macfarlane
The New Lawyer: How Settlement Is Transforming the Practice of Law (2007)

Kimberley White
Negotiating Responsibility: Law, Murder, and States of Mind (2007)

Dawn Moore
Criminal Artefacts: Governing Drugs and Users (2007)

Hamar Foster, Heather Raven, and Jeremy Webber (eds.)
Let Right Be Done: Aboriginal Title, the Calder *Case, and the Future of Indigenous Rights* (2007)

Dorothy E. Chunn, Susan B. Boyd, and Hester Lessard (eds.)
Reaction and Resistance: Feminism, Law, and Social Change (2007)

Margot Young, Susan B. Boyd, Gwen Brodsky, and Shelagh Day (eds.)
Poverty: Rights, Social Citizenship, and Legal Activism (2007)

Rosanna L. Langer
Defining Rights and Wrongs: Bureaucracy, Human Rights, and Public Accountability (2007)

C.L. Ostberg and Matthew E. Wetstein
Attitudinal Decision Making in the Supreme Court of Canada (2007)

Chris Clarkson
Domestic Reforms: Political Visions and Family Regulation in British Columbia, 1862-1940 (2007)

Jean McKenzie Leiper
Bar Codes: Women in the Legal Profession (2006)

Gerald Baier
Courts and Federalism: Judicial Doctrine in the United States, Australia, and Canada (2006)

Avigail Eisenberg (ed.)
Diversity and Equality: The Changing Framework of Freedom in Canada (2006)

Randy K. Lippert
Sanctuary, Sovereignty, Sacrifice: Canadian Sanctuary Incidents, Power, and Law (2005)

James B. Kelly
Governing with the Charter: Legislative and Judicial Activism and Framers' Intent (2005)

Dianne Pothier and Richard Devlin (eds.)
Critical Disability Theory: Essays in Philosophy, Politics, Policy, and Law (2005)

Susan G. Drummond
Mapping Marriage Law in Spanish Gitano Communities (2005)

Louis A. Knafla and Jonathan Swainger (eds.)
Laws and Societies in the Canadian Prairie West, 1670-1940 (2005)

Ikechi Mgbeoji
Global Biopiracy: Patents, Plants, and Indigenous Knowledge (2005)

Florian Sauvageau, David Schneiderman, and David Taras, with Ruth Klinkhammer and Pierre Trudel
The Last Word: Media Coverage of the Supreme Court of Canada (2005)

Gerald Kernerman
Multicultural Nationalism: Civilizing Difference, Constituting Community (2005)

Pamela A. Jordan
Defending Rights in Russia: Lawyers, the State, and Legal Reform in the Post-Soviet Era (2005)

Anna Pratt
Securing Borders: Detention and Deportation in Canada (2005)

Kirsten Johnson Kramar
Unwilling Mothers, Unwanted Babies: Infanticide in Canada (2005)

W.A. Bogart
Good Government? Good Citizens? Courts, Politics, and Markets in a Changing Canada (2005)

Catherine Dauvergne
Humanitarianism, Identity, and Nation: Migration Laws in Canada and Australia (2005)

Michael Lee Ross
First Nations Sacred Sites in Canada's Courts (2005)

Andrew Woolford
Between Justice and Certainty: Treaty Making in British Columbia (2005)

John McLaren, Andrew Buck, and Nancy Wright (eds.)
Despotic Dominion: Property Rights in British Settler Societies (2004)

Georges Campeau
From UI to EI: Waging War on the Welfare State (2004)

Alvin J. Esau
The Courts and the Colonies: The Litigation of Hutterite Church Disputes (2004)

Christopher N. Kendall
Gay Male Pornography: An Issue of Sex Discrimination (2004)

Roy B. Flemming
Tournament of Appeals: Granting Judicial Review in Canada (2004)

Constance Backhouse and Nancy L. Backhouse
The Heiress vs the Establishment: Mrs. Campbell's Campaign for Legal Justice (2004)

Christopher P. Manfredi
Feminist Activism in the Supreme Court: Legal Mobilization and the Women's Legal Education and Action Fund (2004)

Annalise Acorn
Compulsory Compassion: A Critique of Restorative Justice (2004)

Jonathan Swainger and Constance Backhouse (eds.)
People and Place: Historical Influences on Legal Culture (2003)

Jim Phillips and Rosemary Gartner
Murdering Holiness: The Trials of Franz Creffield and George Mitchell (2003)

David R. Boyd
Unnatural Law: Rethinking Canadian Environmental Law and Policy (2003)

Ikechi Mgbeoji
Collective Insecurity: The Liberian Crisis, Unilateralism, and Global Order (2003)

Rebecca Johnson
Taxing Choices: The Intersection of Class, Gender, Parenthood, and the Law (2002)

John McLaren, Robert Menzies, and Dorothy E. Chunn (eds.)
Regulating Lives: Historical Essays on the State, Society, the Individual, and the Law (2002)

Joan Brockman
Gender in the Legal Profession: Fitting or Breaking the Mould (2001)

Printed and bound in Canada by Friesens

Set in Myriad and Sabon by Artegraphica Design Co. Ltd.

Text design: Irma Rodriguez

Copy editor: Dallas Harrison